I0560768

The Origin of Life

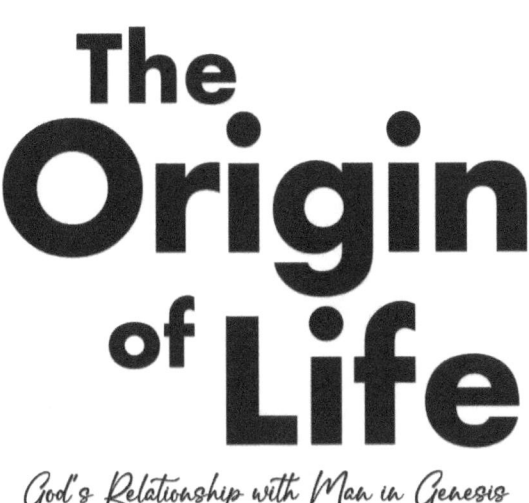

God's Relationship with Man in Genesis

Peter Russell-Yarde

Copyright © 2025 by Peter Russell-Yarde

All rights reserved. This book or any portion thereof may not be reproduced or transmitted in any form or manner, electronic or mechanical, including photocopying, recording, or by any information storage or retrieval system, without the express written permission of the copyright owner except for the use of brief quotations in a book review or other noncommercial uses permitted by copyright law.

Printed in the United States of America
Library of Congress Control Number: 2025918614
ISBN: Softcover   978-1-969213-13-7
            e-Book   978-1-969213-12-0
Republished by: TwinVerse Prime
Publication Date: 09/01/2025

To order copies of this book, contact:
TwinVerse Prime
Phone: (725) 257-6538
clients@twinverseprime.com
www.twinverseprime.com/

CONTENTS

DEDICATION

To the God who called me to serve Him
and who has inspired me to write on His word

BOOKS PUBLISHED BY PETER

Biblical Comment:
The Origin of Life : God's Relationship with Man in Genesis
God Rescues His People : Birth of Nation According to Exodus
The Wilderness Training School : Powerful Lessons in Numbers
Seeing Into the Future : Understanding the Revelation of John
The Path of Wisdom : A Study of Proverbs Chapters 1 to 4
Proverbs 5 to 12
Hosea
Deuteronomy
Epistle to the Ephesians
Epistle to the Colossians
Epistle to the Romans
Epistle to the Hebrews
Epistle to the Galatians
Joshua
Matters of Faith:
Are There Demons? & Other Matters of Faith
Letters to the Seven Churches in Revelation
Lost Souls : The danger of losing sight of God
Covenant & Testament : God's rules for God's people to obey
Belief and Faith : Understanding the Essentials
Ordinary People : Extra-ordinary faith
So You Think You Know About Faith : Learning to Trust God
A Fresh Look at Easter
You Will Receive Power
Assuredly God IS!
Truth & Doubt
Christ IS King : A Guide for Doubters
Law & Grace (Lessons from the Kings of Judah & Israel)
The Return From Exile : Babylon to Jerusalem
Autobiographical:
A Tale of Three Men (Provides background information about how these books came to be written and distributed)
What our faith is all about
The Tent of the Meeting : Illustrating God's Plan of Salvation

PREFACE

1st Edition

Early in the year 2002 my very dear friend Derek, a Jew for whom I had written a number of small articles with varying degrees of success, asked me to write down my comments on the book of Genesis; a daunting task for which I felt particularly inadequate. Being in full time employment at the time I was unable to take up such a challenge. However the opportunity came when I was made redundant in the August of that year.

The book of Genesis was not new to me for I had read it many times and previously studied some parts of it in detail. This time, however, I was in a different frame of mind because God had challenged me late in 2001 with the question "Do you trust Me?" My initial answer was, "Yes Lord I trust you, it's me (and my tendency to make wrong decisions) that I do not trust", and when He repeated the question I repeated my answer.

The number three is important because it signifies Divine perfection and completeness. My answer was neither perfect nor complete because I was denying the power of God to control my tendency to go wrong. Thus when He asked me the same question a third time I had to think about the substance of my answer and change it if my walk with the Lord, which I not only wanted to continue but become more intimate, was to succeed. It is interesting that God required me to repeat my new answer, "Yes Lord I trust you implicitly" to a thrice repeated "Do you trust me?" So five times God had to ask me that same question before

I answered, as He wanted me to answer, that I trusted Him implicitly.

God teaches us and tests us, teaches then tests as we learn of Him. Unless we are prepared to surrender ourselves in complete and confident trust to Him, there is not a lot He can do in our lives. Indeed when others complain about God not preventing disasters where people experience life changing situation either physical, emotional or financial, my immediate response is to ask them if they have ever tried to learn about Him or been in position to call upon Him or listen to Him or respond to anything He said to them whether through the reading of the Bible (if, that is, they have ever read it), from what others have said to them or directly, which has been my experience, particularly in this case. As it was there was a purpose to that question as has become obvious over the years.

Being out of work required seeking other employment. The confusion, however, was:

1.   How much effort should be spent finding other work?
2.   How much effort should be spent in prayer, waiting upon God for the next job of work? The reason for this question was that it had become obvious that God chose the work He wanted me to have no matter how much personal effort was made in trying to find work.
3.   How much time should be spent on this project of writing my thoughts on the book of Genesis, which I was increasingly finding helpful and spiritually stimulating, especially in my situation of being jobless?

My constant prayer for many years had been for my life to be kept within God's plan for me and to be a servant of His as much as His prophets and saints had been, especially those in the Bible who had helped and inspired me, from Abraham through to Jacob, from Moses to Jeremiah and Paul.

In reading the biblical narrative and trying to understand the state of mind of the various characters and their relationship with God and the world in which they lived, it was fascinating to discover, in a particularly dynamic way, that we both experienced the same day to day problems in our walk with God throughout our lives. Such relationships did not depend on particular individuals but the way God, being the same yesterday, today and forever, generally dealt with everyone in a similar way, adapting His approach to each person to suit the needs of that individual according to their characters, just as parents adapt the love and care and discipline they give to their children so that it is specific to each child's individuality.

Although the characters being referred to in the Biblical text had lived in the middle bronze age, I could still clearly empathize with them when they had to make decisions. Some of those decisions, because of my overview of their lives, were clearly wrong; but through recorded scripture the way God was able to nullify or reduce the impact of those mistakes could clearly be seen, such that His servants were able to continue their consistent and close walk with Him. Therefore if, as scripture tells us, God is the same yesterday, today and forever, then surely He is able to have the same impact on the lives of those living in the 21st century that He had on those living centuries before in spite of the tendency of everyone to make wrong decisions.

It was becoming clear that God used Derek to get me to study this first book of the Bible, because He wanted to convey a message and a principle to me at a time of greatest need, for although, as a contractor, there had previously been times when there was no work, this time seemed to be different in that God had become even more intimately involved in my life, through years of spiritual growth; also there was a sense that it was time for a change of direction.

As it was there was no technical authoring work for 23 months, after which there was sufficient work for me until I finally retired on May 6th 2011, in my 72nd year. By 2012 it became more obvious that God was to use me as a writer on scripture as the list above reveals, and the document "A Tale of Three Men" explains. But my writing style is that of a technical author not a that of a theologian or academic. One of my jobs was to write very specific operating instructions for large items of industrial equipment and processes and full coverage was essential. Assuming an operator would know part of the procedure was not allowed, every part of the operation, including safety features and all aspects of preparation and potential dangers had to be included, which is why Derek wrote:

Your way of writing is very precise, this makes it difficult to absorb sometimes, "not easy to read" said your reviewer. God is not easy to understand at all and most of his communications were written down by people so what we think we know is written by Men. Your work 'Explains God' but the reader has to work very hard to understand all the finer points and definitely has to look up the references and pray.

Having found that the various activities of individuals included in the Biblical text could not be treated as either myths or legends, for they are far more alive and believable when treated as actual people experiencing real life issues, it has been inspirational to learn about and seek to understand their relationship to a living and omnipresent God, just as my activities are actual real life issues that tell others of my relationship to that self same God.

In treating the account of their lives as myths or legends there is the clear and very real danger that we will begin to treat God as either a myth or a legend, or remove the person and personal attributes from Him, thus denying us the possibility of a personal intimacy with Him which is, for me at least, the most exciting and realistic element of my relationship with the Lord God of Israel.

The other point to consider is where does myth and legend end and reality begin? I would suggest that settling that point could provide the source of many a discussion, making the acceptance of the reality of the characters a preferred option.

An important lesson to learn is that God is Spirit and they that worship Him must do so in spirit and in truth (Jn. 4:23). A central factor to be accepted, particularly when reading this first book of the Bible, is to approach the Holy Bible as a spiritual book without unnecessarily 'spiritualizing' every aspect because we need practical instructions to live in this practical world. God, who is Spirit, is teaching us spiritual truths that will have a major impact on our lives here on earth if we allow Him to bring to life the spirit that is within each one of us. So many people discard the Bible in general and the First Testament (more commonly known as the Old Testament) in particular because they try to treat it as any humanly written and humanly inspired book, rather than as a God written, God inspired book written for our benefit by Holy Spirit inspired men and women. (2 Peter 1:19 – 21)

Over the years as I have been led to write on scripture it has become very clear to me that unless we can understand and accept the book of Genesis then it is unlikely that we will be able to understand the rest of scripture. This is because Genesis is the foundation, the preface and introduction to the Bible, the key that opens up the secrets hidden in holy writ.

The reason the Bible stands tall over all other religious works is that it is full of prophecies, most of which have come to pass exactly as prophesied with many yet to be fulfilled. Yes men wrote it. But when considering the wonderful truth of the words of the prophets, it is essential to realise that no prophecy recorded in scripture was ever thought up by the prophets themselves; rather it was the direct intervention and inspiration of the Holy Spirit at work within them who gave them the true message from God (see 2 Peter 1:21, 22). Paul speaks of every scripture being given to us by inspiration from God (2 Tim. 3:15 – 17); if that is true then we also must seek Divine guidance and inspiration to read and understand it and apply it to our lives. Thus God not only gave it to us in the first place, but for us to understand its message God must also interpret it to us through His Holy Spirit for us to be able to fully understand it.

How do I know that? Because I have allowed God to work in me to regenerate my spirit so that I can communicate with Him spiritually. That is why God chose me to write, trained me to write and then used me to write on His word through the inspiration of His Holy Spirit. As I have already confessed I am not a theologian or an academic, merely a professional technical author who has turned his attention to writing on scripture. What is particularly interesting is that to write instructions in industry the equipment or process I am writing about has to work according to the design. If it doesn't I cannot write about it. The same goes with scripture. If scripture was nonsensical I could not write about it as I have done.

Derek had kindly given me a copy of the Pentateuch & Haftorahs with commentary some years before. It was edited by Dr. J. H Hertz and published by The Soncino Press. The book and its comments have greatly helped my understanding the account of God's dealings with men from the creation to the death of Jacob and have found it very useful. Although nothing has been quoted word for word, it must be acknowledged that the comments in that book have helped my understanding of the Jewish perceptions of the message of Genesis. On this point I willingly and enthusiastically admit that Israel IS God's first born (Derek is part of that company); a fact that must never be denied.

The Christian gospel is founded on the First Testament, and does not deny it, rather it is a natural progression of it in the plan of God for the whole of mankind. The Gospel message is for the Jew first and then the Gentile. I am grafted into Israel, not the other way around (Romans 9-11). It is my privilege to have been rescued from spiritual death by the Jewish Messiah and am counted as part of Israel by Him.

Some edited notes on the comparison between the life of Joseph son of Jacob and Jesus son of Joseph produced by Elhanan ben Avraham have been nothing short of exciting to my spirit and an edited version has been provided in Chapter 8.

The thoughts in this volume are a result of my current:

1.   dynamic relationship with and faith in God.

2.   situation where I am having to put my complete trust in God for the future and His requirement that I do so without wavering.

3.   understanding of the way God was so inseparably involved in the lives of the key characters mentioned in Genesis.

These are my personal thoughts recorded in the hope that they will be of help to others. They are not the result of studying the writings of scholars except the comments included in the Pentateuch and Haftorahs mentioned above. There is neither a hidden agenda, nor a particular type of person targeted. It is available for those who want to read it!

Since its distribution by email in 2003/4 this book, along with my later books on Exodus, Numbers and Revelation, were translated into Spanish for churches in South America and Chinese, and I was assured by rabbi Aaron, who came to believe in Jesus Christ as his Messiah through my books and worked for a number of years in China for the Lord, that over 400,000 Chinese have studied these books.

2nd Edition

It is now 2015. Derek, who has been studying this book for about eleven years on and off has finally exhausted all that it had to offer and has given me permission to rework the text, probably in the hope of my discovering new things within the biblical text that would allow him to study it in depth further. In this second edition a new section on God has been added and various parts expanded to hopefully bring more clarity to the text.

3rd Edition

New chapter on Lot has been added (2018).

My books do not sell in sufficient quantities for me to be able to afford a proof reader therefore there could well be typographical errors and other mistakes. However, according to Janet Chittock's review (Jan. 2015) on Amazon – she stated that the first edition was great for group study and very challenging. My hope is that with the additional chapter on Lot this third edition will be even more challenging.

4th Edition

Font raised to 12 point and a full edit carrier out.

6th Edition - Evolution

Chapter one has been totally rewritten because the mention of evolution was becoming a distraction. The emphasis for such an important book as this must be about the miraculous creation which was created out of nothing, the awesome creator, and about man's growing relationship with God, his creator. There is no denial intended concerning the findings of archeologists about the apparent development of man. There are no details of how God created man available, except that only He alone could have create all that we see around us and above us, because He alone was present at the time. All we know for certain is that it took millions of years to develop, not six days as we know them, as explained in chapter 9.

It is interesting that in Genesis, which is the introductory book to the whole Bible, chapter 1 to chapter 2:3 ascribes everything to the living God. Mentioning evolution means a flat denial of Divine revelation, for one must be true and the other false. All God's works were pronounced "good" seven times, which denotes spiritual perfection.

Man starts with nothing but a completely new spirit within a new body. He begins his short life in helplessness, ignorance and totally without memory and experience. His whole life is therefore subject to an evolutionary process which applies only to human affairs, an evolution can mean either progress or failure, depending upon the influence of the environmental powers each person experiences.

Whereas man has evolved from living in a cave to a hut and then houses, and travelling by foot then cart and now a powered vehicle and even fly, birds still fly and build nests, foxes and badgers burrow in the ground and feed on what they were programmed by the creator to do. The moment we enter the Divine sphere no trace or vestige of evolution is seen. There is preprogrammed growth and development within the creation, but no passing, dramatic change or evolution[1] being transferred from one to the other.

All God's works are perfect, for He Himself is pure perfection. Within Himself He contains all the wisdom of the world plus much more that has not been or has yet to be revealed, for He is also the creator of the spiritual world of which we know very little, nor do we know anything about the wonder of His habitation, which is for the moment hidden from us.

We will never properly understand the reason for the dinosaurs, or the theory of the emergence of man brought about by the finding of skeletal remains which suggests that man evolved. However we interpret those remains, there is no definitive proof that the theory is valid, for it is just that, a theory.

Evolution is primarily a theory and is very limited in its scope because someone had to be behind the creation purely because the world and the universe are so complex, with every part, both miniscule and gigantic being dependent upon one or more other parts. Saying

---

[1]   *Evolution means the process by which different kinds of living organisms are believed to have developed from earlier forms. That is completely different from living things developing like a caterpillar turning into a butterfly which is predesigned into them.*

the appearance of the world and the universe just happened tests the intelligence of the majority of the population of the earth. It does not answer the question of how and why and what happens in the future, particularly with the growing problem of global warming.

What is for sure is that God was the only being present at the moment of creation, and we have a proven record of God's involvement with man throughout the millennia and the intensity of the love He has shown man throughout that time.

It is important to remember that man is the pinnacle of His creation and that God created man in love so that He could work with him throughout his lifetime. The whole of the history of Israel is all about their willingness or unwillingness to serve their God, and all that happened to them when they tried to do things their own way. The other remarkable thing is that almighty God should tie Himself to the nation of Israel by being known as the God of Israel.

This earth is a testing ground for man. The initial test was the choice of the fruit of the two trees in the centre of the garden. The current test is to remain faithful to our Lord and saviour and with His help, putting on the whole armour of God, withstand all the fiery darts of the Devil.

Genesis is the essential introduction to the Bible, not only because it tells us what happened when God created the earth and the universe, but the reason why Satan has such a hold on the world and what we need to do to stay faithful to God.

May the God who is the same yesterday, today and forever be your constant and consistent source of inspiration and fulfilment as you reach out to Him through prayer and the study of His word, the Word of Truth.

Peter

Please do not read this work without referring to scripture, particularly the references.
It is essential that you assure yourself of the truth of what is written here by checking up everything and confirming it with scripture, and through prayer.
(1 Jn. 4:1).

ACKNOWLEDGMENTS

Derek who first got me writing on scripture and continues to encourage me.

Rabbi Aaron who had me write on the book of Revelation and Moses' Tent of the Meeting and became addicted to my writing.

To the Lord my God who called me to write on His word through Derek and has inspired me as I carry out His will.

Pauline Rae of TwinVerse Prime who contacted me through social media and has agreed to publish all 34 of my current list of books

Ramon who has so skillfully designed the cover of this book

INTRODUCTION

This Introduction provides a list of unusual words with interpretation.

This first list will not necessarily be as extensive as it should be but it will be extended as additional words needing such an explanation are brought to my attention.

Word	Meaning
Man	God made man (an individual) first and from a rib of that man God made a woman who was to be a helpmeet for the man (Gen. 2:21-24). The responsibility of the man was to love and take care of the woman as he did for himself for they became one flesh once their bodies had been joined through intercourse. Therefore husbands and wives have their particular and individual responsibilities towards each other (1 Pet 3:1-7; 1 Cor 7:1-16; Eph. 5:22-33; Col. 3:18-19).

Although the whole emphasis of the creation of male and female was on procreation Paul spoke of the advantage to both men and women of being single. However the rule that man was given authority over woman still remained not to belittle or enslave the woman but to treat her with respect, allow her to do her work unrestricted by oppressive rules and look after her for man was given that responsibility by God and it must not be abused.

Word	Meaning

It is true that vertically before God we are the same and both men and women must give an account of themselves to God at the final judgement. However horizontally whilst on earth the position of the man over the woman still remains whatever man might say

Men   **As for Man**

Woman Man covers both sexes. Although the first woman was created as a support the man, that is the strictly confined to their earthbound relationship. As far as God is concerned spiritually men and women are equal and He deals with individuals of both sexes in the same way. All individuals must seek after God and He will appoint them tasks according to the gifts with which He has provided them.

G-d Many Jews, even those who have come into a knowledge and belief in the Messiah, are unable to fully pronounce the name of God omitting the vowel, just as Yahweh and Jehovah can only be used without the vowels because of their respect for His uniqueness and awesomeness. To the true Jew God is unknowable and so mighty and hugely complex that He is indescribable, so they prefer to leave out the vowel when using His name in the text. Where it is not my work, I wish to show respect for the author by using his text, taken from the web and sent to me by a friend, with as little alteration as possible.

Remez "hint" the interpretation of Scripture at the level of allusive implication. For instance, Pidyon Haben - redemption of the first-born - is alluded to by an acronym of the letters of Bereshit, which spell "ben rishon acharei shloshim yom tifdeh" - the first son you shall redeem after thirty days.

One of the paths of Remez is that of Gematria, the search for meaning by evaluating the numerical equivalents of Hebrew words and verses by using the number values of the letters of the Aleph Bet (Aleph = 1, Bet = 2, ...etc.).

2

Tehilim   Psalms – there are a number of Hebrew words used in Chapter 7 for which I have not given an English equivalent. There is so much of worth in what Elhanan ben Avraham has written that I have not be very concerned about providing them.

Some people have told me that it is not an easy or light read; some have called it scholarly, although I am far from being a scholar with my educational background, and others have called it inspired. At first concerned about making it lighter so that more people would be able to read it and understand it, reading through it many times to see how changes could be made, I have found it impossible to do so.

Then I realized that the work reflect my own growing desire over many years for an ever deeper understanding of God's word, and as it was God Himself who, through Derek, inspired me to write what has been written, it would be reasonable to say that the work was not intended as a casual read that could be put down at the end and forgotten, but be an encouragement for those serious about knowing God to seek after truth, opening their hearts to receive spiritual food direct from God through the Holy Spirit.

The emphasis for those who read it must be a hunger for a deeper understanding of not just the Word but for a knowledge and understanding of God Himself, Blessed be His Name.

There is one other important matter that must be taken into account when studying scripture and that concerns the Fatherhood of God. The Lord Jesus Christ, the Jews' Messiah, constantly and consistently referred to the Father who sent Him. Some lay and ordained members of various churches have attempted to teach that God has no gender. I challenge that teaching as inserting into the minds of individuals, particularly those who are young in the faith or just starting out as a believer, an alternative thought, a tactic used by Satan from the beginning. To me the Bible is sacred text, therefore if the Son of the living God refers to God as His Father then I believe in God as Father, Son and Holy Spirit.

Those of us who teach and lead in the universal and spiritual church of God, which the living Lord founded on His death and resurrection and includes all who truly love and serve the Lord, will be judged far more harshly than any other member of that church, Jew or Gentile. So to all leaders and believers I say, be ever prayerful and watchful regarding the truth of what you believe and for which you give witness, because if it does not strictly accord with the truth of God, then there is a danger that on the day of judgement you will be found wanting. Without inspiration from the Holy Spirit who was sent to guide us into all truth (Jn. 16:13 – 15) we will be unable to speak the truth in love.

A Note of Caution

Since the original distribution of this work on Genesis then Exodus Part 1, I have been informed that those who are not able to possess a complete Bible, that is one that contains what is called the 'Old' and 'New' testaments, have been enjoying the Old or First Testament without feeling the need to study the New or Second Testament or enjoying the Second and neglecting the First.

This is very DANGEROUS! Both testaments are essential to our spiritual well being and cannot be separated because they provide us with the complete account of God's dealing with Man as my book "The Tent of the Meeting : Illustrating God's Plan of Salvation" clearly demonstrates.

The Messiah Himself said that He had come to fulfil the Law not destroy it. Romans 9-11 explains very clearly that the Jews are still God's chosen people and those born as Gentiles (non-Jews) through their acceptance of the life, death and resurrection of the Lord Jesus are grafted onto the spiritual Israel, joining those Jews who have accepted the appearance of their Messiah Yeshua (Jesus) and His sacrifice on the cross according to prophetic announcements in their scriptures.

There are some prophecies in the first testament that are still to be realized, as are prophecies in the second testament.

God Himself is not divided so neither should His Word or those that are truly surrendered to Him.

May God, through your dedication to Him in prayer and the study of His word, direct your hearts and minds in the knowledge and love of Him, and may your relationship with Him deepen with every word you read and every moment you open your heart to Him through prayer, both active and passive.

About the Theory of Evolution (see Evolution in the Preface)

Having rightly been contacted by an ardent creationist who disputed my mentioning the theory of evolution in the previous editions of this book, it is important to make it very clear that it is only the fact that we need to realize the creation did not happen in an instance but over billions of years that evolution was mentioned. In response to the dispute I have totally rewritten chapter one.

The problem is, to take God out of the equation, which the evolutionists do, provides no answer as to how and why the earth and surrounding universe was created and its purpose. Indeed what is man's purpose given that the world in this present age is in such a mess, far from the ideal of the original garden of Eden. The world is experiencing wars and rumours of wars, unrest throughout the world and global warming which cannot be sorted out because of diversity amongst the nations which is preventing agreement on how it should be tackled. Only God can unify mankind and correct the disastrous situation of the increasing temperature of the planet He created specifically for man.

In the Holy Bible there is a certainty in the fact that God existed before anything came into being and it was He who, through His absolute power and authority, created the heavens and the earth to provide a place for man who He created in His own image.

What is more the Bible is specific in telling us that this creator cared about His creation and through a chosen nation, wanted to tell the whole of mankind about His love and have them love Him in return. Without that knowledge there can be no meaningful understanding of why the world was created, or by whom. The evolutionists prefer to leave it as an open question because they do not know the answer.

In their ignorance the evolutionists are still seeking to find out how the world came into being and why, searching the heavens and the earth for clues that will satisfy their so far unfulfilled desire to discover its origins and purpose. But how do they explain the waters that covered the rock core of the planet at the beginning? Regarding the big bang, they have no explanation to tell us what exploded or how it exploded. It just happened.

On the other hand those of us who believe in an all powerful creative God have no such problems for through having His Spirit speaking to us through the spirit He implanted into us, we have opened up to us the love and knowledge of God and of why the world, the universe and man were created and His eternal purpose for our existence.

Interestingly, He still has all His creative powers to sort out global warming once man has come to his senses and acknowledge God as their creator and give Him the honour due to His name. For according to scripture the earth still has many more years of existence because the Son of God will reign on the earth for a thousand years.

Man is God's creation. The fact that the Spirit of God breathed His spiritual breath into man raising him above the rest of creation was for the sole purpose of God entering into a meaningful, spiritual marriage type relationship with him, which man had to enter into willingly. Man had a choice. Be bonded to God or live a life devoid of the presence of God.

God provided the world as a testing ground for man, an anti-room to heaven to see how man reacted to Him, with the intention of providing a place of love and purity after their physical death, for those who had willingly enter into that spiritual type marriage relationship with Him during their life.

The focus of this book is therefore on the creation and the initial development of that God-Man relationship, up to the moment God took those he had chosen to be His special people into the melting pot of Egypt, turning a group of twelve tribes into a nation under a national leader at the start of a history of that God-Man relationship, which is all part of this book, for without man there is no point to the earth. It is decidedly not about the theory of evolution which has been generated by God ignorant and unbelieving man over time and neglects to give all the credit that is due to God for this remarkable earth and universe.

God was eternal, is eternal, will be eternal for eternity. He has the power to create, sustain and destroy that creation. Unless we are prepared to acknowledge Him, accept His salvation for our sins and totally surrender ourselves to Him, then we will end up, after our physical death, in that place God has prepared for such people, which is devoid of His presence and therefore of His light and overwhelming love.

It is a place of darkness, where there is weeping and wailing and a gnashing of teeth because of its loveless, lightless oppressive atmosphere. It is a place of regret for those that did not following after the promises of God.

1 OUR CREATIVE GOD

The fool says in his heart
there is no God
Ps. 14:1

In the Beginning God (Gen. 1 & 2)

> *1 In the beginning God …*

No study of scripture can be of any worth unless the person of God, who and what He is, is fully established. After all the Bible narrative begins with God and ends with the anticipated return to the earth of God's true born Son,

> *20 He who testifies to these things says, "Surely I am coming quickly. (Rev. 22:20)*

not as the suffering servant in order to die again for the sin of man, but as the victorious High Priest and King who overcame the scourge of death by dying and then rising again[2] demonstrating His power over physical death. What love for man God showed in that sacrifice of his only begotten Son, who was part of the creational team of Father, Son and Holy Spirit.

Before anything existed that exists God was, a Spirit being with personality, living in endless space, unrestricted by time and space for He inhabited it in His omnipresent state, a concept that is impossible for the finite human mind to fully comprehend, restricted as we are to

---

[2]   *See my book: 'A Fresh Look At Easter'*

time, distance and space.

The Bible is all about God and his relationship with the earth He created, and man who is the pinnacle of His creation; for it has His hallmark throughout. Interestingly, although God gave man authority over His creation particularly the living creatures, at no time does it say that He has surrendered full and absolute control of all of it to man or anyone else, or the support of its operation. Only He has the power to do that.

Paul in his second letter to Timothy (chapter 3) wrote:

> *16 All Scripture is given by inspiration of God, and is profitable for doctrine, for reproof, for correction, for instruction in righteousness,*
> *17 that the man of God may be complete, thoroughly equipped for every good work.*

And Peter in his second letter (chapter 1) wrote:

> *20 knowing this first, that no prophecy of Scripture is of any private interpretation,*
> *21 for prophecy never came by the will of man, but holy men of God spoke as they were moved by the Holy Spirit.*

Therefore from the first verse we have the author identified as both creator and Lord as recorded in this case by Moses who wrote as he was inspired by the Holy Spirit. For who was alive in the very beginning to record what happened apart from God Himself? So the word is the only true record of the events of the creation, which provides us with the principle features of the creation without going into detail about the intricacies of how it was achieved.

It is only curious fallen man that wants to know the intimate details, all the while ignoring the principle teaching of scripture which is all about man's spiritual relationship with his creator. What matters most is for mankind to understand who God is and how we, being part of His creation, relate to Him as our Father for He created us for a purpose which is explained in the rest of scripture. The principles of the creation merely guide us to that truth.

The very first statement is very brief, just four words *In the beginning God.* How many men and women over the centuries have studied the heavens and the earth, seeking to find any information regarding the origin of the world and universe, let alone how life began on the earth and developed over the millennia and never found God? How many naturalists expound all they have learned about life on earth and yet have never acknowledged God as the creator?

It is curious to think that God did not need to create anything for He was at peace within Himself as He was. But He chose to create the universe and at its centre to create the earth on which He would create a being in His image, a being that could commune with Him, for He wanted to love him, and be involved with him, for man was created in such a way that without God in their lives they were spiritually incomplete. And it is knowledge of the spiritual aspect of man that is most critical in our understanding of the act of creation.

It was His choice to create all that He created, and, because He is a God of love, He created it in love for the purpose of love being its central theme. What is more He created it out of nothing, for in the beginning there was nothing whatsoever except Him and endless space.

The word used to describe God is Elohim, which is a plural noun for God, which is used to refer to Him as a mark of respect. It is the basis of understanding that God is more than one. Indeed it becomes evident throughout scripture that there are three individuals who are so united that they act in total unison to achieve a single objective, each knowing their place within the Godhead. As scripture unfolds so each member is not only revealed, but also their purpose within the triune God.

YHWH is God's true name.

Some of the Attributes of God

Infinite — He is self-existing, not created and therefore without origin and, because of His pre-existence, is over all of us. The name Jehovah, which is used some 6,800 times in scripture and often translated Lord God, has as its root self-existing. It speaks of His unlimited strength, His sovereignty over all things and His infinite and intrinsic goodness.

Omnipresent — He is everywhere at the same time even though He exists in limitless space where there are no boundaries. This is something impossible for our finite minds to comprehend.

In the Psalms David wrote:

Where can I go from Your Spirit? Or where can I flee from Your presence? If I ascend to heaven, You are there; If I make my bed in Sheol, behold, You are there. If I take the wings of the dawn, If I dwell in the remotest part of the sea, even there Your hand will lead me, And Your right hand will lay hold of me." Psalm 139:7-10

The reason for this is that God is pure Spirit and therefore has no physical form, which is why God told the Israelites they were not to make a carved or formed image, for he has no form that they can use to represent Him.

He is not a ghost, so we cannot possibly imagine what He is like so we must accept Him as a person in whose image we have been made.

Self-Sufficient — He is self-existing, without origin. God did not need to create anything for He was at peace within Himself as He was. The Father has life in Himself, granting the Son to have life in Himself (Jn. 5:26). This also means that He is self-sufficient in all things such as wisdom and power.

Immutable — He has not changed and indeed cannot change for He is from everlasting to everlasting consistently the same. This means that He is completely dependable, a stable and stabilizing force. His promises are unassailable, therefore we can be entirely confident that the God who promised us everlasting life will provide those who accept the conditions of that eternal life with that life (Ro. 8:325 – 39).

Omnipotent — He is the only source of all power [omni meaning all and potent meaning power), which means that there is nothing that he cannot do in or around the earth and universe (Ps.

33:6). Because he is eternal and totally holy and pure, and the source of all love of the greatest kind, unlike human love, His power can only be used for good.

Omniscient — He is all-knowing. The most telling scripture is found in Isaiah 46:9 to 10:

Remember the former things of old, For I am God, and there is no other; I am God, and there is none like Me, Declaring the end from the beginning, and from ancient times things that are not yet done, Saying, 'My counsel shall stand, and I will do all My pleasure.

God not only knows Himself, but being the originator of all that exists in spiritual and physical form, He knows not only all that is known, but all that it is possible to know, so there is nothing that He does not know.

The comforting thing about His omniscience is that there is nothing about us and our situation of which he is ignorant and has the resources to support us in all and every situation and state of mind.

Glorious — His purity and holiness result in Him having such a brightness that even the angels have to protect themselves. The light of His countenance is of the brightest and purest kind, totally unblemished.

To Moses God said that he could not look on His face, only His back because the contrast of the brightness of His glory and his sinfulness would be the death of him.

His glory is aligned to His other attributes, His radiance and beauty emanate from all that He is and does and man was created for His glory. indeed it is necessary for man to praise God not for God's sake but for man to understand his place in relation to almighty God, to realize the incredible privilege that is His just to be created by Him and to know Him.

Love — There is nothing in this world that has not been gifted by God and love is at the very centre of all that He does, the controlling factor behind all of His actions within the environment of the world.

It was love that paid the ultimate price of dying on the cross to provide salvation for all mankind. God did not

12

need to do it. To become man and suffer spiritually and physically, but it was because of His infinite, compassionate love that cause Him to do it.

Wisdom — Paul in his letter to the Romans wrote:

> *O, the depth of the riches both of the wisdom and knowledge of God! How unsearchable are His judgments and unfathomable His ways. (Ro. 11:33).*

And in Proverbs 2:6, 7

> *For the Lord gives wisdom;*
>
> *From His mouth come knowledge and understanding;*
>
> *He stores up sound wisdom for the upright;*
>
> *He is a shield to those who walk with integrity;*

God is the source of wisdom for he has both knowledge and understanding.

Faithful — God has kept His side of the covenant even though the nation of Israel has been at times totally negligent.

The Creation (Gen. 1 & 2)

1   *In the beginning God created the heavens and the earth.*

In studying this verse we initially discover two things. First the Father (God), and then the Son because He is the Word (Jn. 1:1 – 5). In the second verse it mentions the Spirit of God which reveals the part of the Godhead who does the work of creation.

God did not create the earth from any preexisting materials, for in the very beginning there was nothing, just empty space. So it was out of nothing that the earth was created, and according to Peter in his second letter (2 Peter 3:10), in the end it will all be burned up and return to nothing, just as man is made from the dust of the earth, and at his physical death it is to dust his physical body will return, leaving his soul and spirit to pass on into the spiritual sphere.

So what can we learn about God in the beginning, in relation to what was made?

13

1. He had all the creative powers and abilities necessary, for He is and always has been sufficient in Himself and has existed from eternity and will exist into eternity, for He was never born and will never die[3].

2. He is completely separate from His creation. As creator He also has full ownership of the creation in its entirety, with man the most important element of it, although it is very clear that the earth was made for man not man for the earth.

3. Being omnipresent throughout eternal space, God has the ability to influence His creation at will from within and without, for He has retained full authority over it. But where it says that He will shake the heavens and the earth, He and His abode are completely unshakable, so that the creation is contained within a small area of eternal space, not the whole of it. This provides an indication of the true vastness of eternal space, which is beyond man's capacity to imagine.

4. As creator he has knowledge of all things, in fact there is no subject involved in the creation or otherwise that is unknown to Him for He is omniscient, all-knowing. Indeed there is not a subject used by man that was not from Him.

5. Considering the vastness of the universe, which is beyond the wit and ability of man to fathom, God has shown His unrestricted power to not just create but control the whole of creation, down to the last miniscule item, which is demonstrated by the overwhelming power of the weather, and the environment as a whole.

How great is the Lord and worthy to be praised.

And the Spirit of God moved upon the face of the deep waters.

By this means the third member of the trinity is revealed. So within the first two verses of the Bible each member of the Trinity is mentioned. It also tells us that it is the Spirit of the living God that caused things to happen for He was present from the moment the

---

[3]   *Physical death only came with man whose life spam diminished over time for Adam lived for nine hundred and ten years, and Methuselah for nine hundred and sixty nine years, but after the flood the length of life gradually reduced.*

formless earth appeared and has remained in the earth, although not earth bound for He is omnipresent, throughout the life of the earth.

It is interesting that when the Son was on earth and did things that were not according to the natural happenings, it was the Spirit, with whom He was endowed without measure because the three members of the Trinity can never be separated, who with His creational skills was able to do such things as bring the soul back to the dead thus bringing them back to life, still the storm, heal the sick. He did these things because it was He who caused the creation to happen at the word of the Son, so what happened in the beginning was being repeated during the ministry of the Son. How else could the Son, in His human body, know what others were thinking, but through the Holy Spirit who alone can enter into the body of people and know their thoughts?

It refers to the waters as being deep for the dry land had not yet appeared so all the water on the earth, currently in the seas, rivers and lakes, was above the rock foundation of the world.

3 And God said,

When considering God and all that He did during the creation it must be remembered that God is entirely Spirit and therefore does not have vocal cords like man. Where it says, *And God said*, it is by His intellect and will that He does things. The Father desired light to be created, the Son spoke the word and the Spirit performed the act of creating light. Just like in our bodies, the brain does not actually speak to cause the legs to move, it is an act of unconscious thought and will.

However God can cause speech to be heard, just as the Father spoke to the Israelites from the top of Mount Sinai and after the baptism of His Son by John saying, *This is My beloved Son in whom I am well pleased.* Certainly He has 'spoken' to me or for I have been able to hear clearly what He was saying to me, so that it is legitimate to say, *God said.*

When the Son became flesh to dwell amongst men, He spoke as we speak for He had the body of man. Also in the first testament when the Son appeared to Abraham as Melchizedek he was able to 'speak' as are the angels when they appear to man, for nothing is impossible to God.

3 And God said, Let there be light: and there was light

The majority of what God made requires light for it gives warmth, feeds us with vitamins, enables the eyes to see and the plants to grow. But this was not the sun for that was not created until phase four.

How and where on the face of the earth the light appeared is not recorded but it appeared on the earth, for the heavens and the sky had not yet been created, but it must be understood to be on the highest part of the earth which was still covered by the deep waters. The only other time the earth was covered in water was at the time of Noah when he was in the ark.

4 And God saw the light, that it was good:

God is light and in Him there is no darkness at all, says the word, for light was intrinsic to Him, of His very being. Because He is light, He considered it necessary to create light on the earth, for light is energy. Little happens in complete darkness, everything works at a much slower pace than in the light, for light is not only pure energy, but also imparts energy.

Darkness hides things for it is merely the absence of light, but light reveals; which is why the Word is referred to as light for it spreads light and reveals the works of God and the works of those that prefer darkness rather than light, for their deeds are evil.

And God saw the light, that it was good:

As He was light He desired light to shine upon His newly created earth, which was to be at the centre of His creation. The jewel in the crown of creation. Although there is much speculation about the possibility of there being life on other planets in other galaxies, it is very clear that this word of God, the Divine word of the one and only living God, focuses on just one earth, its creation and what has happened on the earth. So there is no other earth for the simple reason

16

God sent His only Son to be clothed in human flesh and die for the sins of man. The Bible explicitly tells of God's relationship with man since his creation, and includes promises of all that is to come, so there cannot be another earth.

In recording that God said the light was good, it is not saying that God was amazed by it, but that mentioning that He approved of it indicates to man that it is significant and worthy of praise.

and God divided the light from the darkness.

This proves that light and darkness cannot coexist. Light is pure energy whereas darkness is merely the absence of light, for it has no energy within it. So where there is light there can be no darkness, but it was necessary for this to be made clear that God separated the light from the darkness. When an object interrupts beams of light it creates shadows. Today the night comes to one side of the earth for it can only shine on the side nearest to it because light goes in a straight line.

How God separated the light from the darkness without the sun being in position and the earth revolving is unknown, but the light that He caused to shine on the earth moved to create an area of light and an area of darkness.

5 God called the light day and the darkness night.

God called so that the light and darkness could be distinguished from one another because the principle feature of light revealing truth and darkness hiding evil is used throughout scripture.

So the evening and the morning were the first day.

Notice that until light was created darkness covered the deep, that is the deep waters that covered the earth. So the day started in the evening. It was not until the appearance of light that the first day could be acclaimed, which is why the Jewish day starts in the evening. By saying *So the evening and the morning were the first day* establishes what constitutes a day, but during the creation the day was not 24 hours as we know it today, for the sun was not put in place until day four and the time and seasons had not been established until the earth's central axis was tilted.

6 Then God said, "Let there be a firmament

So far God had created the earth and light, the next stage was to create the heavens. Isaiah (40:22) wrote:

It is He who sits above the circle of the earth,

. . .

Who stretches out the heavens like a curtain,
And spreads them out like a tent to dwell in.

And Psalm 104:2 talks about God stretching out the heaven like a curtain.

in the midst of the waters, and
let it divide the waters from the waters.

That means there was a separation of the waters covering the earth, some being used to create the sky (the firmament) and provide the earth with clouds which water the earth (2 Peter 3:5). Interestingly there is no mention of the waters covering the earth in the *beginning* in the theory of evolution.

According to the Biblical account of the creation, the air was in the midst of the waters separating the clouds from the standing water.

8 And God called the firmament Heaven.
So the evening and the morning were the second day.

This activity ended another 'day', or phase in the creation of the earth and heavens which was not the 24 hours that we know today.

9 Then God said, "Let the waters under the heavens be gathered
together into one place, and let the dry land appear"; and it was so.

This was when the surface of the earth buckled and shifted to provide land mass for the continents and mountains, hills and valleys and vast valleys for the oceans. It was helped by much volcanic activity, for the centre of the earth is exceptionally hot. Many islands were created by hot molten ash spilling out of openings in the earth's surface.

10 And God called the dry land earth, and the gathering together of the waters He called Seas.

This was His creation and God was taking ownership of it by naming everything; the land and water, earth and environment. What is interesting is that man can live without food for some time, but the absence of water can cause dehydration very quickly.

And God saw that it was good.

We are now seeing form beginning to appear out of the chaos of the first and second days. Gradually the earth is beginning to take on the shape of things to come.

11 Then God said, "Let the earth bring forth grass, the herb that yields seed, and the fruit tree that yields fruit according to its kind, whose seed is in itself, on the earth"; and it was so.
12 The earth brought forth grass, the herb that yields seed according to its kind, and the tree that yields fruit, whose seed is in itself according to its kind. And God saw that it was good.

What is so interesting is that God willed and it was done, not in a chaotic but structured manner. The vegetation that appeared did not grow from seed for no plant had previously grown to produce seed. *the herb that yields seed, and the fruit tree that yields fruit according to its kind, whose seed is in itself, on the earth,* these parent plants appeared as if out of nowhere.

The answer to the question, Which came first, the chicken or the egg? is the chicken, for a live chicken, hen and cock, had to be first to lay the egg for how else would the egg appear and be kept warm to hatch? And how did the chicken appear. It was created by God, just as the first man was created and only when the woman was created could children be born to them.

It was the earthly light that encouraged the plants to grow and mature. Because it says *Let the earth bring forth grass* it is reasonable to assume that it grew from nothing to produce seed that would produce the next crop

13 The evening and the morning were the third day.

The third day had passed by which time light had appeared, the waters had been separated into the heavenly waters, causing the firmament to appear which we see as the sky, and the waters covering the earth were separated into seas, lakes and rivers. So on the second day the heavenlies were created through the medium of the waters covering the earth.

How interesting that there should be water covering the surface of the earth and through the separation of the water on the earth by using some of it to create the spiritual world and the universe. On the earth water is the most essential ingredient in plants and people, for those starved of water perish, but they can go days without food.

The crust of the earth is miles thick and it has been discovered the further down into the crust man has ventured the hotter it gets to the point where it is unbearable, so how can a big bang have achieved that? Also consider the power that was required to cause the crust of the earth to move. But God caused it to happen along with volcanic activity to create mountains, hills and valleys with the waters covering the earth being segregated into seas, lakes and rivers.

So the cycle of the movement of water began, with it being sucked up into the sky from the seas to produce clouds, the water descending as rain watering the ground and filling the rivers which flow to the sea.

Also the appearance of grasses, plants and trees which all took up moisture from the ground. This was the first appearance of created life that could reproduce itself.

The earth had progressed from unformed rock with a moulten core, covered in water into a well-organized entity. After creating the spiritual heaven, and causing the surface of the earth to buckle creating mountains and valleys to confine the water into separate areas, dry ground was revealed on which living things started to grow[4].

God was now ready for the next stage of His creation.

> *14   And God said, Let there be lights in the firmament of the heaven to divide the day from the night; and let them be for signs, and for seasons, and for days, and years:*
> *15   and let them be for lights in the firmament of the heaven to give light upon the earth: and it was so.*
> *16   And God made two great lights; the greater light to rule the day, and the lesser light to rule the night: he made the stars also.*

On the fourth day the sun was unveiled in all its glory and began to shine, continuing the night and day cycle previously established, with the moon reflecting the light of the sun during the night, the lesser light, and the sun, the greater light, shining by day. The tilting of the axis of the spinning earth introduced the seasons along with time, because for the first time regulated days and years were established.

What is interesting is the clear and airless vast distances in the cosmos allowed the light from the fiercely burning sun to pass unrestricted over vast distances lighting up and warming the earth and all other planets in our solar system which appear to us as stars. And the sun has not been reduced in size or brightness over all the years it has been burning.

> *17   And God set them in the firmament of the heaven to give light upon the earth,*
> *18   to rule over the day and the night, and to divide the light from the darkness: and God saw that it was good.*
> *19   And the evening and the morning were the fourth day.*

This introduced the physical firmament of the sun and planets, which appear to us as stars, the formation of which initially guided people travelling over land and sea in ancient times. And again in naming everything including the night and day, seasons, days and years God established His ownership of the developing earth.

---

[4]   *It is interesting that after about a year under water, the dove Noah sent out of the ark brought back a leaf. How did plants appear after all that time under water?*

Living beings Appear

It is the sun, the greater light, that encourages life by giving it light and warmth and vitamins. The moon reflects light from the sun and is responsible for the tides and much more.

> *20 And God said, Let the waters bring forth an abundance of living creatures, and fowl that fly above the earth in the open firmament of heaven.*
> *21 God created great whales, and every living creature that moves, with which the waters abounded, after their kind, and every winged fowl after its kind: and God saw that it was good.*

After setting the heavens in order, it was now time to focus on the earth and the lower parts such as the ancient waters, which were now confined to specific areas of the earth, and the air, which now contained oxygen and other elements to sustain living creatures.

God now entered into creating active life, creatures that moved rather than the static plant life, starting with fish in the sea from great whales and all life such as molluscs and other creatures that live in the sea, along with fowls that flew in the air above the sea and land.

God was clearly beginning to prepare the earth for the introduction of man.

> *22 And God blessed them, saying, Be fruitful, and multiply, and fill the waters in the seas, and let fowl multiply in the earth.*
> *23 And the evening and the morning were the fifth day.*

The plant life produced seed to replicate themselves, whereas with these living creatures it was necessary for the male and female to get together to reproduce, hence God blessed them saying , *Be fruitful, and multiply, and fill the waters in the seas, and let fowl multiply in the earth.* Indeed it is interesting that creatures have an inbuilt desire to mate and reproduce.

> *24 And God said, Let the earth bring forth the living creature after his kind, cattle, and creeping thing, and beast of the earth after his kind: and it was so.*

*25 And God made the beast of the earth after his kind, and cattle
after their kind, and everything that creeps upon the earth after his
kind: and God saw that it was good.*

Finally God dealt with creatures that live on the land, that breath air.
In verse 24 the beast is mentioned last but in verse 25 it is mentioned
first which possibly indicates that no creature is preferred.

In regard to the creatures living in the water, the sky, and the land
some lived off others in a pecking order and others lived off greenery
in the sea or dry land.

About Dinosaurs

It cannot be denied that amazing creatures first walked on the earth,
swam in the sea and flew in the air, because fossilized remains have been
discovered over the centuries as the earth gives up its stored secrets.
Charles Darwin, who at no time said there was no God, was a scientist
and observer who, in considering the data he had accumulated, came
to certain conclusions.

What is interesting is when touring the Galapagos Islands, we saw
how a newly formed island of magna produces grass and shrubs, as
though the creation process was still on going.

The word Dinosaur was first coined by a Richard Owen in 1841, but
previous to that it is possible that fossilized remains of creatures given
up by the earth were called dragons. It has since become a science in
its own right.

Christians cannot ignore the hard facts exposed by the earth and
must somehow equate these facts with the Biblical account which
is sparce. In verses 20, 21 and 24, 25 the creation of all the living
creatures is covered merely by saying that God created them, which He
undeniably did because of the first verse where it says, *In the beginning
God created the heaven and the earth*, and because of tested truth of the
Biblical account of the development of man and the accuracy of the
history of the human race, centred on Israel.

God does not lie, He has no need to for He has nothing to hide
and is from everlasting to everlasting and is the only one who could
have created all things out of nothing. His powerful influence is still

experienced today by those that believe in Him.

So the fact that God created the heavens and the earth out of nothing through His own ability is in no doubt. What we need to do is to try and understand how He did it, which we will probably not fully know until we are with Him in His place of rest, for as Paul wrote to the Corinthians (13:12), *For now we see in a mirror, dimly, but then face to face. Now I know in part, but then I shall know just as I also am known.*

It is well known that the earth is billions of years old and that man appeared very much later than the foundations of the earth were laid. What happened in the very beginning is unknown and without inspiration from the Holy Spirit is likely to remain unknown.

The Creation of Man

> 26 *And God said, Let us make man in our image, after our likeness: and let them have dominion over the fish of the sea, and over the fowl of the air, and over the cattle, and over all the earth, and over every creeping thing.*
> 27 *So God created man in his own image, in the image of God created he him; male and female created he them.*

Paleoanthropology is the part of science that studies human evolution, but it is all based on the study of skeletal remains. In short, the conclusions are down to supposition by humans about their origin. Yet in spite of all the so called evidence, only God was there at the time of the creation, so His word must supersede man's flawed research and guess work.

What really matters is not only our personal spiritual experience of being united with God through the shed blood of our Lord and Saviour, Jesus, but the proven record of the way in which God has involved Himself in the life of man in general and in the personal lives of individuals such as the patriarch, prophets and disciples in particular as recorded in scripture, proving beyond doubt that the eternal God who created all things is very much alive and active in the affairs of men.

Whilst it is true that the limited information in the Bible does not give us all the answers, and the factual findings from the earth seem to clash with what the word tells us, it is essential that we deal with the known truth that God exists and is all powerful and seeks to be spiritually bonded with those that believe.

Why bring doubt through the lack of Biblical information regarding fossils and skeletons that have been found, when man's relationship with God can lead to eternal life through a dynamic spiritual relationship with Him.

The Bible, which is Holy Spirit inspired, tells us that God created man in His own image or likeness. In other words man was specially created to be compatible with God from the start, for man was to be the culmination of His creation, the pinnacle of His achievement.

In Genesis chapter 2 we find out *the Lord God formed man of the dust of the ground, and breathed into his nostrils the breath of life; and man became a living being.* With God being pure Spirit, it was essential for man, if he was to be compatible with God, to have a spirit so that Spirit could communicate with spirit. How else could God communicate with man?

Man + breath of God

BODY SOUL SPIRIT

To put it another way:

Body	Soul	Spirit
Flesh	The person's Character and controller of the body.	Spirit communes with God

So in creating man, God designed in him a need for His involvement. Just as the three members of the Godhead are bonded together so that they think and act as one, so God wanted the same relationship with man. (Jn. 17:21) True life can only be achieved when Man is willingly in total spiritual union with God, for why else would God breathe the breath of His Spirit into the nostrils of man.

Just as Jesus came to do the will of Him who sent Him. So too is man bound to God in such a way that he too must do the will of God, as Jesus said:

"Not everyone who says to Me, 'Lord, Lord,' shall enter the kingdom of heaven, but he who does the will of My Father in heaven. (Matt. 7:21)

Undoubtedly God knows best. That does not mean we are to become robots, for we are required to live our own lives, make our own decisions, but as we are guided by God for we need His help to guide us through life. To help and bless us. In our lives we all meet with difficulties, for many of which we do not know the answer, but God does. He is there to guard and guide us through the difficult times and bless us in the good times.

This is what God told the children of Israel through Moses (Deut. 30:19, 20):

I call heaven and earth as witnesses today against you, that I have set before you life and death, blessing and cursing; therefore choose life, that both you and your descendants may live; that you may love the Lord your God, that you may obey His voice, and that you may cling to Him, for He is your life and the length of your days; and that you may dwell in the land which the Lord swore to your fathers, to Abraham, Isaac, and Jacob, to give them."

Earth is a testing ground for heaven. God offers us life and blessing and all we have to do is to be a loyal son or daughter and love the God who created us, and obey His instructions on the best way to live our lives so that when we die, He will look after us and provide us with a place of eternal rest. We are to be family to Him, to live within the family of God, owing our allegiance to Him as our Father and the head of the family, who always knows what is best for us. And having been focused on loving God all through my life I can say that life becomes a joy when lived under His loving care.

It is interesting that when God created the dry ground the Bible says, *God said, "Let the earth bring forth*; when the seas were created, *God said, Let the waters bring forth,* when the earth was to be filled with living creatures *God said, Let the earth bring forth.* But when man was created we are told, *God said, Let us make man in our image, after our likeness.* It was a join decision of the triune God to *make man in our image, after our likeness,* so that man is like the Father, Son and Holy Spirit. Not the same as, but like them, with decision making, speaking and spiritual attributes.

Man was to be the only created being that stood upright, had of himself flexibility in movement, dexterity so that he was able to perform complex tasks, had a mind that could work out complex equations, could organized himself into communities and nations, a soul and, very importantly, a God breathed spirit within him (Gen. 2:7) with which he alone of all creation could use to communicate directly with God.

He was to be able to think for himself, make decisions, be in control of himself, be creative and able to assert his God given authority over the creation. But more than that, man was to be able to relate to God, for he was born of Him for His good pleasure.

God made man with the sole intention of him being in an intimated relationship with Him, so that they could work intimately together for the good of the whole of creation. Building a world according to God's initial design and purpose.

God, as his creator, was to be Father to man throughout his life, with a Father/son relationship being developed between them, for God created man in order to be directly engaged in his life on the earth.

Yes God gave man independence of thought and will, but that was so that man was not an automaton, automatically doing what God told Him would not create a living relationship based on love. The relationship between God and man had to be through mutual respect, a willingness to be spiritually bonded together and for man, in his own way, and by his own will, to be obedient to the will and purposes of God for himself.

How could almighty God bless the man He loves so much except he acknowledges God as His maker and master. The Israelites were given the option between life and death (Deut. 30:15), sadly so often they chose disobedience and death.

In the very beginning we read that God walked with man in the cool of the day (Gen. 3:8), so the first man actually saw God, through being spiritually attuned to Him. But then sin got in the way, so a Messiah was sent to repair the relationship between God and man, a restoration made possible by God alone, a restoration that man had to accept or reject; with no possibility of being undecided.

The new relationship could never bring back the same pure intimacy that Adam experienced at first when he was still in his pure state, when God walked with him in the cool of the day, but an intimate relationship nonetheless which was based on the intimacy of Spirit with spirit until we are actually in the presence of God in our risen spiritual state.

So the acceptance by man of God's offer of eternal salvation meant man entering into an intimate spiritual relationship with his creator, for as the Messiah prayed (Jn. 17):

> 20 *"I do not pray for these alone, but also for those who will believe in Me through their word;*
> 21 *that they may all be one, as You, Father, are in Me, and I in You; that they also may be one in Us, that the world may believe that You sent Me.*
> 22 *And the glory which You gave Me I have given them, that they may be one just as We are one:*
> 23 *I in them, and You in Me; that they may be made perfect in one, and that the world may know that You have sent Me, and have loved them as You have loved Me.*

This oneness was to be a spiritual marriage, a bonding together of the Spirit of God with the spirit within man, which required man to be completely obedient to the will and purposes of God for him.

For God did not create the earth for Him to then sit back and allow things to happen. No. He had a purpose for the world, to prepare man for entering into His eternal place of rest. Remember the earth and the universe did not fill the enormity of endless space, for God had a space of his own so that when He says He will shake the heavens and the earth, the sea and the dry land, he did not include that part of space which was His abode.

That is how special man was to be to God.

> *31 And God saw everything that he had made, and, behold, it was very good. And the evening and the morning were the sixth day.*

So the creational process came to an end on the sixth day with God blessing the man He created telling them to, *Be fruitful and multiply; fill the earth and subdue it; have dominion over the fish of the sea, over the birds of the air, and over every living thing that moves on the earth.*

2 MANKIND IN CREATION

My son, if you receive my words,
And treasure my commands within you,
So that you incline your ear to wisdom,
And apply your heart to understanding;
If you seek her as silver,
And search for her as for hidden treasure;
Then you will understand the fear of the Lord,
And find the knowledge of God.
(Prov. 2:1,2,4,5)

The Temptation of Man (Gen. 3)

Appointing Adam and his wife Eve as the gardeners in His garden in Eden, God gave them complete freedom in it. However, as a test two trees were planted in the middle of the garden, the Tree of Life and the Tree of the Knowledge of Good and Evil. As vegetarians, Adam and his wife were allowed to eat of any fruit in the garden, the only exception being the fruit of the Tree of the Knowledge of Good and Evil. No restriction was placed on eating the fruit of the Tree of Life.

The picture being painted in Genesis, starts with the background of a perfect creation that God was pleased with, and man in perfect spiritual union with God. The first two chapters of the book focus on God and His time of creating the world and the universe in which it was positioned.

But this was all to change for although it was originally created illustrating the heights of man in perfect communion with God, it was soon to change introducing the darkness of evil and the depths of his fall due to his own fleshly desires. What Satan did to spoil the idyll was to appeal to man's baser instincts of wanting knowledge and being 'as God' to know good and evil.

Who is Satan?

From the very beginning of the life of man we are immediately confronted with a character called the serpent who beguiled Eve and caused Adam to sin. But who is this serpent and how come he has attracted to himself the names of Lucifer (Son of the Morning), Satan (primarily meaning "to obstruct, oppose") and the Devil (described as a fallen angel, the father of lies Jn. 8:44).

He was possibly the first and therefore the most senior angel to be created, who was not satisfied with his position before God and wanted to be God. No matter how Satan lost angelic dignity, in eminence of reason and subtly of nature, possibly because of his standing in the hierarchy of the angelic host, he surpassed not only all other creatures but humanity itself. Indeed he uses his ability to hide himself whilst influencing the thoughts of people by suggestion, and has the ability to appear to people posing as an angel of light. His ability to deceive is renown, which is why he hates the book of Genesis and the book of Revelation which tells of his permanent demise

With no creational skills, and tasked with promoting the praise and worship of the creator God, through his rebellion he became the promoter of evil and chaos and commands other fallen angels called demons that have the ability to embed themselves into various objects, particularly idols made of various materials and also humans giving them strength far beyond their normal natural strength — as in the case of the demoniac whose name was legion (Matt. 8:28, 34; Mk. 5:1 – 20; Lk. 8:26 – 33).

In Revelation a new character is mentioned, the dragon, which is a combatant in the war in the heavens that has spilled over onto the earth:

> *"And war broke out in heaven: Michael and his angels fought against the dragon. The dragon and his angels fought back, but they were defeated, and there was no longer any place for them in heaven. The great dragon was thrown down, that ancient serpent, who is called the Devil and Satan, and has deceived the whole*

*world; he was cast out of heaven and thrown down to the earth,
and his angels with him." (Rev. 12:8 – 10)*

In order to fully understand the biblical text, it is important to know the characters that are part of the account of God's relationship with man, not only in Genesis but throughout the whole Bible. We have already obtained a brief understanding of God. The other major player is initially introduced as the serpent but by considering other passages of scripture a fuller picture is painted of this unfortunate but important angel. The remainder of this section headed 'Who is Satan' is an extract from my book, 'The Tent of the Meeting : Illustrating God's Plan of Salvation':

God trusted man and gave him authority over all the living things of the earth (Gen. 1:26). At some time, however, in the spiritual sphere of God's creation a rebellion occurred. An archangel referred to as Lucifer, called *"Son of the Morning"*, who was probably the most senior and greatest angel God created decided he wanted be take God's place and be God. He is described as being the *"seal of perfection, full of wisdom and perfect in beauty" (Ez. 28:12)*. Such was his radiance that he was said to have been covered in precious stones and gold, his musical prowess was with timbrels and pipes; this had been prepared in him on the day he was created. He was appointed the guardian angel for the world as it was at the beginning. He is said to have been perfect in all his ways, with unrestricted access to God Himself, and he wielded great power over God's angelic host (Ez. 28:12 – 19). Such was his power and authority that when the archangel Michael disputed with this same angel (the Devil) over the body of Moses, Michael did not have the authority to accuse him directly but called on a higher authority saying, *"The Lord rebuke you!"*. Although the passage in Ezekiel 28 concerns the King of Tyre, the reference to Eden, the Garden of God, gives the true identity away for it was this angel, Lucifer, who appeared to Eve as an angel of light to convince her that to eat of the forbidden tree was good and not really against God's instruction to Adam.

But how did this remarkable cherub, so blessed by God, end up by being brought so low? The text tells us that his heart was lifted up because of his beauty. It is worth recording here that in the context of scripture the heart is considered to be the centre of a person's will and intellect. Not satisfied with the gifts of looks and music and the position of power he held in God's kingdom, (which he received from God when he was created and did not have to earn it for himself), he wanted more and turned his wisdom to corrupting ways for the sake of his splendour. It must be emphasized that all that he had was not his by right; it had been given to him when he was created. It is essential for each one of us not to allow ourselves to be puffed up before God, particularly if we have an outstanding skill or talent for you have received it as a gift from God for the good of all men.

Let us consider this passage carefully, for it tells us a great deal; not only about the prince of this world but also about his influence on men, in this case a king ruling in Tyre (which still exists today). He was probably called Ethbaal and had been a priest before taking the throne from its former occupier. Ethbaal, who gave his daughter in marriage to Ahab, started the worship of Baal in Israel. He considered himself a demi-god and even wiser, in his own opinion, than Daniel whose fame had spread north to Tyre (Zech. 9:2b – 4). His wealth through trade was very great and his influence over the surrounding nations was extensive. This attempt to destroy God's plan of salvation through distracting Israel away from the truth through the worship of false gods was a typical sign of his continued influence and work in the world.

We cannot allow ourselves to be deviated from the central theme of scripture which is all about God's relationship with this world that He has created and the people that inhabit it; and conversely man's relationship with God and the spiritual world that He created along with the world of the flesh. We must recognize the fact that He created all things and that His power over all of His creation is undiminished through time as men's power decays; this means that we must take God seriously. Hear what Isaiah has to say on this matter:

"Have you not known from all that you see around you
and the events that have occurred?
Have you not heard God speaking through His prophets
and all that He has created?
Has it not been told you from the beginning in the Torah
When the earth was formed and came into being?
Have you not understood from the foundations
of the earth how night follows day
And the seasons do not falter?
It is God who sits so high above the circle of the earth
that the people appear small and insignificant like grasshoppers.
Be assured it is God who stretches out the heavens like a curtain
Using them as a tent for Himself.
He has absolute power over all men that rule with power over others
Able to bring their schemes to naught.

It is He alone who distributes power to the weak
And those seemingly insignificant in the eyes of men.
Those who try to live in their own strength shall grow weary,
But those that seek the Lord with all their heart,
Desiring to know Him and serve Him
shall continually renew their inner spiritual strength:
Indeed supplied with His power
they shall mount up on wings like eagles
That use thermal up draughts of air to fly to great heights
They shall run and not be weary
They shall walk and not faint.
(See Is. 40:21 – 31 Consider Ps. 34)

It is essential when considering all these things that we maintain in the back of our minds the realisation that the God who made all things is still the same supreme God to whom we must direct our obedience. The thoughts and devices of unbelieving men will undoubtedly come to naught; for they are here one minute and departed the next and their influence and life products disappear and have little or no effect on future generations.

The greatest danger for anyone is to believe that they are

greater than they are, for from the dust our human bodies were made and to the dust our bodies will return. It is only the God gifted spirit within us that will live on, at which time our influence on the earth will have ended and we will be completely at the mercy of God. For it is His decision alone that will allow us access to heaven, where He lives, or to hell, the place where He is not, according to His rules and not our interpretation of those rules.

In speaking through the prophet Ezekiel, who had been appointed to speak to God's people Israel, particularly in exile (Ez. 2), and referring to the Prince of Tyre God says:

> "... *your heart is lifted up,*
> *And you say, 'I am a god,*
> *I sit in the seat of gods,*
> *In the midst of the seas.'*
> *Yet you are a man, and not a god."*
> *(Ez. 28:2)*

So what are the facts surrounding this king that will help us understand something of what God is saying to us?

The king had his headquarters on an island off the coast which was considered to be sacred to the god Hercules; to the extent that the colonies, the peoples in the surrounding area, considered Tyre to be the mother city of their religion and also of their particular political existence. Such a situation encouraged the king to gain an inflated opinion of his position, coming to the belief that he was a god, even believing that he was God. Daniel's fame had spread to that area and the king thought he was even wiser in his own opinion of himself than Daniel, yet Daniel knew that his wisdom came not from himself but from the Lord God of Israel, the God he had, in obedience to the Torah, committed himself to loving with all his heart, mind and strength.

The king was very clever and had great wisdom in trade so that his riches increased. But he allowed those riches, the beauty of his possessions and his powerful position (not only in his own kingdom but amongst his neighbours) to lift his heart, so that he thought he had attained the high level of a god. God is saying in this scripture that He would show this ruler with an inflated ego that he was as frail as everyone else and would die at the hands of the aliens God would send against him. The very seas that he thought protected him would be the scene of his demise. For God asks him through the prophet Ezekiel, "Will you say before him who slays you, 'I am a god'? You shall die the death of the uncircumcised (unsaved heathen) ..." (Ez. 28:9, 10)

There is an intrinsic danger in scripture in taking literally what is expressed figuratively, and figuratively what is meant to be taken literally. Such is the information contained in the lamentation for the king of Tyre. But there is a matter of equal importance which is the fact that two creations co-exist and operate side by side. The cherubim (above the mercy seat) and seraphim (Is.6:2) were representatives of a different creation and were continually in the presence of God and man on the earth. In this lamentation there is a bringing together of these two creations for what happened to Lucifer is reflected in the manner of the inflated, self opinionated pride that led to the fall of this king (Ez. 28:11 – 19).

> *"You were the seal (the completion) of perfection*
> *Full of wisdom and perfect in beauty."*
> *(v12)*

Such was his rank within the spiritual realm that no one could bring a charge against him except by calling on a higher authority such as in the case when he was there to make accusations against Joshua the high priest; the angel had no recourse but to call on the Lord to rebuke Satan (Zech. 3:1, 2).

Indeed Satan had complete access to Eden, the garden of God, and the holy mountain of God. He was most magnificently attired and provided for on the day that he was created; for it must be realized that Satan is a created being who was anointed to be before the Lord to be the worship leader of the heavenly host. This guardian cherub with overshadowing wings was blameless in all his ways until iniquity was found in him. Such was his beauty and the glory of his person and the power of his position (which he had not earned for it was all provided for him on the very day he was created) that he wanted to trade on all that he was and had in order to achieve the highest goal which was none other than the throne of God Himself.

"You have said in your heart:
I will ascend into heaven,
I will exalt my throne above the stars of God;
. . . .
I will be like the Most High."
(Is. 14:12 - 15)

Remember that man was the pinnacle of God's physical creation, and His delight. For Satan to achieve his ends of becoming like the Most High what more did he have to do but to take authority over the world which would allow him to rule the centre of the universe creating for himself considerable power and influence outside heaven. In order to do that Lucifer needed to gain authority over man to whom God had given authority over every living thing on the earth.

With a proud heart and an inflated ego he corrupted the wisdom that he had received from God because of what he saw in himself. In so doing Satan had defiled the sanctuaries in which he had authority and would be brought low. His desire for power, played out by taking power for himself over man, did not turn out as he had imagined, for although God had given authority to the man He, as creator, had never given His ultimate authority over His creation as a whole. Man was required to be obedient to his creator and could only do that which was within the bounds God had set. Satan too was a created being, even a cherub of the highest order, but he was still under the authority of God (Job 1).

> *"How are you fallen from heaven*
> *O Lucifer, Son of the Morning!*
> *How are you cut down*
> *you who weaken the nations!*
>
> *... you shall be brought down to Sheol*
> *(the place of the dead)*
> *To the lowest depths of the Pit"*
> *.(Is. 14:12b, 15; see Lk. 10:18)*

Like the reference in Ezekiel, Isaiah prophesied against a ruler, in this case the King of Babylon. However the underlying message is for Satan (also known as the Devil) who is still working quietly in the background through those who have rejected God, and who want to gain power in this life. Unfortunately such people forget that all men will die and have to face an eternity in the spiritual world, finding out when it is too late that what they will face and experience will not be to their pleasure but to their grief. Satan raises men up in order to bring them low, whereas God brings men low, to the point of repentance, before raising them up to great and unspeakable joy.

This is perhaps the most important and essential lesson that anyone interested in coming into a true and real and dynamic relationship with God must understand and have fixed in their hearts. God wants men and women to seek Him face to face. Satan, on the other hand, does not want them to know who he is but hides himself; except when he appears as an angel of light, believing it will have a greater effect on his victim. He prefers to put suggestions in the mind of an individual and direct their attention away from the things of God to the things of the world that he has perverted.

Satan's Deceptive Methods Exposed

The account of the temptation of Adam and Eve, being part of the word of God, cannot be ignored; indeed it is the basis of all that happened to man from being separated from his Spiritual creator God to being provided with a once and for all sacrifice for sin through the person of God's Son and our Saviour Jesus Christ.

It focuses on the fruit of the tree they could not eat, that is the Tree of the Knowledge of Good and Evil, which was put there as a test of their loyalty to God and their willingness to be obedient to His will. After all, as his creator God knows what is best for man, every individual, and it is only when we allow God to oversee our lives that we find fulfillment and happiness.

The diversionary tactics Satan used in his determination to take over control of the physical creation from God by obtaining man's allegiance, were first to cast doubt on God's word, *"Did God say?"* and then to oppose it outright, *"You shall not die"*, a tactic he still uses today. What Satan has never been able to achieve, however, being a created being himself and therefore lacking the creative skills of God, is total control of the earth and its environment. Only God owns that power and ability.

In coming to the woman, Eve, Satan asked her, *"Are you sure that you are not allowed to eat any of the fruit in the garden?"* Such a restriction would mean that a whole range of foodstuff would be denied them, but that was not what God had said. It can be seen from *"You may eat of any fruit except fruit from a specific tree, that is the Tree of the Knowledge of Good and Evil"* that God put a restriction on just one tree to test man's willingness to be obedient to Him. Had Adam and Eve eaten of the tree of life then the picture would have been totally different and sin would not have entered the world and caused the devastation it has; but that, as they say, is conjecture.

Eve replied, *"Of course we can eat of any tree, but we are not to eat from the tree in the centre of the garden* (but there were two) *or touch it* (an embellishment) *or we will die"*.

"It's a lie", hissed the serpent, *"You will not die, for God knows that the instant you eat it you will become like Him* (they were made in His image so they were already at that point), *for your eyes will be opened and you will be able to distinguish good and evil* (not however from the aspect of good but, because they would be in defiance of God and unwittingly transferring their allegiance to Satan, from the aspect of evil)."

Satan's work is to challenge, contradict, and then offer an alternative explanation to God's Word.

So what was on offer?

39

- Eyes opened – which means that God was supposed to be withholding information from them, but they would only see their nakedness and the problem of sex would dominate human relationships instead of being something very natural.

- Be like God – powerful and all knowing perhaps? Although God created them in His image, they were created, earth bound beings in which the breath of the Spirit of God had been breathed, but without God's creational powers so they could never be like God.

- Being able to distinguish between good and evil – which suggests they would have the spirit of discernment, but that could only be given by God as a special gift. In fact by them eating the forbidden fruit Satan would have a greater hold on them and there would forever be a battle within them to live a life worthy of God their creator, particularly after God gave the Law to the Israelites on Sinai.

To better understand just what was about to happen when Adam ate of the fruit, we need to consider the impact of what that was to mean to those that followed. To the Romans Paul explained it in this way (Ro. 7 esp. 14 – 25).

Conflict Between Two Natures

We know that the Law [spoken by God to the Israelites] *is spiritual* [because God is Spiritual], *but I am a creature of the flesh* [carnal and unspiritual because sin has prevented my God breathed spirit from being active within me], *sold into slavery to sin* [held under its control].

For I do not understand my own actions. I do not practice what I want to do, in fact I find myself doing the very thing I hate, yielding to my human nature, the worldliness within me that is my capacity to sin.

Now if I habitually do what I do not want to do, meaning I agree with the Law, by confessing it is morally good.

If that is the case, then it is no longer I who do the disobedient thing which I despise, but the sinful nature abiding within me.

For it is confirmed that I know nothing good lives in me, that is, in my human nature, the worldliness within me that is my capacity to sin. For although there is a willingness to do good present in me, the actual doing of good is not.

For the good that I want to do, I do not do, but I practice the very evil that I do not want. So if I am doing the very thing I do not want to do, I am no longer the one doing it, that is, it is not me that acts, but rather the nature to sin which lives in me.

So I find by the law governing my inner self evil is present in me, that is the one who wants to do good. For I joyfully delight in the law of God in my inner self with my new nature, but I see a different law and rule of action in the members of my body with its appetites and desires, waging war against the law of my mind and subduing me and making me a prisoner of the law of sin which is within my members.

O wretched and miserable man that I am! Who will rescue me and set me free from this body of death, this corrupt, mortal existence?

Thanks be to God for my deliverance through Jesus Christ our Lord! So then, on the one hand I myself with my mind serve the law of God, but on the other, with my flesh, my human nature, that is the worldliness within me which is my capacity to sin, I serve the law of sin.

Sin is insidious. It is like a virus that attacks from within our bodies. It infects the innermost nature within the souls of men causing them to rebel against God, His laws and statutes. Throughout their history, God was sympathetic towards the people and encouraged those determined to love and serve Him however ineffectually, knowing that others fell completely under the power of Satan and his demonic forces, causing mayhem to those round them.

Let us be of no doubt, Satan's real aim in fooling man was to gain for himself the authority God had given to man over His creation and ultimately to usurp the throne of God. Because Adam and Eve accepted Satan's word in defiance of God's specific instruction, they were ejected from their utopia and mankind has been searching for it ever since, yet all the while still accepting Satan's way to the exclusion of the true way of salvation.

The three elements of Satan's strategy, which are based on the lust of the eye and flesh and the pride of life, are as follows:

Deception   Satan was here revealing himself as the first confidence trickster. The arch deceiver. He has not changed and like many who have been duped, Eve did not ask the question, "How do you know what is in the mind of God?"

ElevationHow can that which has been created be the same as the creator? It is impossible! It is like saying that having created something the created can then create something in its turn.

Mankind from Eve and Babel have been seeking to be more powerful and more important than God, not realizing that in so doing all their efforts were enhancing Satan's power over them. God wants us to submit to His authority and obey His will so that He can love us and reward us with His special gifts.

Special Knowledge   Knowing is one thing; having the ability to use that knowledge is quite another.

The future described by Satan may have appeared exciting but it was an unknown future for which Eve and Adam needed a true guide. What Satan was not going to tell them was that he was more than just a guide, he was their master and enslaver. They had removed themselves from the care of a loving creator God and put themselves at the mercy of one who would elevate deception, fear and suspicion amongst them to an art form.

This account of the fall of man must not be accepted as a story but reality; indeed, it is because so many have been persuaded that it is only a story that its impact and significance has been diluted.

A principle that I was taught by a Jewish believer is that throughout scripture it is important not only to look back, but also to look forward.

In looking back we must never forget what happened in the garden, especially with regard to the deceptive ways of Satan and the fact that it was there in that garden of joy and peace where God and man enjoyed each other's company. It was in the garden that sin entered into the world resulting in man being ejected from it, causing the way in which we could relate to God to be irrevocably changed.

It is also imperative that we never forget the fact that it was immediately prior to God ejecting the man and woman from the garden that God promised a way of salvation through the shedding of the blood of prescribed animals, and then in due time introduced that way of salvation according to the prophetic utterances of His servants throughout the intervening centuries.

In looking forward we see the eternal rest which He has also promised and will provide, and we are privileged to have had it revealed to us.

In the meantime there is a significant verse (Gen. 3:15) that will explain much of the terrifying things that have happened in the history of the human race, especially with regard to the chosen people of God, the Jews, and those Gentiles who have truly believed in Him and not become merely members of a particular cult or religion. There is no purpose in saying I am a member of a particular Christian denomination, for none of those organizations can save you; the most important factor is if you have had a life changing experience of the Saviour Jesus and entered into an active relationship with Him.

It is the blood of Jesus alone that can cleanse a person from sin and it is only God who has the power to send the non-believer to hell (Matt. 10:28; Matt. 25:31-36; 2 Cor. 5:10).

"And I will put enmity
Between you and the woman
And between your seed and her Seed;
He shall bruise your head,
And you shall bruise His heel."
(Gen. 3:15)

There has been enmity between Satan and his followers, both demonic spirit beings and human, and the true followers of God throughout world history. The Anti-Semitism seen throughout human history, and even today, is evidence of that enmity, the increasing

43

opposition against the non-catholic, true believers in Jesus, particularly in places such as Malta, is another indication of that enmity which will increase the nearer we get to the second coming of the Lord Jesus.

Our love and acceptance of the Lord's people, both Jew and Gentile, Roman Catholic and non-catholic is the only sign that we are right with God for the simple reason God still loves His people Israel and all that truly believe in Him and will never let them go. Indeed His plans for the future have Israel at the heart of them.

If we hate, or merely object to the presence of God's chosen people in the Holy Land of Israel (the Roman Emperor Hadrian called the land Palestine, in memory of Israel's greatest enemy the Philistines, in response to the rebellious Jews who fought against his occupying troops) that God gave to His people in perpetuity, and even consider that the Holy Land belongs to those opposed to the presence of Israel in it, then we are not of Him who created all things and the Spirit of God is not in us.

Ask yourself the question, "Where in all the world will the Messiah arrive at His second coming?" Surely it is to the Mount of Olives in the land of Israel. Now ask yourself the question, "Whom does the Lord consider owners of that land?" Is it not His own people to whom He will return? "Although they have been a thorn in the side of the surrounding Arab nations, have those nations ever been able to get the better of the people of Israel?" No. And why not? Because God Himself is protecting them with His mighty arm.

But the Lord had the last word for He prophesied that although Satan would bruise His heel (the Seed of the woman, the Messiah who would appear in the flesh at the appointed time and was to die through that serpent bite) yet He would crush Satan's head, that is have complete victory over him through His resurrection, thus nullifying the threat that physical death was final for those in whom the Spirit of Christ dwelt.

The spiritual warfare that is being experienced in the world today is a direct result of that moment in man's history when Satan was able to obtain the authority held by man over God's creation. Indeed, during His ministry the Messiah did not once contradict Satan when he claimed authority over the world and is called the prince of the power of the air. But it did not mean that God lost control of His creation or that man lost all authority. As it is explained in Job 2:1 – 10, God holds the ultimate power in His creation restricting Satan in what he is allowed to do.

Promises given in Genesis regarding the appearance of a Saviour were realized with the appearance of the Messiah Jesus many thousands of years later after God had delivered to the world through His people Israel necessary knowledge regarding man's relationship with Him and how man should relate to Him. Now, with the Messiah's authority, we who have believed also have authority through the Name of Jesus over the one (Satan) who caused Adam to sin.

The dark and stormy clouds of conflict that immediately gained a place on the world's canvas of life, and threatened to dominate it, represented the eviction of Adam and Eve from the garden, the murder of Abel by Cain and the slow degeneration of man in the eyes of God. Adam and Eve received a considerable shock to their system when they experienced the rapid eviction from their perfect world to the harsh realities of toil and hardship and fear in an open and unguarded world.

This must be the most graphic picture of the differences between the God intended joyously peaceful and loving environment in the world he had created, and the harsh, dangerous environment of Satan's world system where evil stalks in the form of deceivers, murderers, liars and cheats, with but a few totally honest, loving God fearing folk.

To Adam and Eve, now separated from the intimacy with God that they had enjoyed, the true nature of Satan was revealed. Satan was making his mark on the picture of world history that had started with such promise. Fortunately, God would ensure that a golden thread of light ran through the picture, a thread difficult to see in places but that would, at times shine brightly to dominate the clouds of darkness.

The Divine creator is identified by two names in the first two chapters of scripture:

- Lord (translated from Adonay) is the prescribed traditional reading of the Divine Name expressed in the four Hebrew letters YHWH which is never pronounced as written. The Hebrew route of the name means 'to be', and expresses eternal existence. The Divine Name is spoken of in close relationship to men or nations and expresses the Lord's loving kindness.

- God (the plural Elohim) emphasizes His justice and rulership.

The Midrash says, *"Thus spoke the Holy One, blessed be He: If I created the world by mercy alone sin will abound; if by justice alone how can the world endure? I will create it by both."*

This is important to all true believers for it emphasizes the promise of salvation that God offers them and which they have accepted. What is a true believer? It is one who has taken the first commandment to heart and have given (dedicated) himself wholly and without restriction to God in His service.

Evicted from the Garden

God said, *"Man has become one of us"* or rather man has gained significant knowledge through disobedience and that knowledge could outstrip not only his capacity to handle it but his willingness to submit to the original Divine Laws of Creation that were established to bring harmony and reason to life on earth. The history of man throughout the centuries provides ample proof of the debilitating nature of sin in man and just how lawless and ruthless man is capable of becoming. Without that breathed spirit within man being active, then man is no better that members of the animal kingdom, even given their greater intelligence.

God had already promised the woman that He would greatly multiply her, although giving birth to new offspring would incur pain and travail, but she would also submit herself to the man. It is interesting that the sentence metered out to the woman does not include the word "cursed" as in the case of Adam and the Serpent. But God pronounced the fruitfulness of man a blessing in which woman's pain and travail is inextricably bound up and that is her woe, her reminder of Satan's deception.

Adam, on the other hand, would have to labour to provide food for himself and his family, *"Because you have disobeyed Me by listening to the woman and have eaten of the fruit of the forbidden Tree … cursed is the ground … in toil shall you eat bread"* (Gen, 3:17, 18).

God knew only too well, that if through his new self-importance urged on by Satan, man ate of the Tree of Life he would secured entrance into His place of rest. Through the breath of the Spirit of God breathed into his nostrils, man had already received spiritual immortality, but it was where He was destined to go for eternity was dependent upon his relationship with his creator. In his sinful state, consider just how explosive a cocktail could be created, if through men and women breeding godless children, none of whom would die, being able to enter into the purity and brightness of His glory. That is why God had to refuse man a second choice.

Certainly the prophetic message of Jesus that there would be a continuation of mankind's inhumanity to man with wars and rumours of wars provides, in some small way, a glimpse of what life on earth would have been like; an earth where the weak and vulnerable would exist in a living hell whilst powerful and ruthless men would be battling it out continually to gain the upper hand, spurred on by Satan who is the architect of chaos.

In expelling man from the garden, God took the only course open to Him to keep the man away from the Tree of Life that had been available to him from the beginning. Access to the tree, which would never die, was to be denied to man only for a time. We read of the tree in the book of Revelation, providing fruit every month with leaves that will provide for the healing of the nations with its roots in the river of life.

There is the story of the vine at Hampton Court in London, which stopped fruiting for some time. Then suddenly it started fruiting again. At the same time that this happened the Thames nearby was being dredged. Along with the mud the dredger brought up was a mass of roots, which turned out to belong to the vine. The roots of the vine had reached the river and they were drawing water from it to feed the fruit. Such is the tree of life by the river of life, which flows from the throne of God.

Thus God drove man out of the Garden. To prevent man ever gaining access God placed cherubim at the east of the garden and a flaming sword that guarded the way to the Tree of Life. It is only through obedience to the call of God to repent and accept the salvation that He has provided in His Son that the tree of life will once again be available for us to enjoy.

We are told that God is spirit and they that worship Him shall worship Him in spirit and in truth (Jn. 4:24). Jesus, when tempted by the Devil said that, *"man shall not live by bread alone but by every word that proceeds from the mouth of God" (Matt. 4:4)*. In line with this Jesus also said that the message He gave came from the Father and therefore His Word WAS Spirit (Jn. 6:63b).

This means that to understand the words and message of scripture we need to be in the same state that the first man was in before the fall, which means we need to be in a regenerated state whereby our spirit is revived by the Holy Spirit and we are therefore born again in the Spirit (John 3:6b). Those untouched by Jesus, and therefore not reborn by the Spirit of God, will not understand the Word of God and the scriptures will remain a mystery to them.

It is clear that the warning of death that God gave to man should he eat of the tree of Good and Evil did not mean physical death because he lived to tell the tale and we are alive today to confirm that.

To understand the warning and its affect on man, the statement the Lord Jesus gave to the tempter makes clear that physical food is not sufficient for man, because the spirit breathed into him by the Holy Spirit requires spiritual food and such food can only come from our Spiritual God, therefore *"man shall not live by bread alone but by every word that proceeds from the mouth of God" (Matt. 4:4)*.

This means that we need both physical food that will feed our physical bodies and spiritual food that will feed out spirits. Thus it is evident that when man ate of the forbidden tree and was evicted from the garden he died spiritually and his access to God was terminated.

It was in the Garden that the man and woman were created; it was in the Garden that God, the pre-incarnate Christ, walked with man and communicated with him easily; it was in the Garden that man defied God and forfeited any bond of trust between them. This surely is why God insists that to receive salvation men must be ready to enter fully into an intimate relation with Him and be willing to lose their lives in Christ through total commitment and completely surrender themselves to Him to inherit eternal life.

In that way, and in that way alone, can we possibly have a relationship with God that will have any true and lasting meaning, and we can then receive regeneration and be reborn spiritually, with a new freedom to communicate with God personally.

Now if man's communication with God through his spirit was severed through spiritual death when they were evicted from the Garden, how come righteous Abel was able to please God? The power to bridge the gap that had appeared between a Spiritual God and fallen and unregenerate man was and always will be with God. It has meant that many men and women throughout the ages have responded to God because He has touched them, knowing that they would be responsive to Him. Abram being a prize example.

Righteous Abel was the first of the children of Adam and Eve to come into a knowledge of God and responded to Him in such a way that he understood what God required in worship, for he alone knew the requirement for the shedding of blood to receive forgiveness (Heb. 9:22); something that Cain could not understand because he was totally unresponsive to the spiritual call of God.

In rejecting Cain's offering God knew full well the anger that was in his heart and spoke to him saying, *"If you do well will you not be accepted? And if you don't do well sin lies at the door. Its desire is for you but you should rule over it." (Gen. 4:6)* Be of no doubt that God will not test us beyond what we are able to bear. Unfortunately Cain's mind and heart were far from God and he had set his mind on killing Abel.

It is essential that the people of today realise just how important the book of Genesis is to our understanding of salvation and how we can not only communicate, but also enter into a relationship, with God that will allow us to receive heart-peace through the regeneration of the spirit within us, even in the most traumatic of experiences, and receive eternal life that we might be with God for eternity.

God was right and Satan wrong. Man did die, not physically but spiritually, which means that a spiritual chasm appeared between God and man.

> *"It is the Spirit who gives life; the flesh profits nothing. The words that I (Jesus) speak to you are spirit, and they are life." (Jn. 6:63)*

Surely this is the same Spirit that brooded over the waters and caused the creation of the world from the instructions given by the Word (Jesus) that He received from God (the Father)?

Therefore read the scriptures, because in them they display their own authority. Consider this:

> *"All scripture is given by inspiration of God,*
> *And is profitable for doctrine, for reproof,*
> *For correction, for instruction in righteousness,*
> *That the man of God may be complete,*
> *Thoroughly equipped for every good work."*
> *(2 Tim. 3:16, 17)*

And this:

> *"... Knowing this first, that no prophecy of scripture*
> *Is for any private interpretation,*
> *For prophecy never came by the will of man,*
> *But holy men of God spoke*
> *As they were moved*
> *By the Holly Spirit."*
> *(2 Peter 1:21, 22)*

Even this volume is the result of inspiration I have received from God. Unless believers read the scriptures diligently, seeking after truth, praying over every word and phrase and message they will not be enlightened or come into a full and precious experience of the True and Living God; regenerated by the Spirit of the living God.

The True "New World" Order

The deception, fear and suspicion introduced into the world by Satan has not gone away; rather it has intensified. The first clear evidence of Satan's rule was the killing of righteous Abel by Cain; an example in personal relationships where the fallen, sinful nature of a man, had got so out of communion with God that jealousy and hatred was allowed freedom to take root and grow in the heart of Cain. Although God had shown him a way out of the situation, Cain was unwilling to respond to God's advice, indeed Cain rejected God completely and went on to live a completely Godless life.

Just as the contrast between the righteousness of God and the darkness of evil is so great that they cannot cohabit, so the contrast between those without God and those in communion with God has the potential to become dangerous because the evil seeds of jealousy and hatred when sown in fertile ground grows up to produce violence.

Paul warned the Ephesians of wolves who would come from within the church to lead many astray (Acts 20:29, 30). Men and women who have no relationship or true knowledge of God, who seek to bend the rules laid down by God for true righteous living according to His righteousness.

Those completely out of touch with God who seek to impose their idea of the Christian gospel onto those within a Christian community, interpret God's rules in a way that bears no relationship with the word as recorded by His servants the prophets.

Where God's word is not allowed to go from being head knowledge, that is where truth about God and His salvation is realized and the repentant sinner first seeks after God, to become heart knowledge, it can be said that the seed falls on the hard ground and either does not germinate or germinates but does not last.

I have known many ordained and lay preachers who have not known the word of God as they should have done and their messages were spiritually dead. Totally un-inspirational.

In the 20th century many have poured scorn on the reliability of the scriptures, and with the ascent of liberal theology any thing goes, even to the acceptance of active homosexuality, which goes against all that God has created and has said in His word. How can two males or two females multiply by having sex with each other?

When God said that it was not good for man to be alone, did He make another man? No, He made a woman from one of Adam's ribs and they became joined together both physically and emotionally. Yet some tell us that the marriage of same sex couples is approved by God and they can be accepted into the Christian Church.

Why do women preachers say that God is female when even the

Son of God, our eternal saviour, calls Him Father? All these things gradually, almost imperceptibly, divert us from the truth about God and are demonic.

The word of God belongs to God and He holds the original manuscript, and it is by that original wording we will all be judged in the final judgement as mentioned in the book of Revelation.

Satan is clearly at work in the church today gradually drawing those members who are not spiritually reborn and therefore not able to read or study the scriptures with understanding, far away from God. Yet that same Word is the spiritual food and sustenance of all those who are spiritually reborn of the Holy Spirit.

It is important to realize that Saul was like all other religious leaders of the Jews until God physically blinded him, took him aside and opened up the scriptures to him. That was the reason Saul became Paul the apostle having done a complete U turn. In his state of blindness God's Holy Spirit worked with Saul to help him understand all that he had been missing in the scriptures so that as Paul the apostle to the Gentile he had had his spiritual eyes opened to the truth. God worked through him to provide the basic Christian doctrine still used in the church today.

It is a fact that far too many preachers are not preaching the truth because they have not had the spirit within them regenerated or their spiritual eyes opened to the hidden truth within the word of God.

Have you ever considered the question, "Why should Satan be so keen to have Christians neglect and even deny the truth of the first Testament?" Because He does not want them to know or understand either his deceptive work on the first man or methods of working as disclosed throughout the first testament, which would enable them to be on their guard to prevent him deceiving them (1 Pet. 5:8, 9). But more than that Satan wants to achieve total dominance in the world and ultimately usurp the throne of God, an objective he will fortunately never achieve.

In this present day it is noticeable that almost the entire world is against Israel, the promised home of God's chosen people, which is the only true democracy in the Middle East. Jesus, when He comes again, will come to the Mount of Olives and nowhere else. Biblical prophecy says quite categorically that God will, in the end time, restore

Israel to the land He gave them (that is the Promised Land). That started to happened in 1948.

Now just supposing Satan is able to crush the nation of Israel so that it is no more! Would Jesus Christ be able to come to the Mount of Olives as promised? Although He has complete power, that is not God's plan.

Satan will try, with the help of the nations of the world, to crush Israel, but as you will see from my book "God Rescues His People : Birth of Nation According to Exodus", and "Deuteronomy", Satan was not able to achieve it when Israel was at the mercy of the Egypt Pharaoh.

It is therefore clear that Satan has no hope of achieving it, for God is protecting Israel in spite of their continued errancy. Because of his holy name and eternal plan for mankind, and because of the remnant of true believers. God is greater than Satan and all the deities still worshipped throughout the world. Though the world is against Israel, God is greater that all the nations of the world combined and will keep Israel safe so that when the Son of God comes again, Israel will still be in the Promised Land.

It is true that the plethora of religions is all part of Satan's deception of mankind with the object of diverting man's attention from the true Word. This situation also brings conflict between the various religions causing chaos.

Only the believing remnant of the people chosen by God (Israel) and those who have come to believe in the God of Israel and have been grafted onto Israel, have knowledge of the real truth. Those of Israel who have rejected their God, have rejected the truth and the way of life leading to the Tree of Life, which has not died.

After Genesis 3 there is no further reference to the tree of the Knowledge of Good and Evil. It did its job testing man in the garden. Now we have the message of salvation and the cornerstone of true faith, which is the Jewish Messiah, Jesus, who is a stumbling block to those who refuse to believe the truth, causing them to be confused and irritated by the Second Testament. The message of salvation leads us all to the tree of life, which will give us eternal life by continually feeding us in the New Jerusalem.

It is important to know that an ineffective church is no threat to Satan. Indeed it can be said that a church that is not targeted by him is in fact on his side. For example a convention was held in a city in England with Christians from various denominations coming together in one of the main churches in the city (neither the city nor the particular denomination is being mentioned here for obvious reasons).

The convention was considered a tremendous success because the gospel was preached and many people were directly affected in various ways by the activity of the Holy Spirit. For the most part those who have truly given their hearts and lives to the Lord Jesus and have received the baptism in His Holy Spirit (that is when the Holy Spirit enters into and begins to directly influence that believer) know instinctively which spirit (good or evil) is working around them, because the Holy Spirit is able to tell them.

Unfortunately the minister and elders of that church were so blind to the working of Holy Spirit, and so insensitive to Him that the following day, a Sunday, before the services started, they went round the church exorcising the Spirit that had done so much good the previous day, demonstrating just how far from the knowledge of God the leaders of some churches are.

No man is completely free in this world! Either he is under the authority of God, carrying an easy yoke and ultimately bound for the glories of heaven, or he is under the authority of Satan, carrying a heavy yoke and ultimately bound for hell. Both heaven and hell are real places and the reason we can be sure of that fact is explained by the parable Jesus told of Lazarus and the rich man (Luke 16).

What is clear is that the message to Cain was that if he had done what he should have done he could have overcome. The warning to Cain that sin was waiting to attack him and longing to destroy him is a warning to which we too must listen and act upon.

We are told that Satan is like a roaring lion seeking whom he may devour (1 Pet. 5:8). We know that God can provide us with a way of escape and all the help we need to overcome (Eph. 6:10 – 18) if, that is, we are willing to accept His help. Cain rejected that way and pursued his own vendetta to his eternal regret.

The Importance of the book of Genesis

Genesis is the one book where the spiritual (particularly the Holy Spirit and Satan) so clearly operates in the affairs of men but is never absorbed by it. The spiritual and physical are two separate entities that are essential to each other and work closely together but are never merged together as one whole, for one is temporary and the other eternal.

> *Now it happened, when men began to multiply on the face of the land, and daughters were born to them,*
> *that the sons of God saw that the daughters of men were beautiful and desirable; and they took wives for themselves, whomever they chose and desired. (Gen. 6:1, 2)*

For example it is intimated in the verse above that angels see how beautiful the women of men are and marry them, but the reference to angels has more to do with men of abnormal strength and ability on the field of conflict or in the hunt who were considered by the ordinary people to have the power and ability of angelic beings rather than being real angels entering into the affairs of men.

Angels are God's spiritual messengers, performing one function at a time and able at times to make themselves appear before humans as men or women. But in reality God made the angels spiritual beings from a different mould, with different characteristics and purpose. Indeed it is said that angels do not marry amongst themselves (Matt. 22:30) so, being without a physical body, how could they marry humans with whom they are unable to have a physical relationship?

For the benefit of the reader, throughout Genesis there is spread a handful of key characters whose relationship with God is of vital importance to our understanding of the character of the Almighty and how individuals relate to Him. It is easy to think of each one as unique or super human. Yet apart from perhaps Adam, each one was an ordinary person born in the natural way, whose heart was malleable and responsive to God.

Each one heard God's voice in a distinctive and special way that suited their character and lifestyle, responding to it in an act of total obedience, setting aside their personal desires and aspirations for they knew that as their creator, God had their best interest at heart.

As God is the same yesterday, today and forever we must assume that His attitude to individuals has not changed.

Satan's fall from his unique place in heaven, as God's master musician and leader of angelic worship, was caused by pride and his desire to usurp God's throne, taking God's place and bring into the world his own system of control and government, which is the reverse of the principle on which it was founded.

This was not based on God's inspired love, but on hatred and deception, which has inevitably led to chaos and confusion. The behaviour of some national leaders towards others is sometimes described as inhuman; but what is the difference between human and inhuman behaviour? Very little. This is because since sin entered into the world, the pure God focused behaviour of men has been corrupted by sin to varying degrees.

Therefore, apart from the behaviour of those whose hearts are truly focused on God and, through the engagement of the Holy Spirit in their bodies and lives, are in a marriage relationship with their Lord, all men are to varying degrees influenced by Satan and therefore their behaviour is less than the perfect created human behaviour God had intended them to display.

God had given man control of His earthly creation even to the extent that Adam named the animals. To take control of the earth, therefore, all Satan had to do was to take it from man's hand by taking authority over man.

The difference between God's way and Satan's way is that God brings men low so that they can come to realise their sinful state and dire need of a Saviour to cleanse and heal them, not only of sin but of the effects of that sin, so that He might raise them up to glory; whereas Satan's method is to raise them up with pride, self-interest and self-satisfaction so that at a later date he might imprison them under his stiflingly oppressive control, and bring them down into a sub-human state.

Indeed the principle governing the people of the world today is for individuals to have, and if necessary fight for the right to have, the best things in life to satisfy their carnal (worldly, fallen) nature because they think they are worth it.

Today the world under Satan's tyrannical rule believes him. The doubt about God and His Word is as strong today as it was in the days of Adam and Eve. All around there is suspicion regarding the accuracy of God's Word. Many leading clerics in the Christian church argue constantly about the accuracy of this or that section of scripture, clearly demonstrating that Satan's control of the human race, even to those within the Church, has not slackened.

The advent of animal sacrifices foretold the full release of mankind from Satan's control. But this has been dealt with in more detail in my book, "God Rescues His People : Birth of Nation According to Exodus"

It is only when those who would believe in Jesus Christ as Saviour and Lord seek out the foundation of their faith by searching all the scriptures that Satan's true role in the subjection of mankind to his worldly system can be discovered, as we are now doing. It is also the only way the true power of the salvation from sin offered by the Lord Jesus Christ can be really understood.

Noah and the Flood (Gen. 6 – 9)

The re-creation of man was rendered unnecessary when God found Noah, a righteous man, and made him the centre piece of this first major act of His salvation of mankind. According to our measurement of righteousness he could well have not been considered righteous, but God saw that in his day Noah had a heart for Him and a way of right living owned by no one else at that time. It was therefore in Noah that God brought man back from a state where he was spiraling down into the abyss and up to a higher plane of life.

God's regret in having to take such drastic action is understandable. All that He had created in the beginning and the way in which He was delighted with it all, particularly with the ultimate creation of man must have been a great delight to Him. But then the disaster as all His work had been contaminated by man with his enthusiasm for sinful ways.

The way man so quickly deteriorated through an increasingly immoral lifestyle that would ultimately have destroyed him will have been exceedingly sad for God, yet God's love for man caused Him to provide a plan to rescue those who would be willing to fully turn to God, an once more become spiritually alive.

For 120 years Noah, under God's direction, preached to the people and gave them a testimony to his trust in God by building an ark for a catastrophe that was to come. For a farmer to build a sea going craft must have been unique and rather dramatic in its day. But everyone laughed it off as being the brainchild of an eccentric.

Even Noah could be forgiven if at times during the great build he wondered if he was wrong and everyone else right. When finally the ark was completed and the animals were gathered together to enter it, Noah will have had his trust in God confirmed.

Noah, his family and all the animals with their food entered the ark as the Lord commanded them and the Lord shut them in, meaning either that the Lord shut the entrance door to ensure it withstood the violence of the storm, or a beautiful figure of speech signifying Divine protection.

Three significant stages are noted: The lifting of the ark, the floating of the ark and the covering of the tops of the mountains by twenty two and a half feet, so that the earth was completely covered with water, as at the very beginning. No land was visible whatsoever. God fulfilled His promise to the letter.

There are a number of significant points that need to be considered:

1. Where did all this water come from and where did it go when it receded to reveal the dry land once more?

2. By rough calculation, from the first rains until the land was dry was one whole year of twelve months in today's measure (that is from the second month of one year to the second month of the next year). During that time the whole population within the ark had to be fed and watered and effluent discharged.

3. When the Dove went out for the second time she brought back an olive leaf, yet the earth had been flooded for a year?

4. The ark was without any form of propulsion (no sails) or steering, so how did it stay in the same area?

5. What happened to all the remains of the drowned humans and animals? Were they consumed by the fish that, presumably, had not been affected by the flood?

As God was in charge of the whole situation, miracles were a matter of course.

What is interesting is that whereas Adam was restricted to plants and fruit for food, Noah and his family, once they were reestablished on dry ground, were allowed to eat the flesh of animals, providing the blood had been completely drained out. As a result animals would be frightened of man.

So Noah, his family and all the creatures that had been saved were instructed to populate the earth.

Noah's first task was to offer burnt sacrifices in thanksgiving to God for their salvation and survival. These would have been totally burnt up with nothing left for the offerer. In response the Lord God promised never to bring about a worldwide flood of that catastrophic nature again, but that did not rule out specific and localized punishments in response to the evil inclination that dwells in the heart of men such as the action God took against Sodom and Gomorrah.

It is sad how quickly this new beginning is infected with the unfortunate situation of Noah's indiscretion and Ham's unfortunate reaction. Noah planted a vineyard, squeezed the fruit and drank the fermented juice. Whether Noah knew what would happen, or he was ignorant of the effects of such liquid refreshment, we have no means of knowing. But he obviously drank too much and ended up naked and in a drunken stupor in his tent.

Somehow Canaan is implicated in what happened next but no specific details are given. When Ham got to hear of something that happened to his father, instead of quietly covering him up and keeping the matter to himself, he went and told his brothers treating it as a matter of amusement. In response his brothers took an outer cloak and, without looking at their father's nakedness, covered him up.

Shamed by the state he had allowed himself to get into, on sobering up Noah was furious with his middle son and Canaan whom he consigned to continual servant hood, he and all his offspring. It was firmly held in ancient times that a blessing or curse, which the father pronounced upon a child, affected their descendents. Therefore here we have in effect a forecast of the servile and degraded nature of the Canaanites.

Children of all ages should show respect to their parents, even when there is evidence of faults and errors. It is at times like these that we all need to remember that none of us are perfect, indeed we have all sinned and come short of the glory of God, there is none perfect, no not one.

Noah's pronouncements over his other sons were blessings rather than curses. Shem was to be the main recipient of his father's blessing just as Isaac blessed Jacob. Japheth receives the blessing of worldly prosperity and widespread dominion but he was to dwell in the tents of Shem meaning that there would be friendly relations between them. But Canaan would be the servant of both. It is interesting that there is no mention of Ham or his other offspring, only Canaan.

The generations from Noah (Gen. 10) are itemized almost like a shopping list. Inserted into the list is the account of the introspective enthusiasm that resulted in the building of a towering monument reaching up into the heavens at Babel (Gen. 11:1 – 9).

Although the building methods of the day would never have permitted it to reach the height of a modern skyscraper. The aim was to maintain the unity of mankind and celebrate its supreme importance in the world, and in the process totally abandon all thought concerning its dependence upon the God who created all things and gave man the breath of life.

But the project had been confounded and disunity introduced by God who caused the people to speak a profusion of languages and acquire particular national traits, which finally caused the people to fill the earth as God originally required them to do.

Today, however, we see God allowing the countries of the world once again to act as one as the rapid advance of high quality communications and the variety and speed of transport make every corner of the earth accessible.

A unifying language (English) has been provided and a unifying purpose to make the world a safer place in which to live is leading to the prophesied one world government that, like the mind behind the tower at Babel, will not have the Divine Creator as its objective.

Rather it is Satan's second and last fight in his effort to usurp the throne of God. Working invisibly as he does, mankind has not realized the evil mind driving it towards his goal of confrontation.

Unfortunately much of Israel and the Church have seemed blissfully unaware of the spiritual battle God's angelic army is waging against the forces of darkness. But this is now changing with God shaking the nations with Covid-19 and financial chaos.

Even the glimpses of the battle God has allowed into scripture are in danger of being totally ignored by many of those purporting to have an interest in the Christian message. Only those who either have, or will become spiritually aware know the dangers which every true believer, whether of Jewish or Gentile origin, faces.

Finally the list of individuals making up the generations from Noah extends to the family of Terah and the appearance of Abram.

3 LOT

Who was Lot?

Lot, was Abram's nephew, the son of Abraham's brother Haran who died before his father Terah left Ur of the Chaldean's. Lot played a minor, but no less important role in the life of Abram and was the cause of Abram showing his real character in times of trouble.

When God called Abram to leave the town of Haran and go off on a journey to a land He would give his descendents, Lot went with him rather than stay with Abram's other brother who became the father of Rebekah, Isaac's wife. Perhaps Lot was excited by the opportunity of travelling, it certainly had nothing to do with any relationship he had with the God who had spoken to his uncle Abram.

As God blessed Abram so Lot was also blessed and became very rich in livestock and servants. But we need to consider that it was not Lot who was close to God and serving Him because a man's relationship with God is personal, and this is illustrated by the relationship Jacob and Esau had with the God of Abram and Isaac. All that Lot acquired was because of Abram.

As we shall see later, Jacob ultimately became close to God as the result of his personal search to understand the relationship his father and grandfather had with God. As a result of this personal search for God, God drew Jacob to Himself in a unique way over a long period of training and personal experience.

It is important to realize that just because Jacob went on that journey to 'find God' for himself it did not mean that his sons would automatically enter into the same personal relationship with the God. Indeed it became very clear with the experiences Joseph went through, that they were far from God and after the death of their father Jacob were still only vaguely in tune with God.

Lot would have been no different all those years before the birth of Jacob because it is clear Lot had no personal faith which is made evident through the decisions he made.

It became obvious that the two men with so much livestock and servants could not possibly co-exist because of the limited amount of pasture land available to them. As the senior Abram had every right to tell Lot which area of land was his choice, but Abram was gracious enough to allow Lot to make his choice and he would go in the other direction.

Throughout scripture it is made very clear that the easy life is, or at the very least has the potential to become, the best means of a man to lose his faith. It is only when a man is faced with problems that seem not to have an obvious answer that the only true way to find a way forward is to ask a wiser person for advice. King David put his whole trust in God his saviour and whenever he had a problem he immediately asked God what he should do. That has always been the means of keeping a man close to God.

What Lot obviously did not do was to seek advice from the God who had called his uncle Abram and through whose grace and mercy he had received all that he owned. Looking with human eyes from his vantage point he saw the lush green meadows in the well watered Jordan valley and thought of all the benefits of settling down with plenty of food for himself and his livestock, avoiding the need to live a nomadic life looking for enough grass for his cattle and food for his family and servants. So he chose the plains for himself and those dependent on him.

The Misfortunes of Lot

Abram's life of trusting God, a life of hardship in which God was to train him and draw him closer to Himself, was to continue. The Lord Jesus spoke about not looking with the eyes and worrying about what we should eat or drink or wear because life is far more than being concerned about such things.

As Adam and Eve found out to their cost, life is all about our relationship with God, which is *the* most important matter in our lives on earth.

If God created each and every one of us, along with all that we see around us, clothed the lilies of the field and fed the birds of the air, then as the pinnacle of His creation, will He not provide for us if we but trusted Him enough?

Our physical needs force us to trust Him. If we have all that we want, we have no reason to trust God for our next meal, or the means to buy clothing or somewhere to live. Having received so much through being with his uncle, Lot looked with his eyes to see the goodness of the land in the Jordan valley and all that it could supply him and his tribe without any regard to the God of Abram who had been so generous to him through the service of Abram. What he did not see, however, was the life of corruption lived by those living in the nearby cities of Sodom and Gomorrah. The wealth of the land led them to a life of ease and that led to corruption.

During a local war Lot and his household were captured (Gen. 14) with all their possessions. One escapee managed to reach Abraham to tell him about the situation. Lot's wealth and well being had been as the result of Abraham's acceptance of God and his continued faith even in times of difficulty. Now Abraham's concern for his nephew ignited in him a desire to recue his own kith and kin.

Using clever tactics, Abraham rescued Lot and his possessions and return him to his home. And so Lot continued to live in that same area with his daughters growing up and becoming engaged to two local young men. What is not clear is the size of his household, the number of servants and livestock since his rescue by his uncle.

Now a new problem arises for Lot (Gen. 19). The situation in Sodom and Gomorrah with its sin and corruption became known to God. It is interesting that although Lot knew about the decaying situation, because of something the men said, such as, *"Who do you think you are? We let you settle amongst us and now you are judging us and trying to tell us how to behave?"* It seems he had tried to live a righteous life in that situation but sadly saw no reason to move away, to separate himself and his family from such depravity.

When the two angels arrived at Sodom, Lot was sitting in the gate of the city and greeted them. Although they were prepared to spend the night in the open square, something that in many other towns and cities might have been perfectly normal and safe, Lot knew they would not be safe there and urged them to come to his house where they could refresh themselves and be safe.

What is of concern is that although Lot was at heart a righteous man,

> *"for that righteous man, living among them day after day,*
> *was tormented in his righteous soul by their lawless deeds*
> *that he saw and heard"*
> *(2 Peter 2:8)*

he did not at any time see fit to withdraw his family from such a depraved town when he became conscious of just how bad the depravity had become. He had started as a tent dweller, but over the course of time decided to blend in with the surrounding population by building himself a house thus making his stay permanent. Such acceptance of evil behaviour is detrimental to our relationship with God. Evil and goodness cannot coexist.

For example, homosexuality is of Satan not of God, of that there can be no doubt whatsoever, and therefore inexcusable to true believers. Indeed it is part of the decline in moral standards initiated by the consequences of Adam's rebellion against God and his being removed from the Garden of Eden.

Constantly and consistently through scripture we read of the moral decline of all those who give up on God, even though God never gives up on them.

Such was the decline in moral standards that the male residents of the whole city came out in force to 'have their *carnal* (physical sex) way with the strangers'!

What is astonishing to us today is that when Lot went out to remonstrate with the crowd he was prepared to sacrifice his two daughters in order to keep his guests safe. Now the safety of his guests should have been a priority, but his willingness to sacrifice his two daughters to the baying crowd was a very sad admission.

God's way from the start has always been that a man should unite with a woman to produce offspring. This is the only natural function of mankind. For those in a relationship that is not of God the only way offspring can be produced, physically or by *artificial* insemination, which is a means of getting round God's design for the production of children.

Love must be at the centre of the relationship between the man and the woman which induces the desire for the pure, natural bodily contact method, which is the way God designed us to produce offspring.

When the Bible says that the couple will become one flesh it means that when the man is coupled to the woman in sexual-intercourse they indeed become united as one flesh. Any alternative relationship came after man's rebellion against God. Such arrangements are of Satan and not of God.

See how the crowd accused Lot of acting as a judge to their depravity (v9)? so the angels resorted to supernatural means to prevent the crowd gaining entry into the house.

We can see the pleadings of Abram taking effect when the angels urge Lot to gather his family together prior to them fleeing for their lives. Once the men threatening the house had gone, it was safe for Lot to meet with his sons-in-law to urge them to come with them in fleeing, but they cynically thought to their cost he was joking, because they were unbelievers.

In the early morning the angels insisted that Lot and his family go quickly, before the punishment was initiated. They even had allowed Lot to flee to the nearest town on the plain rather than into the mountains because he was frightened of the dangers that might be lurking there. The one condition laid down by the angels was that they should not look back.

In the Christian life looking back over our lives is sometimes a good thing because if we truly have been putting God first then we will be able to see the hand of God in all that we have done. In this instance, however, God's instruction was not to look back, but to focus on getting away from the danger zone, of not witnessing His judgment because of the effect on them.

From being a man of wealth with many possessions, here we see Lot and his daughters leaving with just the clothes on their backs. Sadly Lot's wife, who is not named, disobeyed the specific instructions of the angels and through her delayed response she felt the effects of the deluge of fire and brimstone from heaven and was suddenly no more than a statue, frozen in time. Why she delayed and looked back we shall never know, but one thing is for sure, God has presented us with the opportunity to receive the gift of salvation. If we delay accepting it and our life is taken away from us unexpectedly then we will suffer the same fate.

Thus did Lot loose everything because his heart was not fully with the Lord as was Abram's heart. Surely it is a salutary lesson to us that if our hearts are not loving and obedient towards God being obedient to the will and purposes of God for us by not communicating with Him, then we could lose our treasure on earth and not experience a place that might have been reserved for us in heaven.

4 ABRAHAM

God Calls Abram (Gen. 12)

The uniqueness of Abram is his willingness to turn his back on a world that had once again got sidetracked from the focus of Noah's saving faith. A continuation of the strand of gold, that would weave its tortuous way through world history, reappears in the black clouds of a world that had once again forgotten God; seeking instead to produce its own homemade variety of deities that they could worship with little effort. These were Devil inspired false gods which had no power to save.

Today it is a case of employing religious people who will preach comfortable and comforting words to worshippers, preaching peace, when there is no peace (Jer. 6:4; 8:11).

Experience and knowledge gained through scripture clearly indicate that God responds to those who, disillusioned with the empty spiritual and non-spiritual offerings of the world that cannot satisfy the Divinely designed soul of men and women, seek after the truth. Not knowing what the truth is they cry out through the spiritual darkness that surrounds them in an impassioned plea to the one God they believe must be present somewhere in the universe who can fill their emptiness and hunger for completeness and purpose.

Surrounded by idols that he realized had no power or ability to do anything but to sit where they were placed, Abram was just such

THE ORIGIN OF LIFE

a person who called out to the one true God, ignorant at the time of just who He was. But God saw in him someone He could work with to create a vehicle through which He could reach out to the people of the world with the message of salvation. A nation built from the foundation of one man that would be a focal point, a living, dynamic notice board by which God could not only tell people about, but also demonstrate His salvation to all mankind through all earthly time.

Thus began a comprehensive history of events and personalities that together provided a coherent and cohesive historicity that has held true in spite of a continuing, concerted and consistent attack on its actuality and reliability from all quarters, even from those who profess membership of the chosen people of God or claim a knowledge and sense of His salvation.

Accusations of myths and legends turn the fact of God and His dealings with real people into a storybook that might or might not have any relevance to each succeeding age. Unsure of what is true and what is of doubtful origin they pour scorn on those who have, with diligence, searched for and found the life changing knowledge and personal experience of God that empowered Abram to leave all that was familiar and journey into the unknown world of the land of Canaan. A land promised to him and his offspring, but that he could never own himself. His one possession was the personal seal of approval of God Himself coupled with the knowledge of life in eternity with Him.

The greater the reliance on intellectual human thinking to understand scripture, the greater the potential for a distorted understanding of what God is trying to say through it.

Many intellectuals have demonstrated their lack of a true understanding and experience of the person of the Divine Deity that impregnates scripture by utterings and murmurings. They cast doubt on the events and personages within the scriptural text, thereby tearing the heart out of the Word of God.

In his book "Foolish to be Wise: A Scientist Comes Face to Face with the Miraculous" (printed 1991 and sadly no longer in print) Professor Roy Peacock, who apparently had part of a jet engine named after him, explained how he had to set aside his learning in order to understand profound scriptural truths, relying instead on the enlightening of the

Holy Spirit to help him understand the true meaning behind each scripture.

In his book Paradigm Shift (Oct 2013) Professor Peacock relates how science and faith hung in the balance for one atheistically inclined scientist, until his life was turned around by events he can only categorize as miraculous, which launched him into a powerful Christian ministry alongside his professional work. A personal memoir of events that shaped the life of a practical scientist.

The book tells a story, and along the way explores the synthesis Roy Peacock found after he came to faith in Christ. Testing the claims of the Bible in the same way he would any other truth-claims, he found that God acts as dramatically and speaks as clearly today as he did in Bible times.

As Roy learns to trust God increasingly in every area of his life, people are healed spiritually and physically through his ministry.

What Roy and so many technically minded people have found is that, compared to his maker, man's wisdom is severely limited. As a technical writer I have had to understand the operation of a variety of equipment and processes in order to produce operating instructions and maintenance manuals and even training documentation, in fact I had to know as much as it was possible to know about the equipment I was writing about in a safety critical environment.

If it did not work I could not write about it. The same principle is involved in writing on scripture. If it does not work in practice there is no point in writing about it, proving the point that faith in God works, and that a life surrendered to Him is the most practical way to leading a fulfilled and joyous life.

To set aside rational thinking and instead prayerfully search the scriptures under the tutelage of the One who inspired each contributor to our Bible, will open up a treasure trove of spiritual gems, a true understanding of what God is saying to mankind in general and to each receptive individual in particular.

One thing is for sure, God never rushed His call to an individual. With the ability of the Holy Spirit to speak to a person within their minds, it is intriguing to know how God persuaded Abram to believe in Him and trust Him. But everyone's experience of God is unique, and tailor made.

How and when Abram heard God speak is not recorded. But it was significant enough in Abram's mind for him to take dramatic action and respond to that call. Such a willingness to act on a command from someone it is not possible to see must be an example to all those who, having found God for themselves, seek a closer and more meaningful relationship with Him. In a world where God was, for all intents and purposes, ignored, whether such an act of total trust and commitment affected those of his day who heard him or met him can only be surmised.

What is certain is that Abram became the founding father of a new and living way where God is put in His rightful place as head of the individual, family and nation. From Abram/Abraham is descended both the physical seed (the nation of Israel) and the spiritual seed (those who have made a decision to follow the God of Abraham). He is the beginning of a new chapter in the annals of the human race and is also unwittingly a focal point of the conflict in the Middle East today. For both sides believe they are legitimate sons of Abraham, the father of many nations.

However true that may be, God's chosen nation, and His first-born, is clearly Israel, the only nation to which He gave the laws and statutes, and through which He determined to reach out to the world.

It is unfortunate that the human arguments as to who is and who is not the chosen of God, which is currently fuelling the conflict, is irrelevant because it is God and Him alone who has the power to chose. Any argument that in any way detracts from the Word He has revealed to mankind is merely reiterating Satan's challenge to Eve, *"Did God say?"* and *"You shall not die ..."*.

Abram's nomadic lifestyle was not free of trials; this is because faith needs to be exercised just as the muscles in the human body need to be exercised to build up muscle strength and therefore be useful.

Also the mind that is not used soon loses knowledge and the ability to function. But at the centre of Abram's life was the worship and understanding of the God who had called him out from the ways and practices of the world into a way that leads to an eternal future (Heb. 11:8 – 10).

His practice of raising an altar and sacrificing to his God as he wandered around the promised land, his witness to the presence of

God in his life and his discourses on the special relationship he had with God will have had a profound effect on his immediate family, on those employed by him, those he gained through acts of generosity by kings and leaders he met and those within the wider community of travellers who had caught something of the powerful message emanating from this leader of men.

Men touched by God in a special way, such as Abram, who were willing to commit themselves to a self-denying and self-effacing venture with God, cannot but be progressively changed. The glory and purity within the presence of God are of themselves life changing, being so powerfully different from anything that is found on earth.

For example Moses' face glowed when he had been with God on the mountain such that the Israelites were overawed by it and he had to hide his face from them until after a while the reflected glory faded away. And the only way we can be uplifted and our lives enhanced is by continually seeking to be close to him who is our all-in-all, our all sufficient support and sustainer.

The fall from grace first caused Adam and Eve to cover themselves, suddenly made aware of a nakedness that had previously been accepted through a purity of vision. The fallen nature of man throughout history has provoked a range of responses from embarrassment at Moses' shining countenance to the killing of many prophets and holy men who, shining like a beacon with the reflected glory of God, drew out the Satan inspired evil in those often unwittingly opposed to all true servant of the living God. The writer to the Hebrews say of them, *"of whom the world was not worthy" (Heb. 11:38a).*

The severity of the response depended on the degree to which the respondent was filled with the evil of a world over which Satan reigned, just like those members of the Sanhedrin who stoned Stephen. All believers in the Most High are encouraged to test the spirits to see if they are from God for many impostors, wolves among the sheep, will continue to work under the banner of God until Satan is finally defeated.

Scripture fortunately does not hide the flaws in the characters of those whose lives are exposed to the view of the readers of scripture. Abram's trust in God's protection, for example, sometimes faltered. When coming to a city where the king or governor had the power to do away with a husband if he took a fancy to the man's wife, Abram asked Sarai to say that she was his sister, which in truth she was (being the daughter of his father but not his mother), because of her beauty. But each time she was taken into the care of a ruler's harem God protected her, for out of her would come Isaac the chosen of God and ultimately the Messiah.

Against Pharaoh, for example, he directed a plague, an illness that could not be explained until the "religious men" came to the conclusion that the problem was with Abram and Sarai. Pharaoh's reaction was that of one found out for the self-satisfying, cruel and predatory activity in which he was engaged.

Realizing that a higher power than he was involved, and with the whole matter so widely broadcast, all he could do was to cast Abram and Sarai, with all the possessions they had accumulated, out of the land over which he maintained an autocratic rule.

Thus the lesson is learned that God can overcome our weaknesses and it is not necessary for a believer to be perfect, which is just as well when we learn that there are none righteous no not one. Rather His power to rescue us is there for our benefit if it leads us to a more meaningful walk with Him.

Abram and Lot Separate (Gen. 13)

Abram's nephew Lot had been with him on all his travels since he left Haran. During that time Lot had also been blessed establishing a household for himself alongside that of Abram. By now, however, the flocks owned by each had become so large that grazing had become a problem, causing friction between the herdsmen and shepherds of the two men, and a parting of the ways had become a matter of urgency.

On leaving Egypt a decision about Lot and Abram going their separate ways became inevitable. Although as the senior man in age and rank Abram was entitled to make the choice, he graciously passed the choice to Lot who then could not come back and complain that he had had to take second best. It also gave Abram the chance to put the matter before God who he believed would guide him, fresh as he was from God's intervention in the Pharaoh affair.

Unfortunately Lot looked with his physical eyes to identify the best grazing, blind to the dangers that would eventually rob him of all his wealth and family, with the exception of his two daughters.

Abram, on the other hand, still on high ground was in a far better position to see the full extent of God's promised blessing of both land and a people to fill it. Although the grazing would not have been so plentiful, he knew God's provision. Had he lifted up his eyes to look down into the valley he would not have seen beyond the mountains to the East and West. But God kept him on the mountaintop where he had an unrestricted 360 degrees of vision.

The first of Lot's trials came when he was captured along with the other inhabitants of Sodom. On hearing of the attack Abram, with conspicuous courage and decisiveness, got together all the men born in his house and went to the rescue. Dividing his men into several groups and attacking by night from several directions, Abram's forces were able to surprise the larger enemy force and throw it into a panic. God later led Gideon to use the similar tactics very effectively against the Midianites.

Unlike Lot, Abram did not trust the King of Sodom and would take nothing from the spoils of war, accepting only that which his men had eaten and a tithe to the King of Salem, lest at any time the King of Sodom should claim that he had helped Abram get rich. His witness to the King of Sodom was that he had lifted up his hands to the *"Lord God Most High, Maker of heaven and earth"* promising that he would not take so much as a thread or shoe latchet from the spoils that he had brought back.

The Significance of Melchizedek

The most significant occurrence in this drama is the first appearance of the priest king Melchizedek, who was both King of Salem (later to be called Jerusalem) and priest of the Most High God. He came out to Abram with bread and wine for his sustenance. In a book (the Bible) in which symbolism plays such an important part, the offering of bread and wine, although given for sustenance at that time, would inevitably be seen as significant considering the later connection between this king and the Messiah. Abram in giving the king a tenth of all the spoils he had taken also has implications for the authority and standing of the

Aaronic priesthood in relation to the priesthood of Yeshua (Jesus)[5].

Because Aaron had yet to be born of a descendent of Abram, and because Melchizedek was honoured by Abram as his senior, Melchizedek was also senior to Aaron, which means that the priesthood of Melchizedek was greater than that of Aaron. According to the writer of the Hebrews the uniqueness of this king is that he was without father or mother and without ancestry, beginning of days or end of life, but resembling the Son of God he continues to be a priest without interruption and without a successor.

This meeting would have implications on the new covenant between God and mankind when the Messiah to the Jews came as prophesied in Yeshua (Jesus). He became a priest after the order of Melchizedek, that is a uniting of the roles of king and priest in one man, being also king of righteousness and also king of peace.

The record of Abram's meeting with Melchizedek (Gen. 14:17 – 24) is one of those pieces of information that is very easily glossed over without realizing its significance. The offices of priest and king can only be combined in God. King Uzziah, all the time he was under the tutelage of the priest Zechariah, (2 Chron. 26:5) sought after God, and God blessed him during that time. It is reasonable to assume that at some time Zechariah died, and even though it was God who had blessed him as king, Uzziah was not satisfied with just being the King of Israel and tried also to usurp the priestly function because of pride (2 Chron. 26:16 – 21) and therefore suffered from leprosy for the rest of his life. It is particularly interesting that the leprosy broke out on his forehead where the high priest would have worn the engraved plaque "Holiness to the Lord", emphasizing the God given right to that office of the person God chose to occupy that office.

The significance of Melchizedek, is that he is called both the king of Salem (Peace) and priest of the Most High God. Elsewhere Melchizedek is referred to as being without father or mother, without ancestry, or beginning of days or end of life, but resembling the Son of God he continues to be a priest without interruption and without successor (Heb. 7:3). It is to this king and priest that Abram gives a tenth of the spoils of a war that he knew God had enabled him to win, and a tenth is only given by a lesser man to a greater one.

____Therefore Abram, the founder of the Hebrew race and therefore

[5]   Read Hebrews 7, 8

of Israel, for the twelve leaders of the tribes were in his loins at that time, was acknowledging the greatness and uniqueness of this king and priest above him and all his offspring.

We cannot leave this matter without connecting the appearance of this remarkable man with the Messiah, the Lord Jesus Christ, who was made a priest after the order of Melchizedek. Why? Because it can be shown that the man Abram met with and who provided him with the bread and wine was the pre-incarnate Messiah.

Through His suffering and death and resurrection, such is the vital nature of the role the Messiah is now fulfilling in heaven as our advocate (Heb. 7:24, 25; 1 Jn. 2:1, 2) that it is unreasonable to assume that the priestly line of Melchizedek that He inherited was established by someone unknown, particularly a created human being or even, for that matter, a created angelic being. God the Father does not go in for delusion or allusion, particularly when it concerns His most precious Son the Messiah, Jesus Christ. The whole matter is far too serious.

The Father has appointed His Son as the heir of all things, for the Son is:

> *"... the brightness of His glory and the express image of His person, upholding all things by the word of His power. When He had by Himself purged our sins, sitting down at the right hand (the side of power) of the Majesty on high having become so much better than the angels, as He has by inheritance obtained a more excellent name than they ..."*
>
> *(Heb. 1:3, 4)*

With such historic and all encompassing credentials, the fact that the Messiah was made a priest after the order of Melchizedek in a sworn statement by God the Father, must mean the position of this Melchizedek, who was priest of the Most High God, had himself to own credentials of similar worth to that of the Messiah.

Consider the exalted position of the Son of God, both before the worlds were made and subsequently in heaven with His Father, after His total obedience unto death according to the will of His Father, in order to save those children of Adam and Eve who were, are and will be prepared to believe in Him. He is and always has been above all creation, both spiritual and physical; the miracles He performed over nature during His ministry on earth confirm His mighty power. Consider also the central and critical purpose of God's carefully and intricately crafted plan of salvation without which there could be no access to the Father by man.

How could we possibly consider that either God the Father, or God the Son, would be willing to allow anyone else, who could be neither spirit nor eternal, to establish an eternal Priesthood to which order the Son would be appointed High Priest and therefore subservient to that person? Particularly as it was to be above all other priesthoods?

How could someone other than the Son of God be given the responsibility of establishing such a Priesthood to which the Son Himself would be elevated after His sacrifice and resurrection, particularly as it was established as an eternal priesthood, to be served, not on earth but in heaven in the very presence of the supreme and awesome God the Father? Who else, with equal or better credentials than the Son of God, could have been cast in the role of Melchizedek, king of Salem (Peace) and priest of the Most High God who met God's chosen, Abram, to bless him but the Messiah before He entered into human flesh?

Indeed, why are we trying to put restrictions on what the Son of God could and could not do before His appearance on earth? Why are we trying to consider the true identity of Melchizedek using our earthly and finite understanding and not allow God to reveal that truth to us?

With the Father, the Son and the Holy Spirit being so supremely powerful and in such complete unity before and after the creation, and with the plan of salvation, including the superior position of the Melchizedek priesthood, having been established in finite detail before creation, there is no one but the Son who could have appeared before Abram to ensure the acceptance by man of the superiority of that priesthood over the priesthood of Aaron through the recording of that event in accepted scripture.

Abram's faith in God was unquestioningly solid. Yet all his efforts to serve and follow God, and all the promises of blessing God had lavished on him were meaningless all the while he had no son to continue the way of faith and trust (Gen. 15). As the greatest desire of a woman at that time was to bear children, it is understandable that Sarai should not only feel the shame of her inadequacy but realise that the time when she would be physically unable to bear children was drawing uncomfortably close.

When God said to him,

> *"Fear not Abram, I am thy shield and thy reward shall be great",*

replied,

> *"But Lord what will you give me seeing I go childless and my senior servant will inherit all my house"?*

Abram could not possibly realize that it was just as important to God that he have a son. Relying on Abram's steadfast faith was all part of God's plans to continue Abram's line through to the promised HaMashiach, the Messiah of Israel. Man and God working in harmony. However impossible it might have seemed to Abram, it was essential that he continued to believe that what was impossible to men was perfectly possible to God. Such a focus on the sovereignty and power of God should also be our objective.

God's challenge to Abram to count the number of stars in the heavens and His assurance that the number of his offspring would be just as numerous once again stimulated his faith, and in his heart he believed that God would indeed give him a son with descendants as numerous as the stars and grains of sand. But however steadfast that faith and however patient he was to wait on God's timing, Abram still wanted some sign to establish this promise.

God Makes a Covenant with Abram (Gen. 15:7 – 21)

> God said to him, "I am the Lord who brought you out of Ur of the Chaldeans, to give you this land as an inheritance."
> But Abram said, "Lord God, by what clear sign will I know that I will inherit it?"

The ancient method of making a covenant was to cut an animal in half and for the contracting parties to walk through the portions of the slain animal, thereby they were thought to be united by the bond of a common blood. To assure Abram of the legitimacy of the covenant God was making with him, He used this local method to establish a covenant between them and to give Abram some understanding of future events.

> God said to him, "Bring Me a three-year-old heifer, a three-year-old female goat, a three-year-old ram, a turtledove, and a young pigeon."
> Abram brought all these to Him, cut them down the middle, and laid each half opposite the other; but he did not cut the birds.

Abram slayed the animals as God instructed him, but was forced to prevent scavenging birds eating them, which symbolized the difficulties to be experienced by his heirs when taking possession of the land.

When the sun was setting a deep sleep, similar to that experienced by Adam before his rib was removed to create Eve, came over Abram and a great darkness that stimulated a dread within his spirit symbolizing that the nation that would issue from him would have to pass through bitter times of oppression. The four hundred years relates to four generations before they would be freed from slavery.

> But God said to Abram, "Know for sure that your descendants will be temporary strangers in a land (Egypt) that is not theirs, where they will be enslaved and oppressed for four hundred years.
> But on that nation whom your descendants will serve I will bring judgment, and afterward they will come out of that land with great possessions.
> (Gen. 15:7 – 14)

In the darkness the smoking furnace and the flaming torch, symbolic of the Godhead, passed between the pieces to establish the covenant. So was delivered to Abram a surety that God's promises concerning the future of his tribe and line would be established and also putting on record the prophetic knowledge of what would happen before those offspring would take possession of the Promised Land. Remember that Abram had no knowledge of the future just as we don't, therefore this vision was God's guarantee that that would happen and did happen as we have on record, which should be a considerable comfort to us.

It is interesting that it was Sarai's idea for Abram to lie with Hagar to produce offspring and his decision to pursue it, just as Adam had eaten the fruit of the tree of the Knowledge of Good and Evil Eve had given him. Yet the promises God had given Abram had never failed. Indeed God's promise to provide him with a son had not been rescinded, but was merely being delayed for a future God appointed time.

Such times of waiting for God to fulfill His promises has been the lot of believers from time immemorial, and can be considered in two ways. Firstly the promises are given as warnings of things to come to allow the believer to prepare themselves, secondly the delay is aimed at building up our trust in God. After all, after receiving the first promise and then experiencing the delay, any future promises will encourage the believer to trust God more than in the first instance.

Unfortunately as with all man-initiated schemes Sarai had not foreseen nor did she foresee the reaction of Hagar to her when the handmaid realized that she had conceived but her mistress had not been able to do so.

Sarai's sense of guilt of her barrenness was difficult enough to bear without also being despised by Hagar who had proved there was nothing wrong with Abram's ability to sire children. But Hagar's haughty attitude towards her mistress was totally out of order and Sarai rightly chided her husband for allowing it to happen seeing that Hagar's position within the family had changed now that she bore his child.

This incident was a fall back to the Babylonian way of allowing the husband to take a concubine as a second wife, if his first wife was barren, but he was not to place her on an equal footing with his first wife.

Abram gave Sarai permission to take whatever action she thought fit to bring Hagar back into line. Unfortunately Sarai over stepped the mark by dealing with Hagar so harshly that her only option was to flee from her mistress. Such action, and the dangers she would have inevitably faced as a pregnant woman on her own, demonstrated the excessive nature of Sarai's scorn.

Full of concern for her own safety and that of her unborn child, Hagar was to experience first hand what she had previously learned concerning the reality of the God Abram worshipped. The angel of the Lord appearing to her and giving her a prophetic message concerning the son she was to bear for Abram had such a profound effect on her that she willingly returned to face Sarai's wrath. That the angel's prophetic word to her came to pass will have established her faith in this living God of knowledge.

So Abram sired a son at the age of 86 and named him Ishmael. Whether or not Hagar related to Abram what had happened to her during her absence we are not told, nor if she suggested to Abram the name for her son. God was quite capable of putting the name into Abram's mind.

No further communication between God and Abram is recorded until he reaches the grand age of 99, 13 years later. By which time Ishmael was established as the heir to Abram and loved by his father.

God's covenant with Abram was now to enter a new phase:

1. The names of Abram and his wife Sarai were to be changed to Abraham (Ab meaning father and raham meaning multitude) and Sarah (bringing out more forcibly the meaning Princess than the archaic form Sarai).

2. The outward sign of the covenant was for ALL males within Abraham's household to be circumcised whatever their status, from Abraham and all under his authority to the most lowly servant and anyone else living freely within his household who had neither been born or bought into his house.

3. The promise of a son for Sarah. For this promise Abraham must have been overjoyed for he laughed with joy, knowing as he did by then that the ability of God to work miracles should not be questioned.

The covenant sign of circumcision was an outward identification mark of an inward decision to willingly serve God, as indeed, Abram had so clearly demonstrated over His life since leaving Haran. Jeremiah called on the men of Judah to circumcise themselves to the Lord and take away the foreskins of their hearts, because the external mark was of no value if their heart was not right with God.

The position of Ishmael with regard to his being a successor to Abraham now a matter of principle. He was the product of an arrangement between Sarai and Abram to produce an heir, the son of a slave woman who had no place in God's plan of salvation.

Unfortunately the human tragedy of Ishmael's rejection is with us today. Mankind, in interfering with God's plans, only succeeds in bringing additional problems upon itself.

God had promised Abram a son and, because Sarai was Abram's only wife, it should have occurred to them that at the appropriate time God would cause Sarai to become pregnant and give birth to a son. It was they who were looking at the biological clock and thinking that God was leaving it a little late. It was they who took matters into their own hands to assist God. But their action was wrong.

Once again God demonstrated to both Abraham and Sarah that He was not tied to natural processes or time scales. Their true son Isaac was to be a son according to the promises of God, conceived at a time when it would not be natural for them to produce children. And the sex of the child was also preordained, further demonstrating the power of God in all matters within the world He had created[6]

It is essential that those who receive promises from God remain faithful to Him no matter how bad things appear to look, and how unlikely the fulfilment of the promise seems to be.

Abraham Visited by Three Angels (Gen. 18)

Three angels now appeared as men to Abraham. Seeing them afar off and concerned for their welfare in the heat of the day he ran to meet them and encourage them to return with him to his tent. God sends out each angel on a single mission. On this occasion one was sent to tell Sarah she was to have a son, one to destroy Sodom and Gomorrah and the third to rescue Lot. Notice that although three had left Abraham, there were only two to whom Lot gave hospitality.

[6]   Consider what Paul wrote to the Galatians concerning the two sons of Abraham (Gal 4:21 – 31).

The message of Sarah's impending pregnancy having been delivered amid her laughter, the men needed to be on their way.

God had chosen well when He selected Abram. Since his decision to trust God for his future he had become a 'noble' man in the true sense of the term. He cared about the welfare of the angels, he cared about the training of his son Ishmael by getting him to select and prepare the animal for the feast, he oversaw the meal acting as a servant whilst they were his guests. Nothing was too much trouble. He then saw them on their way, seeking justice before the Lord for all the righteous that were in the two debased cities God was preparing to destroy.

Abraham's stature had risen to the point where the Lord was not only prepared to discuss with Him a proposed action, but allowed him to argue about a particular aspect of that action. In this incident in his life, Abraham demonstrated just how humble he was before God, yet bold enough to press a case of possible injustice with Him. But it also tells of God's understanding of individual created beings in that He had already dispatched an angel to save Lot and his family in answer to Abraham's request before it was voiced.

Lot was unwittingly fast approaching the point where he was to pay the full price for choosing the lush plains of the Jordan valley rather than seeking God for direction. The apparently easy path can be deceptive. A man of considerable substance when he arrived, he was willing to turn a blind eye to the corruption he saw around him and settle into a community with morals so diametrically opposed to those he had been taught during his upbringing and his time with Abram that he should have felt nervous in their company and settled elsewhere. Indeed his assimilation into the local society was such that his daughters were engaged to local men.

The depths of depravity to which the inhabitants had fallen was clearly shown whilst the two men were guests in Lot's house. Lot was not unaware of the dangers of strangers sleeping out in the central city square else he would not have been so insistent that the men accompany him to his house.

What was of even greater concern was the ferocity with which the lustful crowd surrounded the house and the danger they posed to the inhabitants. To defuse the situation the angels blinded the eyes of those who were bent on causing damage.

Early in the morning, when warned by their father-in-law of the impending destruction of the city the two prospective husbands laughed and ignored the warning, which said little about the witness Lot should have given to the two men regarding a faith in the living God. Witnessing to our faith is a precondition of salvation, for if we are not willing to speak to others about Jesus, He will not speak our names to the Father.

His reluctance to flee gave evidence as to just how much he and his family had been assimilated into the life of the city, although it is clear Lot did retain an element of his original uprightness. His wife was so reluctant to leave this den of sin that she disobeyed the men's warning not to look back and became a pillar of salt; a similar fate was to befall lingering refugees fleeing Pompeii when they were overtaken by the brimstone and fire from which others escaped. Only Lot's daughters stayed with him.

Lot persuaded the men to allow him to flee to nearby Zoar rather than the mountains that were at a greater distance, continuing to pursue the easy option in life, so unlike his uncle Abraham. Later, in his own time, he went to the surrounding mountains with his daughters, possibly concerned that what had happened to Sodom would also happen to Zoar.

It was whilst in the mountains that his single daughters, unwilling to find other husbands or go childless as would have been accepted by women of a higher moral standing, got their father drunk from wine stored in the mountain caves and lay with him to gain children by him demonstrating that the spirit of the culture of Sodom lived on in them. Thus was born the originator of the tribe of Moab (me-ab – from a father) and Ammon (Ben-ammi – the son of my people or the son of my father's kin). Both tribes were to be enemies of Israel.

With all that had happened to him with regard to the promises given by the angels relating to Sarah's pregnancy and his own future as the father of nations, Abraham could have been expected to be certain of God's protection. But the promises of God do not always assure His servants, especially when faced with the threat of physical danger, of complete safety.

Consider all that happened to Job at the hand of Satan, although his life was saved and his end was greater than before his ordeal. At such times a disconnection occurs between the physical and spiritual causing decisions to be made that seem to obviate any assurance that has been given.

Abraham, again concerned for his life because of his rejuvenated newly pregnant wife, feared what Abimelech would do to him to obtain Sarah for his harem, forgetting what had happened to Pharaoh when he ventured into Egypt. Once again God intervened by means of a dream to prevent the area Egyptian governor contaminating the line of promise within Sarah. Abimelech had been prevented from going anywhere near Sarah and all credit to him for arguing his innocence with God to save his life and of all those in his household.

"Lord, will you slay a righteous nation (or 'innocent folk')?"

He had accepted the misleading information given to him by Abraham. Obviously frightened by the dream and the consequences that could have been incurred, Abimelech handed Sarah back to Abraham with many gifts of sheep and oxen and slaves in recompense and, in a separate transaction, a thousand pieces of silver to make eyes blind to the wrong that had been done to her. Both men were at fault; Abraham for not declaring the all important fact that Sarah was his wife, thus putting her at risk, and Abimelech for perpetuating the disreputable practice of acquiring concubines just because of their beauty, making them widows if they were already married.

In all this God Himself is seen to demonstrate His power within and over His creation and His faithfulness in protecting not only Abraham and Sarah, but also His chosen offspring from the errors and devices of men.

In a similar situation Herod too was unable to kill the infant Jesus, for God directed the wise men to go home by another route and Joseph to take mother and child to Egypt out of the way of the tyrant king.

Unlike Pharaoh, in whose land God was not disposed to allow Abraham to stay, Abimelech realized that there was a powerful God blessing Abraham and could well have seen a benefit to himself and his people by allowing Abraham to stay in the land.

The Birth of Isaac (Gen. 21)

When Abraham reached 100 years of age Isaac was born with great rejoicing to a woman who had previously given up all hope of motherhood. It is to his credit that Abraham, apart from the error of agreeing to lie with Hagar, remained faithful to one wife. But Sarah's error was now coming to plague her.

On seeing Ishmael rejoicing along with everyone else at the birth of a brother, Sarah realized that he was still the first-born. To her earthly and new maternalistic view, Ishmael had changed from being an irritant, reminding her of her barrenness, to become a threat to her own child becoming her husband's heir.

The severity of her call to Abraham for Hagar and her son to be banished from the household seemed heartless and cruel to Abraham because he had grown to love the lad and had spent nearly 13 years training him in the ways of a leader. The man who had pleaded with God to save the righteous living in Sodom and Gomorrah found it impossible to agree to his wife's wishes.

However, God's plan rested on the fact that Isaac would become heir to the covenant He had made with Abraham and Ishmael made that impossible all the while he remained with the patriarch. So God intervened giving Abraham assurances about the continued well being of the lad. It would be very strange if Abraham had not uttered a blessing over the two of them and given them some assurance of the protection of the God he served before sending them off into the desert with bread and water.

Throughout scripture it is evident that God often allows matters to get to an extreme when all hope has been exhausted before entering into the lives of those who cry out to Him. Once again Hagar finds herself in an impossible situation. With the water and bread supply exhausted, she settles Ishmael under a shrub to protect him from the fierceness of the sun and withdraws herself a little distance away so that she does not witness the dying moments of her only son. It was not her fault she was given to Abraham or that she should bear his child. They were both the physical evidence of a human plan gone wrong.

It was at that point that God stepped into her life again, showed her a supply of water close by and gave her further promises regarding the future of her son. These promises she would not casually turn aside because of all that she had witnessed whilst with Abraham and her previous desert experience.

We do well to remember these events, not as readers of a book, but as if we were there experiencing the harshness and sense of hopelessness that would have gripped Hagar and Ishmael as they truly believed death was very near them. Such an entering into the physical and emotional turmoil of the moment, empathizing with their sense of rejection and hopelessness, will help us understand the effect of God's wonderful saving grace, even when all seems lost.

Abimelech, after the experience of the dream he had regarding Sarah, observed Abraham and saw that there was something special about him and his whole way of life (Gen. 21). Can those observing us come to the same conclusion? This view was crystallized with the miraculous birth of Isaac.

To prevent any animosity in the future Abimelech, with his army chief of staff Phicol, sought to enter into an alliance with Abraham. This gave Abraham an opportunity to voice a grievance he had with some of Abimelech's servants over a well.

To confirm the alliance Abraham gave sheep and oxen to ratify the agreement; it also reminded Abraham of the gifts he had received that accompanied the return of Sarah. The separate gift of seven ewe lambs was given only in regard to the recognition by Abimelech that the well belonged to Abraham preventing a repeat of the violent action by Abimelech's servants. The name Beer-sheba was a double etymology; the well of seven (lambs) and the well of swearing.

Although the calling into existence of nature's elemental forces at the beginning of creation was a major manifestation of the Divine power and rule over all things, such matters are restricted to the first two chapters of Genesis. The highest and most detailed manifestation of the Divine will and purpose is seen in the hearts and souls of men, in the personal lives of those who do justice, love mercy and walk humbly with their God.

The account of Hagar and Ishmael, faced as they were with a slow death by starvation, and Abraham and Isaac facing death in different circumstances shows just how personally and intimately God desires to be involved with each one of us. The key factor is undoubtedly the willingness of the individual to reach out to God, humbly and with an open yielding heart that allows Him full control.

What is also clear to those willing to offer themselves to God in such a way is the overwhelming love of the Divine that is free to permeate the dynamic relationship.

God's Supreme Test of Abraham's Faith (Gen. 22)

Infant sacrifice, indeed any human sacrifice, angered God. In Leviticus God says,

> *"You shall not give any of your offspring to pass through the fire in sacrifice to Molech, and so profane the name of your God: I am the Lord"* (Lev. 18:21).

Molech or Milcom was an Ammonite god where human sacrifice was an essential part of the worship and sadly Israelites were worshipping that god (1 Kgs. 11:5, 6). Yet here He calls Abraham to sacrifice Isaac as a burnt offering. The life of this miraculous, God given only son, so symbolic of the One to come, through whom all the promises of God would be fulfilled and, unknown to Abraham, central to God's plan of redemption for the whole of mankind, was to be put at risk at God's command.

The tumultuous emotional storm raging in Abraham's breast can only be imagined. These players on the world stage were real people, the script being written as it was acted out and uttered, the final outcome known only to the One to whom all things are known.

Although the text does not mention Isaac during this dramatic moment in his life, he must not be ignored. His respect for his father must have been total because there is no mention of him resisting when his father bound him and prepared the sacrifice. Certainly this experience meant that his faith in God was fully established to become the foundation of his future life.

Abraham did not argue with God, or play for time, or try to dissuade God from this drastic course of action but obeyed promptly, rising early in the morning. There could well have been a sense of reluctance within his spirit, but God had shown Himself to be a friend and a purveyor of miracles and one can only assume that Abraham had such a profound faith in God through all that he had experienced since leaving Haran that there had to be some special meaning in what God had asked Him to do. Up to that time God had never let him down and Abraham must have been convinced that He would not let him down in the future.

Something of his trust in God was evident in his reply to Isaac,

> *"God Himself will provide the lamb*
> *for the burnt offering my son".*

During the final approach to the sacrificial site, it must have dawned on Isaac that he was the sacrifice. Previously his father had already chosen the luckless animal that would be used for the sacrifice. It was unlike him to come unprepared. What then would have been going on in Isaac's mind when he realized he did not have long to live? And what of his testimony not only concerning his relationship with his father but also concerning his relationship to the God of his father. Just as Abraham had to submit to, and be obedient to God, so Isaac had to submit to and be obedient to both God and his father.

The urgency in the voice of the angel in telling Abraham to stop revealed just how willing Abraham had been to completely obey the commands of the living God. Tested to the limit, God accepted the profoundness of Abraham's faith.

This also said much about God's view of the abomination of child sacrifice that was rife amongst Semitic people and their Egyptian and Aryan neighbours. So in spite of the trauma God's command was for Abraham, its purpose was to test both Abraham's faith and be a vivid demonstration – emphasized by the urgency of the angel's voice – that the practice of human sacrifice was infinitely abhorrent and could have no part to play in His worship.

Moses was to emphasize this as he warned the children of Israel not to serve God in the manner of the surrounding nations,

> *"For every abomination to the Lord, which He hates, they have done*
> *unto their gods; for even their sons and their daughters they have*
> *burned in the fire to their gods." (Deut. 12:31)*

The eyes of such heathen were directed to earthly things; being completely blind to the spiritual in spite of the fact that they were worshipping a demonic angel. As for the God of Abraham, it was the complete physical and spiritual surrender [mind and heart] that He required of Abraham.

All the Lord's prophets alike shuddered at the hideous aberrations of the methods of worship employed by the godless, and they do not rest until all Israel shares their horror of this savage, intensely evil custom. It is through the influence of their teaching of this matter that the name Ge-Hinnon, the valley where the wicked kings practiced this horrendous rite, became synonymous with hell, where there will be a weeping and wailing and a gnashing of teeth.

But the importance of the binding of Isaac (known as Akedah) and the willingness of Abraham to obey God even in death, has been supremely exemplified in the lives of the prophets and ordinary people who were willing to suffer the trial of mocking, scourging, imprisonment and being stoned to death for refusing tempting offers to renounce their faith. They were sawn asunder, tortured and hung by the neck; beheaded, gassed, experimented on, mutilating both their body and their minds, starved and worked to death; they went about in skins of sheep and goats, in rags sewn together with string, utterly destitute, oppressed, cruelly treated, people of whom this world is not worthy (see Heb. 11:37 – 40).

Many have refused fortune and honour and sacrificed their own careers and those of their children whenever these involved disloyalty to the God of Israel. Few chapters have, and should have, such a lasting influence on the lives and souls of men (read Hebrews 11).

God now knew for a certainty that Abraham's faith in Him was unquestioning. Whereas, up to the moment of the intervention of the angel, Abraham was focused on obeying God, now his eyes were opened to the ram caught in a nearby thicket. An animal for sacrifice, already prepared by God for this very moment, was offered as a substitute for Isaac just as the promised Mashiach (the Messiah Jesus) was provided and prepared as our substitute on this very hill where successive temples were erected.

This ground, the seat of Zion, was the location of Jerusalem the city in which this self same God placed His Name forever. This was the centre of the land promised by God to Abraham, Isaac and Jacob in perpetuity, and the continuous focus of all Israel throughout their history and ultimately that of world attention, as it is today.

It became identified and spotlighted as the place where the chosen of God was tested to the limit of his faith. Unknown to Abraham, this act at this place would become the touchstone for all future believers, whether of physical or spiritual descent from him.

Its accumulated history has provided the world with all the information it needs to be sure of the existence and power over world events of the God of Abraham. From Melchizedek, to David's recapture of it, to the successive temples, starting with the glorious temple of Solomon, to the murder of the Messiah, to its renaming by the Emperor Hadrian, who proclaimed that the name Jerusalem would never be mentioned again, to its decline to be a smelly little market town under Turkish rule. However, in spite of Hadrian's declaration and desire, the city is today known throughout the world as Jerusalem, and it is continually at the centre of world attention being the center of the conflict between Satan and the One true creator God.

But it is that same God, the Supreme Deity to whom everything seen and unseen belongs and from whom it has come, who first brought prominence to this hill and has had His hand upon it through every age and whose influence, denied by the ignorant, is as awesome today as at the time of Abraham. It is He who must be at the centre of our worship in the spirit of Abraham who first demonstrated what the ideal worshipper should be like.

It is an accepted fact that sworn statements are always done through a recognized higher authority. But when the Lord swore an oath He could swear by none other than Himself, declaring that there is none higher than He. So to Abraham God said,

> *"By Myself have I sworn, …. In blessing I will bless thee and in multiplying I will multiply thy seed …; and thy seed shall possess the gates of his enemies."*

> *"Remember this and consider,*

recall it to mind, you transgressors,
remember the former things of old;
for I am God, and there is no other;
I am God, and there is none like me,
declaring the end from the beginning
and from ancient times
things that are not yet done,
saying, 'My counsel shall stand,
and I will fulfil all my plans',"
(Isa. 36:8 – 10)

This is the reason why God is able to swear by Himself, there being no one who can contradict Him or overrule Him. In such a position He alone has the authority to declare that *'thy seed shall possess the gates of his enemies'* for in those days to possess the gate was to have command of the city.

The story of Abraham's testimony, warts and all, has been a blessing down through the ages. By the changing of one vowel, says the Midrash, the word for blessing becomes a spring of water. Even as water purifies the defiled so even the name of Abraham is able to attract those far from the knowledge of God. And such has been the role not only of Abraham but also his descendents.

The scriptures provide us with the history of a chosen people on account of their tumultuous relationship with God. Amid the doom and gloom of rebellion and wickedness has consistently run the golden thread of the faithful and determined remnant that provided a constant and consistent source of hope.

God, exasperated at times with the hardness of heart of so many, would have started again with another Noah, or another Moses, but was dissuaded by faithful followers (such as Moses) who saw the future only in the survival of the whole of Israel even in its imperfect state. This is to the benefit of those who have wandered from the truth yet have been brought nigh unto God again by those who cannot let Him go but tenaciously cling to the truth.

Be in no doubt that with every step he took and with every decision he made, Abraham was entering into the unknown, like a traveller travelling in the darkest night under a starless sky. Without his faith as his insurance, Abraham was vulnerable to all the pitfalls of wrong paths and erroneous decisions just as we are today.

Now that he was getting old, and Sarah his wife had died, he needed two things; a burial place for the family to use to bury their dead and a wife for Isaac. For the burial place he bought the field of Ephron at Mamre with the permission of the national council of the Hittites meeting in the gate of the city as observed by passersby (Gen. 23). A wife for Isaac was a more difficult task.

Neither Abraham nor Isaac could leave the Promised Land, as it would not have been politic to do so. That left Abraham's most trusted servant as the only one who could go on a mission to Haran and choose a wife from the offspring of Abraham's brother Nahor, thus avoiding marriage with the idol worshippers of the nations around them and the contamination of the true worship of the Almighty God.

The problems experienced by the Children of Israel stem from the intermarrying that went on from time to time. In the time of Ezra, a purification process was carried out because it was the only way of preparing themselves for a return to the worship of the true God. (Ezra 9)

The Search for a Wife for Isaac (Gen. 24)

The account of Eliezer's commission and journey is precious because it provides an illustration of the effect Abraham's faith had on those immediately around him. By placing his hand under Abraham's thigh, the servant's oath not only applied to Abraham but to all the children that had not only issued, but would issue from the thigh in accordance with the understanding of the means of procreation at the time.

Also, by swearing in the name of the God to whom Abraham had surrendered his life, and in whom Eliezer also believed, the importance and essential nature of the servant's task was raised to the highest level. Into the servant's hands was placed the future of all the promises of God made to his master Abraham, so it was in Eliezer's own interests to ask a series of "What if ?" questions.

To Abraham, the faithfulness of God was beyond question and he was sure, because of the nature of the mission, that just as God had guided him, God would also be with his servant to guide him aright.

Although to aid his servant he agreed that should the "What if?" scenarios not materialize he would be released from his obligations, even though such an outcome was not expected.

Bearing gifts for the prospective bride and her family the servant set out to seek a wife for his master's son.

On reaching the town of Nahor, Eliezer went to the one point where people were bound to congregate, that is the well where the people went to draw water. It was there that he offered up a prayer to the God of his master for the success of his mission, asking for a particular sign that would identify the chosen maiden. It is comforting to see God in action. For He had already directed Rebekah to set off to draw water at that moment so that no sooner had the words been uttered than she was near the well.

As requested by the servant, Rebekah, who we are told had both an outer and inner beauty, was not satisfied with just providing him with water but offered to fetch water for his camels also sealing the identity of the maiden as Isaac's bride. Her task fulfilled she was offered gold jewellery both as a token of gratitude and as a means of obtaining the girl's favourable opinion. Asking for the girl's name and if there was room in her father's house to stay, Eliezer was given the final confirmation he needed that God had indeed guided him to the very family he needed to see and to the prospective bride for Isaac.

This was a time for thanksgiving and Eliezer wasted no time in bowing his head and prostrating himself before the Lord to thank him for the true kindness shown to his master and, on a personal note, for leading him aright. Such a personal experience of the awesomeness of the Divine Deity he had worshipped whilst in his master's service must have had a profound effect on his personal faith.

Witnessing such behaviour by the servant will have been a revelation to Rebekah and being presented with such expensive gifts, somewhat overwhelming, coming so suddenly and happening so quickly, dramatically changing what had started as just another day in her life and that of her family. She ran off to tell her family all that had happened and show them the jewellery. Her brother Laban then went out to look the stranger over and using the servant's own phrase for his God welcomed him into their home.

The procedure was to look after the animals first and then to wash the visitor's feet before presenting them with food. On this occasion his mission was so urgent that after seeing to the animals Eliezer explained to his hosts the purpose of their mission before accepting any food.

Giving a résumé of his master's situation and the birth of Isaac to Sarah in her old age, Eliezer then related all that had happened at the well from his point of view, including his request to his God and his meeting with Rebekah, referring to her as a girl of marriageable age. The negotiations then proceeded, although the involvement of the God who had caused Abraham to leave his home so long ago and had taken such an active part in Eliezer's search certainly restricted their room for maneuver.

It is noticeable that Laban disrespectfully, or precociously, answered before his father, which could well have been a warning of the bullish and insensitive nature that was to cause Jacob so much grief when gaining the hand of Rachel many years later.

With the negotiations over and the success of his mission assured Eliezer once again demonstrated his profound faith by acknowledging the God of Abraham and thanking Him for blessing his search for a wife for Isaac. Gifts were then presented to Rebekah, who had played no part in the arrangements for her future, and her brother and mother. Only then could the meal begin.

Rebekah's New Life

In the morning Eliezer was obviously keen to be off back to his master to let him know as soon as possible that his mission had been successful. After all the journey was a long one and Abraham would be anxious to know if the search had been successful. The family, particularly Rebekah's brother and mother, were reluctant to see her go, knowing that it was unlikely that they would ever see her again. It could be that Laban's possessive nature was showing itself already.

To settle the matter Rebekah herself was asked to make a decision. After a night of reflection she too was keen to be on her way to meet this man to whom she was now betrothed. Like Abraham, Rebekah was ready to respond immediately and this must say something about her character.

Isaac was camping near the well associated with Hagar. In the

95

afternoon, Isaac went out into a quiet place to meditate and pray. Whilst he was there, he saw the camel train approaching and went out to greet it. Rebekah, seeing Isaac approach, dismounted as a mark of respect to a person of importance and asked about the identity of this man. On hearing it was the man she was to marry she followed etiquette by covering her face with a veil.

Eliezer then gave a full account of his travels to Isaac and Isaac took Rebekah to his mother's tent and installed her as the new mistress of the household. The text is brief, ceremonies and etiquette stripped out to reveal two important things. That Isaac had no hesitation in accepting Rebekah as his wife and that he loved her, being comforted by her presence and personality for the loss of his mother. It also shows just how excellent was God's understanding and knowledge of Isaac's needs in a wife. Balance had now been restored to the household with Rebekah's arrival just as Adam was fulfilled with the gift of Eve.

The passing of Abraham to his eternal reward concludes the first glowing chapter in the life of mankind and its relationship to a loving creator God.

Of all the great men who had lived up to that time, Abraham had qualities of character and principles that set him way above the others. He was the pioneer of monotheistic faith. Uninspired by the heathen splendour of a Nimrod or a Hammurabi, he broke away from the debasing idol worship of his contemporaries and devoted his life to the spread of the world redeeming truth of the one true God of justice and mercy.

The secret of his first meeting with God when he heard the Divine voice instruct him to forsake his home and family to journey into the unknown remains a secret. But his willingness to surrender himself joyfully to the Divine-Will, gives all who follow after him a clear example of how a resolute faith can lead to a glorious intimacy with the Divine that enables the believer to overcome any size or type of obstacle.

He set an example to his children to sacrifice the dearest things in life and, if need be, life itself in defense of the spiritual heritage entrusted to their care. Along with his renunciation of his own life and desires in the service of God, he practiced loving kindness towards his fellow man.

Witness his magnanimity in his treatment of Lot; his fine independence in his refusal to accept any of the spoils of war won by the men of his household; his benevolence in his reception of strangers; his stand for justice when pleading for Lot when he learned of the judgement on the cities of Sodom and Gomorrah; and his all embracing human pity, which extended even to those who had forfeited all claims to human pity.

For our comfort, amongst the tremendous acts of faith are sprinkled moments of doubt and anxiety, of concern for personal safety measures, and assisting the Divine plan.

Then in the closing stages of his life, his trust placed firmly in the Divine cause, we see the search through his servant for a God chosen wife for his son. This surely was the climactic co-operation between God, Abraham and a servant who had caught the Divine spark of faith, working together for the sole purpose of finding for Isaac the ideal helpmeet to support him and bear his children in perfect harmony.

With his inheritance firmly in the hands of one who had experienced God's saving grace at first hand and was fully committed to a life of faith, Abraham could leave this world's stage knowing he had fulfilled his commission and passed on the baton of promise.

Abraham is the prototype, the example on which to base our own lives. The command *"Look unto the rock from whence you were hewn … look unto Abraham your father"* is directed at all believers, Jew and Gentile alike, for he was considered righteous <u>before</u> he was circumcised, not afterwards.

5 ISAAC

The Succession of Isaac (Gen. 25:19 on)

A new era begins with the succession of Isaac to the promise given to Abraham, a new patriarch with a different style having gone through completely different experiences of how God had dealt with him through his father. The tribe was now well established in the land. But again the birth of a son and heir is delayed, possibly to emphasize that the children that were eventually born were a gift of grace from God for the fulfilment of His purposes.

Towards the end of the pregnancy, Rebekah was so distressed by the violent activity of the twins in her womb that she called to the Lord who told her that:

1. The two boys represented two nations.

2. One would be stronger than the other and they would be mutually antagonistic from birth.

3. The elder would serve the younger – this was fulfilled when King David defeated Edom.

Esau, the name possibly meaning "long hair", arrived with ruddy hair as a premonition of his love of hunting and the shedding of blood. Jacob arrived holding one of Esau's heels giving the impression of trying to hold Esau back, preventing him being the first-born. Isaac was sixty years of age.

There is no narrative concerning their formative years, although the developed characters of the two young men give enough information about their relationship which only confirms what God had told their mother. Conflict between the two brothers was not helped by the parents each of whom had a different favourite, with Isaac favouring Esau and Rebekah favouring Jacob.

Esau loved the outdoor life shunning any learning except for gaining skills in the hunt. Devoted to his father, he was impulsive and more concerned about the present. He pursued a life style that hardly accorded with the standard of devotion to the Supreme God established by Abraham.

Jacob was far more contemplative and coveted the birthright for purely spiritual reasons. In primitive times when the first-born acceded to the position of head of the tribe, he also became the tribal priest. With Jacob's sensitivity to, and growing understanding of, the promises of God to Abraham and then his father Isaac and their importance to the future well-being of the family, it is no wonder that he was concerned about its continuing effectiveness should Esau succeed to his father's position.

Suspecting that his brother did not value the dignity and privilege of his position as first-born as Jacob thought he should, Jacob bided his time until an opportunity arose when he could put the matter to the test.

It is easy to criticize someone for what is perceived to be the reason behind an action. Without going into the character of that person beforehand and considering the circumstances leading up to an action it is unwise to take any firm stand on what is thought to have been the motive behind that action. Jacob, unlike his brother, is scholarly and non-confrontational.

Withholding food from his brother would not have been life threatening. But with the exaggeration of a hungry man whose main focus was on his physical needs whatever the cost, Esau was ripe for the test.

With no material advantage, the birthright of the spiritual inheritance of Abraham did not command a value as high as a dish of pottage. Even when requested to swear an oath to the transfer of his birthright to Jacob, this fickle and impulsive hunter raised no objections but readily complied with the request, his concentration fully focused on the gratification of his momentary pangs of hunger, oblivious to that which to a man of nobler character would be of transcendent worth.

Just as Adam and Eve's eyes were focused on the forbidden fruit oblivious to the consequences of their action, so Esau, in a similar way, swallowed the food hungrily, eager to be on his way.

When God is referred to as loving Jacob but hating Esau it is not a case of love and hate in the normal sense of the two words but stating a preference. From God's point of view, who would be most able and, more importantly, most willing to take on Abraham's mantle when their father died? Surely it would be the one who was most sensitive to spiritual things and therefore more responsive to Him.

The few chapters needed to cover the life of Isaac illustrate the uneventful nature of his life whilst head of family. Apart from being deflected from travelling to Egypt, like his father, at the time of famine, an abundant crop of cereal at the end of the famine and skirmishes with the Philistines under Abimelech, the main focus of the narrative concerns the growth and development of his two sons; the one a hunter and man of action with a rebellious streak, the other sensitive and devout to whom the importance of continuing the family moral and ethical code and life style were very important.

The blessing of Jacob as the eldest in place of his brother Esau should be seen in context. Jacob, as has already been seen, was a sensitive man and lacked the aggressive spirit of his brother that is required of a risk taker.

Rebekah will have clearly remembered, as only a woman who had gone through such an experience during pregnancy as she can remember such things, what God had said to her at the end of her pregnancy. It is likely that she had heard about the transfer of the birthright from Esau to Jacob and was as distressed as Isaac by Esau taking wives of the heathen tribes in defiance of the family custom and the wishes of God who desired to keep the patriarchs and ultimately the new nation of Israel pure (see the book of Ezra).

Whose Deceit? (Gen. 27)

When Rebekah realized that her husband Isaac was ready to give the blessing to Esau, she took action and hatched a plan to ensure that Jacob received the blessing instead of Esau. She was either more sensitive to, or more aware of, the future needs of the family and its spiritual heritage than Isaac.

Rebekah had realized from the start that it would be pointless to try to persuade her husband to give the blessing to Jacob rather than Esau, such was the strength of family tradition and custom that the blessing should always be given to the eldest son whatever his character might be. But that was not God's way. He chooses those best suited to the position rather than merely those in a certain position within the nation or family by reason of birth.

The man God chose to be the best king Israel ever had was the youngest of seven children; this was because God looks into the heart and knows even what we are thinking and truly believing. Saul was the first king of Israel chosen to demonstrate to the people that their choice of king, relying as it did on his apparent physical features and handsome looks, was flawed. It was when David became King of Israel that the nation grew strong and served the Lord their God.

Not knowing how long it would take Esau to find and kill his prey Rebekah first had to persuade Jacob to go along with her plan. His reluctance was based both on his natural reserve, he was not a risk taker like Esau, and a preference to avoid confrontation along with his knowledge of the physical difference between him and his brother. A meditative man he was all too aware of the danger that he could attract a curse upon himself rather than a blessing. Such an outcome would, in his view, be doubly worse than not receiving the blessing at all. Rebekah's willingness to accept the full force of the curse should her plan fail, probably saved the day.

Using all her culinary skills she made a dish, of which Isaac was particularly fond, that would mimic the dish Esau was going to prepare for his father. She then covered areas of Jacob that Isaac, because of his failing eyesight, would be bound to touch when assuring himself that it was indeed Esau and not Jacob who was before him.

Jacob, to his credit, did not try to change his voice because Isaac easily detected that the voice was that of Jacob but the smell and feel was that of Esau. Nor did he change his use of words, for it was unlikely that Esau would have used the expression, *"The Lord thy God sent me good speed"*.

Even though he went along with the deception Jacob did not try to mimic Esau as a true deceiver would because it was not in his nature to do so. Seeking assurances to the last, Isaac finally gave the irrevocable blessing to Jacob, who left his father's presence just moments before Esau arrived in his father's tent to receive the promised blessing.

Although this is the account of a human family event, because it is at the centre, and therefore an integral part of God's Plan of Salvation, to divorce the spiritual aspect of these events would be to completely remove the critical importance of what happened within this family.

God preferred Jacob to Esau and, because we can see the whole story of what happened laid out before us, it is very easy to understand why. God does not chose just anyone to serve Him. The fact that Esau was 'legally', that is according to human law, the eldest, mattered not to God because He looks into the heart of a person and reads the messages being transmitted by that heart; messages of an attitude towards Him that are hidden from even their closest family members, but completely clear to Him.

Esau, thrilled by the chase and kill which he skillfully turned into a meal he knew his father would love, was full of expectancy as he carried the special meal to his father. But his father's startled greeting of *"Who are you?"* was hardly what he had expected.

There can be little doubt that Isaac soon worked out what had happened. The voice had been that of Jacob but the smell and feel was that of Esau. Thus was the deception realized, though the underlying truth, and particularly God's involvement in it, was not causing the whole episode to be brought down to the human perspective.

With the underlying spiritual truth being, understandably, quickly trodden underfoot by Isaac's anger at being deceived and Esau's immediate false sense of hurt being dramatically displayed, the human record brands Jacob a deceiver of the worst kind.

Yet by what name is the nation of the offspring of Abraham and Isaac called in the rest of scripture but the children of Jacob and Israel,

Jacob's God given name. Whose offspring do Christian believer's celebrate every Easter? The offspring of Esau or Jacob?

It is essential that the spiritual activity within those who were committed to God during their lives as Abraham, Isaac and Jacob were, is brought to the fore. The sub-title of this books is important because Genesis is all about God's relationship to man and how He set His plan of Salvation in motion and caused it to gradually develop through many generations until the birth of His Son. That is why the Bible must be declared a complete book, because nothing can be left out, and the clear evidence of God's hand in the affairs of men accepted, as in this case where the rightful heir of Isaac was given his blessing.

As it was, the man to succeed Isaac was to be the right man for the job of carrying the torch handed down from his grandfather Abraham. God could not afford to trust His long-term plan for man's salvation to someone who was so impetuous and rebellious that the thought of having to don the yoke of responsibility and humility before God would have been anathema to him.

To place the blame for this whole escapade purely on Jacob is totally irresponsible and denies the part Rebekah played and the underlying fact that God Himself preferred Jacob to Esau and enabled the deception to succeed. It is much better to realise there was a higher purpose in the way things worked out.

Esau had no grounds to complain about the loss of something he had considered as of less worth than a bowl of pottage. His tears were those of the sensuous, wild, impulsive man that he was, almost like the cry of a trapped creature, and are considered by some as the most pathetic in the Bible. The blessing Isaac gave to his son Esau was more of a prophecy. He would live by the sword and the lordship Jacob would wield over Esau would be short lived and to this end there is the record in the book of Kings of revolts by the Edomites.

It is at least to Esau's credit that he spared his father's feelings and vowed to wait until his death before avenging himself on Jacob. Although Esau's tears would be as momentary as his concentration would allow, his threat to kill his brother, born out of hate was another matter and could not be ignored.

6 JACOB

Jacob Flees from his Brother (Gen. 28)

Rebekah, not knowing how much longer her husband had on this earth, decided to take action. She needed to prevent the loss of one (Jacob) signalling the death of the other (Isaac) by sending Jacob off to Haran, ostensibly to find a wife.

Rebekah, who had been specially chosen by Almighty God to be a wife and mother within this family, shines like a light in this whole drama; sensitive to the spiritual implications of the decisions being made and more aware than the others of the need to be obedient to the will of God and its impact on the inheritance of the promise of God to Abraham, she took the lead role to ensure the purposes of God were achieved.

This is God in action through individuals. Like Esther (Esther. 4) Rebekah, having given birth to the twin boys, was now instrumental in ensuring they lived to begin the next chapter of their lives.

She had willingly taken up the challenge presented to her by this demonstrably active and remarkable God, first introduced to her by the evident faith of Eliezer, Abraham's servant. Just as Abraham responded to God's call, so Rebekah set off without delay from her family to meet a husband chosen for her, not by her family, but by God. Her understanding of this God grew through learning at the hand of her husband Isaac and experience.

Her promotion of Jacob could not be accounted for solely by her ability to relate more easily with him than his brother. The traumatic pregnancy and God's message to her must have had a far greater impact on her decision to plan and carry out the deception than merely preferring one above the other.

Now, with Esau enraged and muttering violence, her concern focused on saving the life of Jacob and in so doing she realized that he would need a wife to continue the line, and that would mean sending him off to her relatives, away from danger. None of this activity can be meditated upon in isolation. No one, as has already been seen, can separate the experiences and actions of men and the fulfilment of God's perfect plan. To do so would negate the underlying message of Biblical truth.

Did Abraham set off for an unknown destination because of a whim? The binding of Isaac, was that caused by some aberration? His salvation, was that the result of pure chance? If the example of Abraham and all his life's experiences are to be fully understood, separating them from the God he had met, believed in and to whom he had dedicated his life, would be a complete folly. Indeed it would imply that the whole of the plan of salvation depended on the roll of a dice and cannot therefore be considered a plan at all.

An example of the involvement of the Almighty in the affairs of each individual mentioned in this first book, can clearly be seen in the actions of Rebekah and Jacob, which is why Genesis is so important in the way it illustrates God's relationship with man; a relationship that is real, enabling us to learn important lessons from this record of their lives.

This time Rebekah knew she could go to Isaac and proffer the suggestion that Jacob should be sent to their family in Haran to find a wife. She also knew that he would decide wisely without ever knowing the real purpose of the journey or question why the arrangements for his departure needed to be made so urgently. It is perhaps fortunate that Rebekah could not know how long Jacob would be away or that she would never see him again.

Esau, seeing the departure of his brother to find a wife according to his parent's wishes, attempted to gain favour with them again by marrying a bride from his uncle Ishmael's family. In this he used his own logic not realizing the increasing and unbridgeable gap he was creating between himself and his family and the God who intended to bless them and their offspring in preference to his own. A gap that would bring about a conflict that continues to this day.

Part of God's plan is that the offspring of Abraham, Isaac and Jacob should be a blessing to those around them and that includes the offspring of Ishmael and Esau. Indeed it is a matter of rejoicing that Arabs and Gentiles of many nations have had such a profound Abramic experience of the Almighty that in spite of horrific torture and physiological pressure they have maintained their faith and trust in God to the very end.

Jacob's Spiritual Journey

The Biblical text now leads us to a new, action packed phase of God's plan of salvation. Jacob, in leaving the protection and support of his family, starts his training as a leader and successor to Isaac so that he might receive the inheritance of God's promise to Abraham and produce sons from whose offspring a nation would be built.

Jacob's departure from his father's presence was like the salt for savouring food being removed from the kitchen. The influence of this young God believer, who had caught something of the vision that had inspired his father and grandfather, would be sorely missed. There is no indication that he was a perfect child for what child is, but it was his belief in Almighty God, however rudimentary it may have been, that was the key to his character and life.

Esau, now the dominant force in the family, did not have the dedication to Almighty God that Jacob had; this would mean that belief in the God of Abraham would dwindle, being suffocated by the preference for the worship of earthly things and the gods of the surrounding nations; the very thing that Abraham and Isaac had sought to avoid.

Jacob's influence was essential in maintaining the worship of the God of Abraham within the family and amongst the hired servants, however stridently his brother tried to oppose it. By his very way of life Esau sought to draw those around him away to a more 'pleasure centred' life of living for today, of freedom to do what you want when you want it. It is unlikely that Esau himself was a religious man in any way, but it is likely his wives would have brought up his children to worship the local gods. It is for this very reason that the removal of the salt, or the influence, of Jacob's presence would be sorely missed.

The outstanding feature of scripture is how it describes the manner in which God speaks to each individual whose heart is open to Him. It was not enough that Jacob should receive his father's blessing. Having been forced to leave the family home, rather than forced to go to Haran, Jacob suddenly finds himself alone and friendless in a wilderness experience, the hardness and unforgiving nature of his situation clearly illustrated by his use of a stone as a pillow.

This is the opening scene of a new life for Jacob. It did not mean that he would not make mistakes, nor that he would now be perfect, but it did signal the start of a new spiritual experience, a journey that would lead him into a deeper and more intimate relationship with the God he had previously only heard about.

It is at a time in his life when he found himself faced with the stark realities and challenges of being on his own and having to fend for himself, away from the comforts and familiarities of the close family environment he had been so used to that God makes a personal appearance. It could well have been the very first time that Jacob had actually met with God person to person; the first of many as he gradually came into a new realization of the reality of God.

God's purpose in meeting with Jacob at the very beginning of his new life of independent living and practical training in manhood was not only to repeat the promises He made to Abraham and Isaac thereby endorsing the blessing of his father and confirming Jacob's place in the line of accession, but also to establish a relationship with Jacob that would put him on the correct path of service that would lead to a spiritual intimacy between them, vital to his special role in God's plan for his life and the future of the new nation of Israel that would be established through him.

There can be no doubt that our studies into the lives of the three great patriarchs of Abraham, Isaac and Jacob have enabled us to realize just how real was their relationship with God. Undoubtedly Abraham's meeting with God was the most significant because God was completely unknown to him, there was no one to point him in the right direction as it was with both Isaac and Jacob, however it is one thing being told about God, but quite another establishing a personal relationship with someone it was impossible to see with human vision.

Isaac's life could not exactly be described as being particularly inspirational because his experience of God had been through his father Abraham and particularly on the mountain when he was very nearly the sacrificial victim. It is also important to remember that a wife was found for Isaac by his father's servant, he remained in the camp with his father.

Jacob's experience can be seen right from the start as being so different in that he learned about the need for a personal relationship with God at his father's knee and over time, particularly after he had been sent off to find himself a wife, by practical personal experiences.

The issues of life and death are in God's hands alone, it signalled the start of Jacob's personal walk with God that made true the saying, *"The God of Abraham, Isaac and Jacob"*. When Jacob was renamed Israel and his offspring became a nation, there was no need for God to repeat this process of confirmation. And so it remains to this day.

Jacob's dream is a gem of scripture with its profound and beautiful picture of just how close God is to each one of us. Jacob's exclamation, *"Surely God is in this place; and I knew it not"*, could be used by us all. What is so remarkable about the dream is that the angels are described as ascending before descending, meaning that alone and without friends as he was, unknown to him were the unseen angelic protectors and encouragers of this God-chosen 'man of God' in whose line would come the HaMashiach, Jesus Christ the Messiah of the Jews.

It is surely true that these recorded glimpses of the relationship between God and man in action are there for our benefit and encouragement in order to bless and encourage us.

It is these glimpses and the manner in which all 66 books so wonderfully dovetail together and support each other in even the smallest detail that allows the Holy Bible to stand tall above all other recorded scripture. Even more wonderful is the fact that only the Holy Spirit, inspiring the various contributors, could have provided such a book with a single theme and message.

Malachi is no more out of tune with Moses as Isaiah is out of tune with Job, or Paul with Jeremiah. All tell of their relationship with, and received messages from the Almighty God who appeared to Abraham,

Isaac and Jacob. It is as profound and almost as unfathomable as the deepest ocean or deepest space.

Jacob, rejuvenated in his faith vowed a vow that set him on a new course that would unite him and his house with the God he had previously only learned about from his forebears. *"If God be with me … then shall the Lord be my God."* In this way Jacob dedicated his life to the God of Abraham.

Jacob Meets with His Relatives (Gen. 29)

Arriving at Haran Jacob, like Eliezer before him, came to the main watering hole to try to make contact with his relatives, and in a similar manner met his future wife when she came out to water her sheep.

Normally all the flocks needed to be present for enough people to roll away the heavy stone. On this occasion Jacob moved the stone on his own and whilst the flock was drinking was able to introduce himself to his cousin telling her three times that her father was his mother's brother, overjoyed that his journey had been successful.

Rachel told her father Laban who, as previously, came out to meet him and welcome him into their home. This welcome was in stark contrast to Jacob's departure, and whereas here the flocks were attended to by one of the daughters, then he and his sons were required to shear the sheep.

At the outset Jacob seems to have decided not to be indebted to his uncle but to earn his keep through working for him. It is interesting that shepherding became an important skill of the Lord's ancestors. He who referred to Himself as the shepherd of the sheep of Israel was descended from shepherds. Moses was a shepherd for forty years before being given responsibility for shepherding the nation of Israel released from slavery in Egypt.

Without a dowry Jacob was in no position to purchase a wife. When his love for Rachel grew to a point where he wanted her to be his wife the only tangible asset he had was his labour. Therefore he went to his uncle and made a deal to work seven years for her. The six Hebrew words used to describe Jacob's frame of mind during the seven years of waiting for her condenses a world of tenderest love. Such was his love for her that the seven years seemed to him but a few days.

This description of his romance is important as it provides an essential understanding of all that follows, remembering that the narrative gives an account of the life and relationships of real people, in real situations who unlike the reader, had no knowledge of what would happen the following day, let alone the following year. At the end of the seven years Jacob had to remind Laban that he was now due his wife.

Laban hosted a wedding feast for the bridal couple. The deception that follows gives ample evidence as to the deceitful nature of Laban who by now was seeing the effects of benefiting from God's blessing of all that Jacob did. It should not be seen as some form of retribution for Jacob's deception to gain the blessing of Esau, which has been explained in detail above. Such a view of Laban's deception provides him with an excuse that is not legitimate. His actions should be considered on their own account.

It is unfortunate that Jacob has been branded a deceiver, detracting as it does from his genuine search for and willing submission to the God of His fathers. It also tends to hide the fact that he was God's chosen servant.

Laban brought Leah, whose only real beauty was to be found in her eyes, to where Jacob was staying. It was dark when the unsuspecting Jacob went in to her. Leah would surely have known about Jacob's intense love for her sister and her sister's love for him.

It is probable that Leah was not told about Laban's plan until the last moment just in case she gave the game away, though Laban would have had to regulate the timing of the nuptials to suit Leah's periods. Nothing is said of Leah's emotions when used in this way, which could be particularly hurtful knowing that she was otherwise considered unmarriageable. She must have realized, however, that the dawn would bring repercussions.

Jacob was naturally furious at the deception and Laban's excuse about the eldest daughter always being married first could not be taken seriously. If that was the recognized custom why was Jacob not told about it before he started the seven years' service for Rachel?

As Jacob had already married Leah by going in to her there was no way that the clock could be turned back. Laban agreed to Jacob having Rachel also if he was prepared to serve another seven years, thus Laban got the benefit of fourteen years of Jacob's blessing, double what he had previously expected.

Laban's character would suggest that this was the very reason for the ruse in the first place. As shall be seen God so often uses these flaws in human nature for His own ends.

The true character of Jacob is displayed in the fact that he honoured his union with Leah and was willing to give himself to her for the seven days to which she was entitled. Only then was Rachel, the one for whom Jacob had served the seven years, able to become his second wife.

Leah was sensitive, devoted and loyal to the point where she was prepared to totally commit herself to her husband, as will be seen as the story unfolds; to her Jacob's love for her was fundamental and the sons she bore for him were an essential element in her desire to gain more of that love.

At the birth of her first son Reuben, Leah exclaimed that God had seen her affliction, clarifying that she was less loved than Rachel when she bore Simeon. Next came Levi, the originator of the priestly tribe, followed by Judah, that is praise because Leah was full of praise to God for allowing her to give four sons to Jacob. Later she was to provide another two of Jacob's twelve sons making six sons in all. With her heart right with God He was able to bless her abundantly.

Rachel on the other hand, although beautiful and continually loved by Jacob, could not let go of her idolatrous past and focus on the God her husband worshipped and served, nor could she bear the thought of being without children, not, it would seem, because she wanted to gain more of his love and affection through them, but for her own sake, her own sense of shame.

Instead of seeking God's help as Leah had done, Rachel complained to Jacob. Jacob's rebuke, *"Am I in God's stead?"* should have been enough to point her in the right direction, but like Sarah she resorted to a Babylonian custom and offered her maid to Jacob to bear children for her. Unfortunately this led Leah following suit. As it was the contribution the maids made to the family numbers was two sons each.

It would seem Rachel was unable to understand the concept that the issues of life and death are in God's hand alone, even though her husband had learned to rely on this self same God for everything.

It is one thing seeking help from an idol that could be seen but was spiritually dead like the seeker and therefore unable to influence the physical, but quite another to seek after a spiritual God that could not be seen but had complete control over the physical.

We have seen from the lives of both Sarah and Rebekah that God is intimately involved in the lives of His servants. Both were initially barren until God intervened to allow them to bear sons. It is unfortunate that these two women felt that they had to contest for the affection of their husband and this unnecessary tension finally led to a law amongst the Children of Israel preventing a man marrying sisters.

As it was the four women were to provide the heads of the twelve tribes of Israel. God had therefore used the deception of Laban and the wifely rivalry of the two sisters for good. During this stable time, with the women comfortable in familiar surroundings, Jacob's family was built up ready for the rigours of the journey ahead when daily life for a pregnant woman would have been far from comfortable, especially with the threat from Esau and the surrounding nations ever present.

Laban had undoubtedly prospered during the time of Jacob's employment. Flocks that his daughter Rachel could manage had now swollen so that it had become a full time job for a shepherd. Such prosperity Laban obviously did not want to lose. Thus it was that Jacob, still with nothing to bargain with but his labour and the Lord's clear blessing over all that he did, had to enter into yet a third agreement with Laban to acquire wealth for himself.

The sheep in that area would have been predominantly white and the goats predominately black. What better way of distinguishing the flocks that would be his wages from those that were Laban's than for his sheep and goats to be those that were not of the predominant colour. Thus was the agreement made between Jacob and Laban.

Even with the agreement so heavily biased against Jacob, Laban still could not control his greed and had his sons remove from the flock all those that could become Jacob's. Having tended the flocks for 14 years Jacob would surely have known the proportion of those that were not of the predominant colour and could not have failed to have been well aware of Laban's duplicity. Yet it was not until the following year that he made a start to gain stock for himself by using streaked rods near the pregnant ewes so that sight of them would affect the colouring of their lambs. From that moment on he separated the strongest of the newly born spotted lambs and kids from the main flock and bred from them so that there would be a continuing tendency to bear strong and healthy spotted young.

Such was the blessing Jacob received from the God to whom he had committed himself that he prospered greatly gaining large flocks, menservants and maidservants. Not satisfied with the wealth they and their father had gained from Jacob's hand, Laban's sons begrudged this relative, who had become a servant in their eyes, getting any benefit from his labour for himself. The relationship had become strained to the point where Jacob realized that something had to be done.

There is no reason why the thoughts of the patriarch should be recorded prior to him making the decision to leave Laban's employ, but it would be out of character if he had not sought God on this matter because it was God who had brought Him here in the first place and was the engine that was generating his wealth. The growing animosity he detected from Laban and his sons to his increasing wealth could well signal a dangerous reaction from them that could cause untold damage to either him or his growing family.

It might seem convenient that Jacob should suddenly hear a message from God at this particular time instructing him to go back home. But what must never be forgotten is that our daily life and God's plan for us are inextricably linked and the timing of landmark events perfect. If the God of Abraham and Isaac and now of Jacob is real and Jacob's commitment to that God complete, then whatever happens in his life cannot be considered with any degree of cynicism. This is Divinely inspired scripture, not a story book where coincidences might be considered as being useful rather than inspired.

The resolve of every truly committed child of God must be that whatever the cost to themselves no major decision is made other than they seek God's face in prayer, asking Him to guide them. They can then be sure that any decision they make that is in line with the Will of God will be upheld or changed if it is not.

Having received God's message Jacob called to his wives whilst he was amongst the flocks and out of earshot of Laban and his sons. Of all people Jacob's wives knew the service their husband had rendered to their father and the way their father had treated both their husband, especially in the matter of his wages, and themselves since they married Jacob.

The servant master relationship that had developed between the two men had obviously affected the treatment they had received even though they were his daughters. Realizing that there was no longer a place for them in their father's house, they aligned themselves and their children with Jacob and the God who had blessed both him and them.

Jacob's Escape

Laban and his sons were three days journey away shearing the sheep and feasting. It is interesting that Jacob, who was still in charge of managing the flocks, was not invited to the shearing or the feasting. It did however make this an ideal time for Jacob to quietly leave the homeland of Laban and make his way back to the land he had left many years before, returning with a household of his own that included two wives, two handmaids, twelve children, menservants and maidservants and flocks and herds.

Laban was informed three days after Jacob had fled. It then took him seven days of hard riding to catch up with the slow moving Jacob in the mountains of Gilead. Although Jacob was vulnerable from the force of men led by Laban, he was following God's instructions and it was therefore his God who met with Laban to warn him against having Jacob return either by enticement or force of arms.

With his anger and desire for revenge dissipated, Laban stuck a note of injured innocence when he finally met with Jacob. But both men knew that if he had had total freedom to do what he wanted, Laban would have forced Jacob to return with him to effectively become a slave to the Laban household.

Laban, possibly to give vent to his real feelings and the frustration he was experiencing, told Jacob of his meeting with Jacob's God. But there was a grievance he could still pursue and that was the loss of the family gods. Jacob gives him permission to search the camp and who ever had them in their possessions, Laban could punish.

This incident clearly identifies the differences between the two sisters. On the one hand Leah, whose only asset was her eyes, was completely committed to her husband and his God. Her devotion to Jacob, even though she was reduced to secondary status before him, brought God's special blessing that enabled her to present Jacob with six sons and a daughter.

On the other hand Rachel an acknowledged beauty and, in Jacob's eyes, preferred before Leah, was not quite so committed to Jacob and his God for she could not let go of the household gods that she had grown up with and had stolen from her father. As a result she had only been blessed with one son after years of barrenness.

Deceptive like her father, she feigned a menstrual period that allowed her to remain seated in the presence of her father when he came to search her tent, thus preventing Laban finding his lost gods.

With his innocence proven, Jacob gave vent to his indignation over the dishonest way Laban had dealt with him. As a shepherd Jacob had to provide a receipt for the sheep in his care and apart from those lost to wild animals and environmental disaster, losses through his own negligence had to be repaid tenfold. Other than that he was bound to return them with reasonable increase. In achieving the higher than normally expected increase, he had had to suffer the vagaries of the weather from subzero temperatures to the full heat of the day and from drought to very wet conditions.

Unable to counter Jacob's reproaches Laban resorted to repeating the claim based on primitive usage that the head of the family is the nominal possessor of all that belonged to its members. His pretence in being solicitous for the well being of his daughters and grandchildren is made a nonsense by his previous behaviour towards them. However his new concern, now that he had finally realized that a higher power than he and his gods was protecting Jacob, was for his own protection and welfare.

This was a typical bullyboy response to a possible threat, and yet Jacob had never posed a physical threat because he was not an aggressive person. In seeking to make a covenant with Jacob and ensure its effectiveness he was prepared to call upon both the God of Abraham and his own gods as witnesses. Jacob was only willing to call upon the former.

Having feared repercussions from Laban when he caught up with him, Jacob will have been relieved when told that the God he worshipped had intervened in what could easily have been a fatal encounter. His sacrifice was of thanksgiving to God for His protection.

When Jacob broke camp to continue on his way and saw the company of angels he realized that there had been two camps during that time, that is his camp surrounded by the company of Angels and Laban's camp. Thus was the place called *Mahanaimer* – two camps. Jacob was now assured that God was mindful of His promises to him and he could continue his journey free from Laban's powerful influence. However the uncertainty of his reception by Esau gradually occupied his mind the nearer he got the land he called home.

Jacob Prepares to Meet with Esau

To find out if Esau still harboured any animosity towards him Jacob sent messengers to tell Esau that he had gained no prestige for he had merely sojourned with his relatives and was now returning home with some possessions and sought to find favour with his brother. On their return the messengers told Jacob that Esau was coming to meet him with a small army of 400 men, far in excess of anything Jacob could muster, which made him very concerned for the safety of his family.

It is worth noting that even with the assurance that God was with him, and had already been protected from an angry and vengeful Laban, Jacob still showed the same human emotion of fear that we all experience when facing possible danger. We have sight only of the physical, whereas God has sight of both the physical and spiritual, except God reveals to us what is happening as revealed to the servant of Elisha as he looked out from the safety of the city of Dothan (2 Kgs. 6:15 – 17).

Jacob did three things:

1. He divided his retinue and possessions into two camps so that if Esau attacked one camp the other had time to flee.

2. He prayed and put the whole matter before God, *"O God of my father Abraham … O Lord who said to me return unto your country… I am not worthy of all the mercies, and of all the truth, which you have shown to your servant; for with my staff I passed over this Jordan but now I am become two camps. Deliver me from the hand of my brother … for I fear him lest he come and smite me … And You have said surely I will do you good and make your seed as the sand of the sea, which cannot be numbered for multitude."*

3. He took for a present some of his possessions for Esau sending them out before him in several droves with a message that these were a present from Jacob to his brother and Jacob was following on behind. Everyone in front of Jacob was to speak with humility to Esau to defuse any anger and animosity he may still harbour. With space between each drove Jacob would receive ample warning of his brother's intentions and therefore time to flee for his life.

The humility and gratitude voiced in Jacob's prayer demonstrated just how much misfortune had developed the nobler impulses of his heart. Twenty years of fixed principles, steadfast purpose, and resolute sacrifice of the present for the future had purified and enabled him to live a more purposeful life that was dedicated to the God who met him at the beginning of his journey into independence and responsibility.

The experiences of God he had had before reaching Laban had been profound, bringing to life all that he had learned of Abraham's life of faith and his father's experiences. It was that teaching during his formative years, along with his personal experiences during his time away from his family that provided him with an immoveable anchor in the deceptive world of his relatives.

It also demonstrated that the apparent self-centredness was but superficial, disappearing like the mist under the noonday sun. Surely Jacob's life and experiences that we are privileged to read about and study clearly demonstrates that it is possible for the truly penitent sinner to come near to God and experience His presence with them.

On completion of all his preparations and the droves had been sent off towards the approaching Esau, Jacob then sent off the first camp and then sent his wives and children over the river. Exactly what happened to them when they had crossed the river leaving Jacob alone is not included in the narrative for attention now focuses on Jacob himself and perhaps the most significant experience of Jacob's life.

From his vision of the ladder set up from earth to heaven, through his various experiences whilst serving Laban, initially for his wives and then for his possessions, and his protection from Laban after he had fled from Haran, Jacob's faith must surely have been built up and his sensitivity to spiritual realities even more highly tuned.

Now fearful for the future and unable to defend himself from so large a force led by the impulsive and physical Esau, Jacob needed the time and space to think things out.

His experience led him to believe that the most profitable thing to do was to seek his God and search his own soul alone in an unpopulated place. All he could envision for the immediate future was to slay or be slain. Neither option was appealing to a very sensitive man to whom any confrontation was anathema. All the safeguards he had put in place were designed to defuse a dangerous situation.

Jacob Wrestles with God

Now alone with his thoughts and seeking the God who had promised to bless him, he wrestled with a man until the break of day. Jacob was a fit man and this fitness was amplified within him because of his fear of the future. Even when his thigh was dislocated, Jacob's determination to continue the struggle was undiminished. When the angel conceded and asked Jacob to release him he would only do so in return for a blessing.

The change from supplanter to Prince of God (Israel) signals a new and godlier phase in Jacob's life. All the past struggles and learning experiences had led him to that supreme moment of a physical/ spiritual struggle that changed his experiential belief and faith in God to a steadfast and certain faith that, notwithstanding his human weaknesses, was to help him overcome fears and uncertainties. It was the knowledge he had gained, through all his life experiences, of the guidance and presence of God through visions and in hearing God speaking to him, that gave Jacob a certainty within his heart that God was with him no matter how bad the situation in which he found himself may seem. Previously God had to show Jacob that He was present in his trials; in future this would not be necessary. Almost as a symbol, a reminder of this epic meeting with God, Jacob would henceforth walk with a limp.

Just as Abraham's tested faith can be our experience at strategic moments in our lives (a crucial element in this author's life), so Jacob's physical struggle with God is allegorical of every individual's struggles and wrestling with their understanding of, and faith in God when facing up to a forthcoming, or current crisis or major turning point in their lives.

This was a pinnacle experience for Jacob, when the physical and spiritual aspects of his life became in a supreme moment irrevocably united, allowing God and man to walk in harmony. Although he was not filled with the Spirit without measure as Jesus was, yet he achieved a level of spirituality that is an example to all those who want to grow in Christ Jesus.

What differentiates those who have prevailed from those who have not is undoubtedly the extent of their determination given to their searched for God. There is also the matter of their willingness to receive and respond to any overtures from God and their continued wrestling within themselves as the spiritual opens up and the need to believe and accept the transformation that will inevitably occur as the Spirit of God does a work within them.

The inner transformation required from that of non-believer to a believer in the God of Abraham, Isaac and Jacob is significant. God always does a thorough work in reviving the God breathed spirit within. For Jacob it was a spiritual wrestling match that brought about a physical deformity to remind him of that moment of dramatic change from just believing in God to knowing Him personally through an inner conviction that can never be erased.

From now on for Jacob it was all about dedicated service resulting in the acquisition of an understanding and acceptance of the promises of God as possessed by the previous two patriarchs. The individual promises that provided an inheritance and sure foundation for them is equally available in a personalized form for all individuals of subsequent generations, Jew and Gentile alike, who have followed Jacob's example.

The Esau's of this world have their eyes fixed on things they are able to see, feel, smell and hear, oblivious to the greater wonders of God. Just as Esau himself was denied the great life changing happenings of God that Jacob was able to experience, so are they.

Jacob's new name is a title of victory. Collectively his children had become Israelites, Champions of God and contenders for the Divine, conquering not through their own strength but with the strength and knowledge that comes from God, but only while they are in a right relationship with Him.

Exactly who the "messenger" was with whom Jacob wrestled remains a mystery of the Divine, but Jacob's life had been preserved even though he had seen, and had physical contact with a divine being.

With Esau and his men getting progressively closer, Jacob put in place his final defensive strategy. Dividing up his family with the maids and their children first, then Leah and her children and finally the preferred Rachel and her son Joseph, Jacob travelled ahead of them to meet his brother. With all the promises he had received from God, Jacob, with memories of his brother now over twenty years old, expected the worst but hoped for the best not knowing how God would intervene in the matter.

Esau, powerful leader of this large company of fighting men, would have had some experience of God, just as Laban had done previously. With their father still alive it is unlikely Esau would have sought to kill Jacob, rather perhaps frighten him and let him know that he was a man to be reckoned with. The meeting was an emotional one as was the norm at that time; certainly Esau was not one to let Jacob know that God had spoken to him, if that is what had happened.

Esau is presented in the narrative as chivalrous and dignified, full of magnanimity and generosity. With all the gifts finally accepted, Jacob needed to be free of his unstable brother's attentions and giving the need for the animals to be able to go at their own slow pace as the reason for declining Esau's offer of protection, the two brothers parted company. Jacob suggested that they meet at Seir, but they never did.

Jacob Settles Down in Canaan

With the feared meeting with his brother over, he travelled to a place where he built a house and set up shelters for his cattle. The name of the place was Succoth, meaning booths, and is in the territory claimed by the tribe of Dan.

Jacob then moved to Shechem, named after Hamor's son, purchasing the land on which he pitched his tent from the people of that place. He had come in peace and set up his camp with every intention of dealing peaceably with the local people. He set up an altar called El-elohe-Israel meaning God, the God of Israel. This had a two fold purpose:

1. To be a focal point for his family, reminding them of the God he served.

2. As a witness to the local people, letting them know with whom his allegiance lay.

So relaxed did they become in that place that Jacob's daughter Dinah, born to Leah, was allowed to visit the local girls on her own. The accepted custom of the governor of a city to take whatever maiden he wished was to prove fatal to Shechem when he took Dinah and laid with her. Dinah was from a family set apart by God with customs that were unique. Being totally different to the customs observed by the people among whom they were living, such an act was totally out of order.

Shechem's action, even though he later showed a willingness to accept the God of Israel as his own because of his love for Dinah, was not only wrong but morally indefensible. In the house of the Patriarchs, high concepts of morality had been established with Abraham's break with the godlessness of his family and the people amongst whom he had lived. It says much about the comprehensive nature of Abraham's conversion from the ways of the world to the ways of the Almighty God who had led him into a new and totally different way of life.

To the new generation of Israelites, Shechem's action had defiled their father's daughter and their sister, which thing ought not to be done. It was considered an outrage against the family's honour that demanded stern retribution. But two wrongs never made a right, and a second wrong done with malice aforethought is doubly wrong.

A parent's belief is not passed on to their offspring. Each person must make up their own mind according to the information they have available during their lifetime. Abraham made a decision to follow the call of God, as did Isaac. But Ishmael, Jacob and Esau each made their own decision. There is clear evidence that the sons of Jacob pursued their own path rather than seeking God's help in this matter, not having their father's knowledge of God, or his faith.

It was up to Shechem's father, to negotiate for this maiden with the girl's family. Using their own style of seeking a solution by compromise Hamor tried to encourage Israel to allow the two peoples to integrate under the house of Hamor. The sons of Jacob insisted that the only way Dinah could be married to Shechem was for the whole of the male population to be circumcised, but their answer was filled with guile and malice aforethought.

Hamor's idea for the two peoples to integrate in marriage was in fact Satan seeking to dilute the people of God and the laws and regulations receive from God by Moses prohibited such activity[7].

The very idea that circumcision would change the hearts and minds of the people to the true worship of Almighty God was erroneous. Circumcision is but the outward indication of an inward conviction that God is, and that He reigns in the life of the one being circumcised, much like baptism of a mature person by total immersion is a sign of an inner conviction and a willing commitment to God. Merely having the population circumcised would not have changed the inner person and their attitude to the worship of gods; indeed it would most likely have caused conflict and a dilution of the dedication of the people of God as happened with Solomon.

When trying to sell the idea to their people, Hamor and Shechem were not disingenuous, being already aware of the benefits to themselves in having this wealthy family as their benefactors, *"Shall not their cattle and their substance and all their beasts be ours?"* They were after all not participants in 'The Promise' afforded to Abraham and his offspring by God but wanted some of that wealth for themselves.

But this course of action was not part of God's plan when He separated Abraham from his family and friends who worshipped false gods and led him into Canaan and a nomadic existence.

Such an arrangement between Israel and the house of Hamor would ultimately have had the same effect as happened to the Children of Israel when they did not remove all the nations from the Promised Land causing them to intermarry, contaminating the "separated"

---

[7]   *See my book Deuteronomy*

people and turning them from the worship of the one true God to the idol worship practiced by those nations into which they had married. Such a thing was abhorrent to the God of Israel and contrary to the whole concept of the offspring of Abraham being called out of the world; that is to be in the world but not of the world.[8]

This whole incident can be seen as a Satan inspired compromise to solve a difficult situation and initiate a means of gradually turning the people of the Promise away from the path God had assigned to them, that is being in the world but not of the world, separated unto Him for worship and witness. It would have been better if they had taken Dinah from Shechem and moved away. As it was when the men of the city were incapacitated after their circumcision two of Dinah's brothers, Simeon and Levi, slaughtered them saving only the women and children and animals.

The direct result of this action by the two brothers in making the whole population suffer for the sin of one man was to remove the dangerous by-product of the compromise solution and cause Jacob, at God's request, to move on to higher ground and a public display of worship of the Divine Deity who commanded the centre of his affections.

With the swelling of the family with all the women and children from Shechem it was necessary to spend time in purification. All the idols, that is the strange carved gods, amulets and charms, were to be removed from their possession, but would that remove the desire to do what they had spent their lives doing from their hearts? It could well be that the older women would, because of the violence and emotional loss they had experienced, be resistant to any suggestion that the God of Jacob was any better than their gods. Not a good experience for them.

But for the members of the tribe of Israel it was necessary to cleans their hearts from evil so that they might focus on the Almighty God who had led Abraham, Isaac and Jacob in their life's journey.

By bathing and abstaining from any act that would render them ceremonially unclean and putting out of their minds ungodly thoughts, replacing them with an attitude of confession and repentance, they were to prepare themselves for the act of sacrificial worship.

What the attitude was of those who had seen their husbands and

---

[8]   *See my book Law and Grace*

fathers and sons massacred and for themselves to become captives of these different and ferocious people is not part of the narrative. But the question must be asked as to what the mothers told their children as they grew up and whether or not any of them were willing to be assimilated into the life and worship of the household of Jacob.

Jacob himself found it difficult to forgive the actions of his two sons, and although he only rebuked them for opening the family to dangers from the surrounding nations, the scripture allows their actions to speak for themselves.

It should be noted, however, that the dying Patriarch exclaims during the blessing of his sons that, *"Simeon and Levi are brothers; weapons of violence their weapons … Cursed be their anger for it was fierce, and their wroth, for it was cruel." (Gen. 49:5).* Jacob, like his father before him, did not like conflict, and the older he got the less he tolerated it. Indeed the influence of his grandfather Abraham is clearly seen passing through Isaac to Jacob.

Our personalities are with us from birth and there is not much we can do about that, but it is how we cope with those personalities in our dealings with others and particularly with Almighty God that really distinguishes one person from another. For it is interesting that Dinah had six brothers and neither Simeon nor Levi were the eldest. In this tragic incident neither Jacob nor his sons seem to have lifted up their voice to God to ask for His guidance on the matter. *"Vengeance is Mine, I will repay," says the Lord.*

Jacob's concern for their safety was groundless because God put the fear of them into the hearts of all the surrounding nations, thus removing any danger of reprisals.

Jacob Refocuses on God

It is important to remember that all the main characters in Genesis were sinners, just as we all are. The only reason God was able to come alongside them and make them part of His plans for the salvation of mankind was because they were willing to surrender their lives to Him. Being inherently imperfect, each one made mistakes, which gives us confidence that even though we are also sinners, God is able to use us too if we are willing to truly surrender our lives and hearts to Him

At Beth-el (or 'God who manifested Himself at Bethel'), which was another 1,010 feet higher than Shechem (1,880ft), Jacob was directed to build an altar and once more meet with God. He had previously met with God at this place when he was escaping from the wrath of his brother Esau. This time, however, he was the established head of a large company of people, having many possessions and spiritually matured by his experiences of life and particularly of God and His angelic hosts. Jacob made it crystal clear that the God at the centre of his worship through sacrifice was the God *"who answered me in the day of my distress and was with me in the way."*

Here Almighty God met with him to confirm his change of name from Jacob to Israel and his receipt of the inheritance first given to Abraham then Isaac. The everlasting promise from God was that their seed would be separated unto God and receive a homeland that was currently called Canaan. After receiving the promise that a company of nations and kings would come from him, Jacob set up a pillar in memory of that land-mark moment in his life.

On the journey from Bethel to Ephrath, Rachel was due to give birth. It was a difficult labour but Rachel died knowing that she was giving birth to a son, her second. She was buried in the area that is now called Bethlehem. In her dying breath Rachel called her son Ben-oni (the son of my sorrow) but Jacob called him Benjamin (the son of my old age). Jacob erected a pillar to Rachel but nothing is recorded of his grief at the death of a women for whom he had willingly served 14 long years. It is interesting that the narrative gives space to record the death of Rachel's nurse.

Inserted here is an incident that had a profound effect on Jacob and demonstrated how much the ways of the surrounding nations had influenced the members of his family. It was the practice amongst Eastern heirs apparent to take possession of their father's wives as an assertion of their rights to the succession. But as in the case of Shechem and Dinah, Jacob and his family lived by a different set of rules because they had been set apart by God as His own. The code of morality by which they lived did not relate to that of the surrounding nations.

Reuben's action in going into Rachel's maid Bilhah was so repulsive an incident that it is mentioned and then the subject is immediately changed. Rachel's death and the memories held by Jacob meant that this violation, although not spoken about, had deeply offended this man. Both he and his wives had been through a great deal, they had survived many dangers and reverses and become welded together as a result. For this young man to be so insensitive as to force himself on this mother of two of his brothers was totally out of order and became a stain on his character. Come the blessing of his father in his old age (Gen. 49) Reuben received only criticism.

The Biblical stories do not follow in chronological order. The account of the death of Isaac is inserted here for convenience and as there is no mention of Rebekah it must be assumed that she had died. As with Isaac and Ishmael at the death of Abraham, Jacob and Esau jointly performed the last rites for their father. However, now there was no danger of Esau carrying out his threat to Jacob because they were both changed men and Jacob owned God's protection from harm.

With the death of Isaac another era had quietly ended, overshadowed as it was by the dynamic happenings in Jacob's life. Whereas Abraham was an epoch maker whose life was inevitably an eventful one, Isaac had inherited the true belief in the living God almost by default, being involved as he was with the testing of Abraham's faith on the mountain. Isaac's task was to transmit that faith in the living God to the one who would succeed him. A patient and meditative man, strong in affection and love, with domestic virtues that have influenced his descendents down through the ages, Isaac achieved the goal God had laid down for him by passing on a life consuming love for God in Jacob that had inspired Abraham in the beginning.

In closing the patriarchal age, Jacob's life was bound to be rough and eventful. His goal was to give birth to the embryo of the Israelite nation that would finally claim the land promised to Abraham and Isaac. Jacob was not totally in control of the birth of his twelve sons. The rivalry of his two wives, Leah being forced upon him by Laban, saw to that, for they even employed their maids to ultimately produce more children than Jacob would have originally intended. But from these sons came the twelve tribes that are still spoken about today and mentioned in the book of Revelation. And this is where Reuben went wrong, for he thought that just as Isaac followed Abraham and Jacob followed Isaac that he would follow Jacob as head of the household, but this was not God's plan. Out of touch with God, we are all apt to go our own erroneous way.

Esau now separated himself from Jacob for the same reason that Lot separated himself from Abraham. But this was also to allow the fulfilment of the Divine plan that Israel would inherit the Promised Land. Tragically the animosity between the twin brothers was to be perpetuated, for there came a time when Edom (*Esau is Edom – Gen. 36:8*) rejoiced when Israel was being attacked and beaten into submission, but such an attitude incited God's wrath against Edom (Obediah), *"For the violence done to thy brother Jacob, shame shall cover you and you will be cut off forever."*

A complete chapter (Gen. 36) is devoted to the descendents of Esau for it must be remembered that he was Jacob's twin brother, the relationship being totally different from that between Isaac and Ishmael. One of Esau's sons, Eliphaz born of Adah, is believed to be one of Job's friends who was trained in pious living under the eyes of Isaac; it is also believed that the Lord had endowed him with the spirit of prophecy.

The offspring of Esau were all real people who, because of his unwillingness to pursue the God of his fathers as Jacob had done, were led away from the worship and service of Almighty God. As Esau considered his birthright as nothing of importance, it seems he parted company with God taking with him his whole household.

Sadly the sons of Jacob did not follow their father's example in recognizing and following Almighty God, continually drifting away to become men of the world, indistinguishable from the men of the nations around them with the one exception that they were still people of the promise. God's patience with them and us has saved both the day and the souls that are found in Him.

That there has always been a remnant within the people of Israel is clearly shown throughout scripture and it is through such people that God has continually sought to bring the nation back to Himself. It was only when the nation repented and asked for forgiveness that God was able to cause them to prosper. The warning, however, is still being sounded that it is only those who are willing to confess and repent of their sins before God and seek His forgiveness who are saved to eternal life.

7 JOSEPH

Joseph Takes Centre Stage (Gen. 37)

The focus now turns to Joseph who was to be the catalyst for the further progress of God's plan for His people Israel. The life of Jacob, apart from a few glimpses and details of the blessing he was to give to his sons before he died, now faded into the background. This new chapter in the life of the tribe of Jacob, renamed Israel by God, provides details of the progress of the sons of Jacob towards nationhood.

In the furnace that was Egypt, the twelve tribes would be melted and poured into a new mould to become Israel. Entering Egypt as twelve brothers and their families, they came out as the twelve tribes of a united Israel. But first the sons of Jacob had to be dealt with.

This is because all but one were leading a life that would take them away from the God of Jacob. They had to be brought back to worship the one true God, leaving the gods of Canaan behind them because sometime in the future their descendents would be required by God to rid the land of those pagan nations.

It bears repetition that the Biblical account of the life and times of individuals during the development and life of a nation have no meaning without also reading about and understanding God's involvement in the process. He can be seen both as the all-powerful protector and benefactor of the Israelite nation and the devoted father who is not averse to punishing them when needed. Removing God's direct involvement in Joseph's life would only provide a lopsided picture of events that would not benefit the reader.

There is clear evidence in Joseph's life that he had an empathy with God very similar to that of his father when he was younger. His brothers, however, were, like Esau, seemingly oblivious to the importance of staying close to God. Joseph therefore shone like a light in a darkening place.

Jacob must have sensed in Joseph, the son of Rachael who he loved very deeply, a kindred spirit and as a result was seen to love him more than his brothers. This situation clearly illustrates why God 'preferred' Jacob to Esau. What is particularly interesting is that this son of Jacob's wife who could not let go of the family gods should be so passionate about his personal relationship with the God of his father.

The scene that was now opening up took on an unnerving similarity to that of Cain and Able. Cain became jealous of his younger brother when Abel's sacrifice was accepted and his was rejected. Now the brothers, seeing Joseph being loved of his father in preference to themselves, followed Cain's example by allowing jealousy to become established in their hearts.

God's word to Cain was,

> *"Why are you angry? And why are you sad? If you do well will you not rejoice? But if you don't do well sin crouches at the door waiting to master you, but you could rule over it."*

Unfortunately Cain did not look into his heart and in confession and repentance ask God to guide him on how he could offer an acceptable sacrifice. Instead he harboured feelings of vexation which opened the door to the evil passions of envy, anger and the violence that eventually drove him to murder his brother.

Exactly the same scenario was being acted out amongst the brothers. The heat of their anger was increased when Jacob gave a coat of many colours to his favoured son. In those times Semitic chiefs wore such a coat as an insignia of rulership.

For Joseph, one of the youngest of Jacob's sons (Benjamin being the youngest) to wear such a coat marked him out as heir apparent, and it was this symbolic apparel that was the final straw, for it stimulated the envy of the other brothers to a new level, turning it into hatred. But it was hatred without a cause for God was with him.

One of the hardest things to do is recognize the superiority of a younger brother. From his brothers' point of view it was more than they were prepared to tolerate.

The life of Joseph is remarkable in that it has all the elements of a thriller, to be appreciated by everyone from the young to the very old, from the simple to the searching soul and the academic who can find fresh depths of unexpected meaning in it, especially when related to other parts of scripture.

Throughout his life, in good times and in bad, Joseph's unwavering faith in the God of Abraham is an example to all those who are willing to read and believe the God inspired scriptures. From his unwarranted treatment by his brothers, through his descent into the depths, into the pit that was an Egyptian dungeon, caused by the reaction of others to his morally and religiously upright life, to his elevation to rulership, Joseph showed none of the normal worldly vengeful traits that occupied the minds of his brothers.

Even when his brothers were at his mercy, his treatment of them was at all times compassionate, even when teaching them about their sinfulness. *"You meant it for harm but God meant it for good."*

Throughout this account of his life there is a sense of the overruling of Divine Providence and the unwillingness of the main character to question or make a complaint against that Divine Deity in whom he believed and to whom he had so clearly committed his life. In his lowest state he was unbowed and in his highest state he was not proud; a sameness of character that is both inspirational and an encouragement to all those who read it. He was an example to be followed.

The story also shows the sense of guilt that dawned on his brothers and their problem, because of the way their characters had developed, and their inability to understand or cope with true forgiveness; a unique forgiveness with no strings attached.

Because their own guilt ridden, sin stained characters found it difficult to show such forgiveness to others they were unable to receive such forgiveness for themselves. Thus to the end they sought to argue for unnecessary clauses to be included within the terms of forgiveness offered by Joseph to 'protect' themselves against any unseen flaws or deceptive small print in that contract of forgiveness.

It is a story of good in spite of evil intent, a reflection of the Divine in the life of fallen man that happened in the Middle Bronze age (2,200 – 1,500 BC) but is still relevant in the 21st century AD.

> *Joseph, when he was seventeen years old, was shepherding the flock with his brothers Dan, Naphtali, Gad, and Asher, the sons of Bilhah and Zilpah, his father's secondary wives; and Joseph brought back a bad report about them to their father.*
>
> *Now Israel loved Joseph more than all his children, because he was the son of his old age; and he made him a multicolored tunic.*
>
> *That special tunic caused his brothers to realize that their father loved Joseph above all of his brothers; so they hated him and could not find it within themselves to speak to him on friendly terms. (Gen. 37:2 – 4)*

It is not normally good for a parent to love one child more than their other children, for the ones who are loved less will naturally feel unwanted and or aggrieved. But the significance here is that this one son loved God just as his father did and it was the other children who had fallen from grace of their own volition.

It was this difference in spiritual perspectives that caused Joseph to see the errors in the lives of his brothers to a degree that he felt obliged to tell his father. Naïve he may have been, for he was certainly not worldly wise, but there was no vindictiveness, no malice in what he did. In this was demonstrated a type of Christ who brought to the attention of his brothers the sinfulness of their ways.

> *Now Joseph dreamed a dream, and he told it to his brothers, and they hated him even more. He said to them, "Please listen to this dream which I have dreamed; we brothers were binding sheaves of grain stalks in the field, and lo, my sheaf suddenly got up and stood upright and behold, your sheaves stood all around my sheaf and bowed down in respect."*

Recounting such a dream to those who harboured a strong degree of animosity towards you was not aimed at achieving any healing, rather the reverse. In the overall scheme of things it seemed a very irresponsible thing to do, but as it happened this dream was prophetic. Not only that but the brothers would be instrumental in starting the process that would lead to that event happening.

> *His brothers said to him, "Are you actually going to reign over us? Are you really going to rule and govern us as your subjects?" So they hated him even more for revealing his dreams and for his seemingly arrogant words.*

It seems that Joseph could not help himself but could well have needed to share the dreams.

> *Joseph dreamed another dream, and revealed it to his brothers as before. He said, "See here, I have dreamed another dream, and lo, in this dream I saw eleven stars and the sun and the moon bowed down in respect to me!"*
> *He also told it to his father; but his father rebuked him and said to him in disbelief, "What is the meaning of this dream that you have dreamed? Shall I and your mother and your brothers actually come to bow down to the ground in respect before you?"*
> *(Gen. 37:5 – 10)*

Someone once wrote that Joseph was wrong to "tell tales" or to have told his brothers about the dreams he received. Such a view is wrong on two counts:

1. A diminution of his standards would not have allowed him to survive and ultimately to rule Egypt as he did. Not forgetting that God was in charge and it was God who had given him the dreams knowing full well what his reaction to them would be.

2. Had he not "told tales" and described his dreams to his brothers, they would not have reacted in the way they did and this story would not have been told.

Jacob rebuked him for telling them all about the dreams because of the obvious impact it was having on his brothers, but it is interesting that the narrative says that Jacob kept the saying in mind for he became aware that these were prophetic and that Joseph had the hand of God upon him. The repetition of the dream and its obvious implications meant that it was more than just a dream causing Jacob to react, *"Shall you indeed rule over us?"*

Divine protection after the debacle at Shechem had allowed the brothers full freedom to roam the fertile plains to find grazing for their flocks and their conquest of Shechem gave them ownership of those lands.

The scene is now set for the real drama to begin, the envy and jealousy burning away within the minds and hearts of his older brothers was quickly turning to hatred, and the hatred giving birth to the thoughts of violence.

The moment arrived when that underlying desire to vent their pent up feelings arrived when Joseph was sent by Jacob on an errand to see how his brothers were getting on as they tended the flock. In answer to his father's call, Joseph, totally unaware of the degree of animosity of his brothers towards him, replied, *"Here I am"*. His father then gave him the instructions, *"Go now ... and bring me back word"* that would irrevocably transform all their lives.

But for the brothers, the sense of guilt that would follow, for them, the unknown result of their action would blight their lives in a way that even though forgiven by Joseph because God had used their action for the good of the family, the fact that it was triggered by evil intent it left a dark stain on their memories that could never be fully expunged.

When Joseph arrived at Shechem 'a man asked him what he was looking for'. Explaining to this 'unidentified man' that he was looking for his brothers the man was able to direct him because he had heard them say they were going to Dothan.

Seeing him afar off the brothers had time to plot their revenge and decided to kill him, also working out their defense, as do all those embarking on a sinful act, that *"a wild beast had killed him"*. But God had plans for Joseph and the scene played out reveals clear evidence of His restraining hand.

Reuben counselled caution. As the first-born, and being morally responsible for Joseph's safety, he had more to lose from the demise of his favoured brother than did his other brothers. He suggested Joseph was put into a pit out of which there was no escape without assistance. These pits acted as cisterns and would normally contain water but the one chosen by Reuben was dry. In that state, however, snakes and scorpions could have occupied it.

When Joseph reached his brothers they violently stripped him of his coat and quickly put him in the pit as planned. Such an unexpected welcome would have thrown Joseph's mind into turmoil but it is most likely that he would have cried out in protest.

The fulfilment of that collective and profound hatred gave the brothers a sense of achievement that made them callously deaf to his cries as they ate bread a short distance away. (It has been suggested that there is no reference in the scriptures to Joseph crying out; this is possible as he was being put into the pit by his brothers. However, it is unlikely that he remained silent because the Midianite merchants knew that Joseph was in the pit.)

Although Reuben's plan was to rescue the lad from the pit when the opportunity arose and restore him to his father, which would have had the added advantage of promoting him in the eyes of his father, he should have shown leadership by objecting to the evil plot in the first place and accompanying the lad back to his father thus taking him out of harms way. But he was unable to show this type of leadership allowing matters to take a turn for the worse.

With Reuben out of earshot, the brothers sighted an Ishmaelite caravan from Gilead, (such caravans travelled through the land east of the Jordan, across the Valley of Jezreel and along the coast to Egypt). This presented a new solution to their problem. Judah suggested that instead of killing the boy, whether physically or by starvation in the pit, and having to conceal his remains, why not sell him to the caravan, as this would have the same effect of getting rid of what they saw as a menace.

Not forgetting that God was in charge of these events, it just so happened that some Midianite merchants who, hearing Joseph's cries, helped him out of the pit and then, with an eye to profit promptly sold him to the same caravan the brothers had sighted. Joseph was now on his way to Egypt according to God's plan, helped on his way by men outside the family.

When Reuben looked into the pit to rescue Joseph and did not find him he immediately thought that some wild beast had killed him and removed his body to a more secluded place to consume him. With the absence of blood or evidence of a struggle around the entrance to the pit being recorded, this was an unreasonable conclusion to make. It does, however indicate the agitated emotional state Reuben was in at the time.

Although this new state of affairs removed from them the responsibility of making a decision on Joseph's future, they still had to provide themselves with a story to tell their father that explained Joseph's sudden disappearance. What the brothers had not bargained for was the niggling doubt and concern as to what actually happened to their brother that continued to plague them over the years.

Remembrance of the intensity of the hatred and desire for blood that motivated them in dealing so harshly with their brother, coupled with the continuing effect of the death on their father, was finally to lead to Judah's confession before an unrecognized Joseph in Egypt.

Rejoining his brothers, Reuben reported Joseph's disappearance, ignorant of their plan to sell him to the passing Ishmaelite caravan. The brothers quickly hatched a plan to distance themselves from their own involvement in Joseph's apparent demise. Killing a male goat (as a sacrifice, a forerunner to the sacrifice for sin with a clue – considering the circumstances – also of the scapegoat, introduced under Moses), they dipped the tunic in the shed blood to suggest that he had been killed. Then, knowing the extent of the distress the sight of the blood stained tunic would cause their father, along with the realisation that his favoured son had perished, they enrolled the help of others to take the coat to their father.

Jacob's reaction was as predicted. Having loved this one son so much, and gained such enjoyment from their shared love of spiritual things, the manner of Joseph's death made it all the more difficult to bear. Despite the efforts of all his remaining children, Jacob would not be comforted, particularly because he was the son of Rachel who had been the love of his life and therefore a reminder of her.

Meanwhile, unknown to his family, God dispatched Joseph to

Egypt and in particular to Potiphar, the captain of Pharaoh's guard who bought this Hebrew slave from the Ishmaelites. This was an important move for Joseph because Potiphar was later able to be a character reference for him before the Pharaoh when he had been brought up from the dungeon to interpret the dreams the Pharaoh had had.

The two central figures in Jacob's large family are Joseph and Judah. It has already become clear that Joseph was key to the furtherance of the plan of God as He changes Israel from twelve brothers into a nation to be His witness to the world. Without Joseph's love for and total commitment to Almighty God, their journey to Egypt and their position within Egypt up to the death of Joseph would not have been possible.

But after that the tribe of Judah took the lead role, being chosen for the main line of Messianic succession, through David and other significant, but not necessarily particularly outstanding characters such as Zerubbabel who led the return from Babylon and the rebuilding of the Temple, to Jesus the Messiah.

There is a sudden break in the flow of the narrative to introduce an account of the offspring of Judah who himself had erred from the way of his father. It also provides a contrast in the lives of the two main characters to show how each reacted when disaster struck.

A Tale of Judah

In Genesis chapter 39 evidence is given as to just how far from the way of truth Judah had gone, because he followed his uncle Esau's example and married the daughter, who is never named, of a Canaanite man called Shua, and had three sons by her named Er, Onan and Shelah. Judah provided a wife, called Tamar, for his firstborn. Unfortunately Er, having been influenced by his mother, was wicked in God's eyes and died as a result of his wickedness without producing any children.

An established custom in the area called "levirate marriage" required a surviving brother to marry a childless widow and produce children by her. The eldest son of this union would take the name of the woman's first husband and inherit his possessions (see the account of Ruth and Boaz). In line with this custom Judah told his second son

Onan to go in to Tamar. But Onan, being as wicked as his brother, refused to sire children for his brother so he too died.

As the third son was too young to marry, Tamar was sent back to her family to be a widow there and wait for Shelah to come of age. In those days betrothal was as legally binding as marriage. But Judah was fearful that Tamar had caused the death of his two sons and was reluctant to put his last son's life at risk.

In Canaanite society, the levirate custom could involve any one of the male members of a family, even the father-in-law. Seeing her father-in-law's youngest son grow into a man Tamar realized that she had been forgotten about. On hearing that Judah's wife had died and that he was to attend a Canaanite festival at the time of sheep sheering, Tamar hatched a plan that was completely honourable in her Canaanite eyes. To avoid detection she disguised herself as a votary of Astarte, that is a *kedeshah* or a woman dedicated to impure heathen worship. The foulest Babylonian custom is that which compels every woman of the land to sit in the temple of Aphrodite and have intercourse with some stranger at least once in her life. This repulsive custom was common in the area of Phoenicia and Babylonia.

In Deuteronomy 23:17, 18 Moses warns against this practice:

> *None of the daughters of Israel shall be a kedeshah, nor shall any of the sons of Israel be a kadesh.*
> *You shall not bring the hire of a prostitute (zonah) or the wages of a dog (kelev) into the house of the Lord your God to pay a vow, for both of these are an abomination to the Lord your God.*

The fact that Judah was prepared to go in to such a woman clearly indicates the degree of his falling away from the true and living way first established by Abraham. It was also in marked contrast to the uprightness of Joseph.

Judah offered her a kid of the goats for her services but in the meantime Tamar successfully obtained a pledge from Judah that would clearly identify the owner, ostensibly to ensure that payment was forthcoming. The signet, cord and staff handed over by Judah marked him out as a sheik in Canaan and as a man of rank in Egypt and Babylonia.

After his return home, Judah sent his friend the Adullamite to retrieve the pledge in exchange for the promised kid. But not only could he not find the harlot, the local people had no knowledge of a harlot living in the area. To prevent attracting bad publicity and suffering the embarrassment that it would cause him, Judah decided to let the matter pass.

Returning to her widow's clothing immediately after the event, Tamar waited to see if she had become pregnant. As it was when she began to show, Judah was informed that Tamar had acted like a harlot for she was pregnant. The leader of a tribe had the power of life and death over all those he ruled so Judah proclaimed the death penalty for Tamar's apparent indiscretion. At this point Tamar, without revealing the name of the father, merely presented the pledge to Judah, who realized instantly that he was the father. Judah then confessed that his daughter-in-law was more righteous than he, both for his action in not giving Shelah to her for a husband and in going in to a harlot.

The birth of the twins was described in detail before the narrative quickly moves back to focus on Joseph's adventures as a slave in Egypt.

This account of Judah and Tamar only gains a place in the inspired record because with such an ancestry it emphasizes the Messiah had a chequered ancestry[9], even with a citizen of Jericho (Rahab) and a Moabitess (Ruth) as His forebears. Only the God of Israel knew who would come from the loins of Judah, and it was this same God who had a major influence on the production of the scriptures. For how else could so many contributors living at so many different times be able to produce a work that is so consistent in its message?

It also gives good reason why Jacob, knowing how his sons were falling away from the true faith like Esau, favoured Joseph. Just as Jacob tested Esau to ascertain his commitment to the God of Abraham when providing him with a meal of pottage, so Joseph's love of the spiritual and his reports on the lives of his brothers told Jacob about the spiritual state of all his offspring (see Ref. 37.2 in the table below). And it was not good.

---

[9]   *In saying this we must be very careful to emphasize that as the Messiah was the Son of God, Mary merely provided the body for the eternal Spirit that was the Son of God to inhabit during His earthy ministry, therefore the lineage is for the body and His position in the history of Israel, not the Son of God Himself who was born of the Father before the creation. For more details see* The Tent of the Meeting, *and* A Fresh Look At Easter.

It is possible that in Joseph, Jacob saw the salvation of his family and its return to the true path of righteousness, hence his gift of a coat of many colours.

Judah's behaviour in comparison with the life of Joseph clearly demonstrated just how at variance they were. As with Judah so with Reuben when he went in to lay with Bilhah and indeed with all the others whose sinfulness was so clearly shown up by Joseph.

As has been seen from the lives of all the men who have been considered thus far, God was not concerned with the momentary lapses but the inner workings of the man's soul and how malleable the soul needed to be to allow it to change once God touched him.

None of them were pure and without sin. Rather, in spite of that impurity and sinfulness, God was able to influence and direct the lives of some in such a way that He achieved a successful conclusion in each of their lives that had a positive effect on the fulfilment of His plan for mankind's salvation. And it is this fact more than any other that amply demonstrates the profound truth that God reigns in every heart that is open to Him to work His work of grace and mercy. But to those whose hearts are closed to Him there is only death and destruction.

Joseph Enters Egypt

At the time of Joseph's entry into Egypt the Hyksos Kings, Bedouin conquerors of Egypt, were in power. During their dynasty it was an exception for an Egyptian such as Potiphar to hold a high government post. Therefore for him to be the Captain of Pharaoh's Guard the ruler must have had complete faith in his loyalty to them. Such loyalty would have attracted trust and authority.

When Joseph was put up for sale Potiphar would have seen his noble bearing and character and sensed his natural authority shining through and purchased him as a personal attendant. Then the captain, seeing how he prospered through Joseph, promoted him to be the overseer of his whole estate, which included buildings and land.

Indeed such was Joseph's success because God guided and blessed his every decision, that Potiphar did not know the state of his affairs, being happy to put his complete trust in this able Hebrew. All he needed to know was that he was prospering as a result.

The only areas over which Joseph did not have jurisdiction were food and Potiphar's immediate family.

Unfortunately the notorious immorality of the Egyptians of that time reared its ugly head. Potiphar's wife saw Joseph's beautiful manly form and fairness of looks and desired him. It was time for Joseph to move on to the next phase of his rise to the top. Seeing him every day, the desire for him grew within her and although she made her need of his attention perfectly clear he was equally clear in his refusal to be party to it.

As the wife of such an important servant of the royal household, and with servants of her own she would have had time on her hands. Self-centred to such a degree her unsatisfied passion for him made her totally obsessed, oblivious to the matter of his honour and the degree of trust and respect that had been generated between Joseph and her husband.

She was deaf even to Joseph's clear statement that such an act would not only be a great wickedness, for by so doing he would betray his master's confidence. But even worse for Joseph it would also be a sin before his God. Even if Potiphar never found out about the affair, God would have known and that, as far as Joseph was concerned was enough for him because he respected and loved God far too much. With her frustration mounting she bided her time for the right moment to trap him.

One day, finding herself alone in the house with Joseph, Potiphar's wife went up to him and grabbed Joseph's clothing with every intention of forcing herself upon him. Joseph, however, saw the danger and ran for his life. A verse from Ecclesiasticus says,

> *"Flee from sin, as from the face of a serpent; for if you come too near it will bite you; for its teeth are like the teeth of a lion, slaying the souls of men".*

That is exactly what Joseph did.

Frustrated by the failure of her effort to have this handsome man satisfy her physical lust and filled with rage, a vindictive maliciousness motivated her to get at him. Taking on the role of the injured party, and with the evidence of their moment of intimacy still in her hand, she called to the servants and accused the absent Joseph of an indiscretion.

Being of pure ancient Egyptian stock she plays the racial card.

Word quickly got to Potiphar whose anger was immediately directed at Joseph, forgetting the fact that he had received a great deal of benefit by having Joseph oversee his estate. His anger would have been stimulated by his wife's accusation that it was his decision to have this Hebrew alien in their home in the first place with its potential for a disaster such as this and its effrontery to purebred Egyptians.

He could easily have sentenced Joseph to death. But there must have been sufficient doubt in Potiphar's mind, knowing how upright and incorruptible Joseph had been in all his dealings, as to the truth of what really happened, that he sent Joseph to prison instead. As Captain of the Guard and responsible for the king's prisoners through his Keeper of the Prison, Potiphar was able to do this without reference to anyone else. As he received conflicting evidence there was little else he could do. But it was all part of God's plan for Joseph.

Joseph, unaware of what God was up to, will have considered this as a reversal of his improving circumstances. But the character of this amazing man would not let him get down hearted and with a sense of God's presence he was again unable to hide his superior mind and soul. It was not long before the keeper of the prison left all the prisoners in Joseph's capable hands and all that happened to them happened through his suggestions. Just as it was with Potiphar so it was with the keeper of the prison.

There is no suggestion as to how long Joseph was in prison before the baker and butler to the king were put in prison under the control of Potiphar. By this time Potiphar would have been well aware of Joseph's trusted status in prison. As the two imprisoned servants were probably of equal rank to himself, Potiphar instructed Joseph to attend them as a form of courtesy to his unfortunate colleagues.

It is likely to have been some considerable time, 'a season', before the two men had a dream that they could not understand. We will never be able to understand God's timing, but He had the responsibility of getting many things into place, including the cycle of the seasons which resulted in the forth coming years of famine, before he set Joseph's elevation in motion.

Entering their quarters one morning Joseph noted that they were sad. Not a usual event it would seem. Asking the reason for their sadness they confessed that they had each had a separate and specific dream that no one could interpret. It is interesting that Joseph's trust in and walk with God had not faltered, because his immediate reaction was to tell them that all dreams belong to God, then he asked them to tell him their dreams (Gen. 40).

First the butler told his dream and Joseph was immediately given the interpretation, which was that in three days, at the time of Pharaoh's birthday, the butler would be restored to his position. Joseph, wasting no time, asked the butler to remember him when he was restored to his position for he had been enslaved and brought into Egypt, and even in Egypt he was innocent of all charges.

Hearing a favourable interpretation of the butler's dream the baker ventured to tell Joseph the substance of his dream. The baker, in his dream, tried to do his job. However, whereas the butler spoke of three bunches of grapes which he pressed into Pharaoh's cup and presented the cup to him, the baker had three baskets on his head the top one containing all sorts of baked goods. But according to the dream he was prevented from giving the product of his labours to Pharaoh because birds took the bread from the basket on his head.

Sadly for him the outcome would be completely different for he would be taken from prison at the same time as the butler, but would be decapitated and his body hung up in public to be eaten by birds.

Exactly according to Joseph's interpretation, three days later, on his birthday Pharaoh reviewed the petitions of the prisoners and gave judgement. The butler was restored to his position and the baker executed, just as Joseph had told them.

It is reasonable to assume that Joseph had his spirits raised in the hope that when the butler was able to mention to Pharaoh about his case he would soon be free. But the butler, relieved as he was to have been restored to his position and anxious to do his best for his master, forgot all about Joseph.

This sad reflection on man's ingratitude, although quite natural, was also part of the plan of God for Joseph who was to wait another two years before he was freed.

Now it was Pharaoh's turn to have a dream (Gen. 41), or rather two consecutive dreams that no one could interpret. The heathen magic was no match for God's wisdom, which required a godly ear to hear, because, as Joseph had told the butler and baker, all dreams and their interpretations belong to God.

As soon as the Pharaoh mentioned that he had had a dream the butler suddenly remembered Joseph. Going before Pharaoh the butler confessed his fault before the king and his sin against Joseph for forgetting him. He then mentioned Joseph, a Hebrew servant (in prison) who had been able to interpret the dreams of him and the baker interpreting each dream according to its interpretation and each interpretation had proved to be correct.

Joseph Before Pharaoh (Gen. 41)

On hearing about Joseph, Pharaoh, anxious to get to the bottom of these troublesome dreams, summoned him to appear before him. Joseph was immediately brought out of prison, shaved, washed, given a change of clothes and led into the presence of the king

Joseph's position before God is again seen as totally consistent. He would not accept the credit for something for which he depended upon God. Pharaoh naturally assumed, from what his butler had told him, that Joseph was a professional interpreter of dreams, *"I have heard it said that when you hear a dream you are able to interpret it"*. Joseph with courtly deference and honesty in the sight of his God corrected Pharaoh's misunderstanding on the matter by informing the king that it was God alone who could give him the interpretation.

Pharaoh repeated his dreams to Joseph with some embellishments, such as *"I have never seen in all the land of Egypt for baldness"*, to give emphasis and an understanding of its affect on him. Joseph then provides the interpretation that God had given to him, emphasizing that the seven years of plenty will be forgotten because of the grievous nature of the seven years of drought. This, says Joseph, is the reason for the dream being repeated.

But this interpreter of dreams, obviously recognized by Potiphar, was already known as an immensely practical man, both during his time as overseer in Potiphar's house and whilst assisting the keeper of the prison. They were also years of servant hood, invaluable training so that at the height of his rise in power he would remember the God who had chosen him and whom he was prepared to serve faithfully and patiently in apparent good and bad times.

With the interpretation Joseph, without any suggestion that he would be the man best placed to lead the nation at this time, confidently offers the king practical advice on the preparations necessary for this act of God that would happen, suggesting that they find a wise and discreet man to manage first the collection and storing of food before the necessary distribution of it.

Amazed by the interpretation and the sagacious manner with which Joseph puts forward a spontaneous plan for saving the nation, Pharaoh, along with his courtiers, had no hesitation in appointing Joseph himself to the suggested position, such was his bearing and evident qualities of leadership.

From slave to statesman of a rank only just lower than Pharaoh himself, Joseph's sudden meteoric rise launched from the dungeon is astonishing. But, from the start of his enforced journey into Egypt, it was all part of God's plan that Joseph should be prepared for such a role as this; not forgetting that Jacob was still under the illusion that this, his favourite son, was dead.

During his time of service both to Potiphar and during his twelve years in the dungeon, Joseph would have learned the language, social niceties and the less seemly side of life in Egypt. From the butler and the baker he would have learned about life in court. Hungry for intellectual conversation, debate and information, it is likely that he would have used every opportunity, especially whilst in prison, to exercise his mind and intellect.

Pharaoh accepted that a higher being had given Joseph the interpretation for two good reasons:

1. His own wise men and magicians could not understand the dreams.

2. Because of the profound nature of the revelation, which prompted Pharaoh to say, *"For as much as God has shown you this, there is none so wise and discreet as you."*

Joseph was thirty years old when he faced Pharaoh to interpret the dreams.

Several things happened that enabled Joseph to save his own family from starvation and teach his brothers a valuable lesson:

1. He was made Grand Vizier or Viceroy and given total control over the land of Egypt save that only Pharaoh was greater than he.

2. Pharaoh handed Joseph his signet ring to symbolically endow him with royal authority.

3. The authority given to Joseph was publicly endorsed when he rode in the second chariot next to Pharaoh.

4. He was dressed in royal attire, with Pharaoh's signet ring and a golden collar, which was only awarded for outstanding achievement.

5. His name was changed to better suit his new role. Zaphenath-paneah meaning 'food man' – 'of the life' or the Chief Steward in the realm in the face of Famine. This name change helped to conceal his real identity from his brethren when they first came to Egypt. Furthermore, from the immature youngster of around sixteen/seventeen that his brothers knew, Joseph would have changed dramatically in appearance and maturity due to his hard life as a slave in the land of Egypt.

6. He would have his own fine house and servants.

7. Pharaoh gave him Asenath, the daughter of Poti-phera priest of On (On was the centre of sun worship) who bore him two sons, Manasseh (Making to forget - that is for God has made me forget all my toil and all my father's house) and Ephraim (for God has made me fruitful in the land of my affliction).

There is considerable scriptural evidence to suggest such a similarity between the life of Joseph and the Mashiach Yeshua (the Messiah Jesus) to indicate that Joseph was a type of Christ, and for this I am grateful to Elhanan ben Avraham who recorded some of his thoughts on this subject, a copy of which I was able to obtain. (See Chapter 8 for an edited version.)

In the initial discourse Elhanan ben Avraham quotes the sages of the Talmud (Bavli Brachot 34B) *"All the prophets prophesied only of the days of the Messiah."*

Moses, to whom is credited the setting down of the record of Joseph's life and bringing out his bones, is considered as Judaism's greatest prophet. It is to his credit that much of the detail concerning Joseph's life in Egypt is accurate. If there is a truth in the above, then is it not possible that we might learn something of the promised Messiah of Israel from the story of Joseph?

When Ya'akov Avinu (Jacob) was about to die, he gathered his sons around him and said,

"Gather yourselves together that I may tell you that which shall befall you in the end of days," (Genesis/Bereshit 49:1).

Hebrew for *"the end of days"* is achrit hayamim, the same form used in the scriptures to refer to the Latter days, the Day of the Lord, the coming of Meshiach. Jacob then prophesied over each of his sons.

Over Joseph he said,

"Joseph is a fruitful bough, even a fruitful bough by a well, whose branches run over the wall; the archers have surely grieved him, and shot at him, and hated him, but his bow abode in strength, and the arms of his hands were made strong by the shepherd, the stone of Israel; even by the God of your father, who shall help thee with blessings of heaven above, blessings of the deep that lieth under, blessings of the

breasts, and of the womb; the blessings of thy father have prevailed above the blessings of your progenitors into the utmost bound of the everlasting hills; they shall be on the head of Joseph, and on the crown of the head of him who was separated from his brethren."

Was this amazing prophecy referring only to the remaining years of Joseph, the son of Jacob? Or do the prophetic words reach through time and generations to a later "son of Joseph"? And has there been any figure in Jewish history to whom the "blueprint" dynamics of the life of Joseph might point? The same question could equally be addressed to the final prophetic blessing made by Moses concerning Joseph (already long deceased) just prior to his own passing:

"The blessed of the Lord is His land, with the precious things of heaven, with the dew, and the deep lying beneath, with the precious fruits of the sun, with the precious produce of the months, with the best things of the ancient mountains, with the precious things of the everlasting hills, with the precious things of the earth and its fullness, and the favour of Him who dwelt in the bush. Let the blessing come 'on the head of Joseph and on the crown of him who was separated from his brothers.' His glory is like a firstborn bull, and his horns like the horns of a wild ox; together with them he shall push the peoples to the ends of the earth" (D'varim/ Deuteronomy 33:13-17).

The name of Ephraim was often used for the ten northern tribes of Israel because it speaks of being fruitful — Ephraim (for God has made me fruitful in the land of my affliction).

Joseph Meets His Brothers

When the famine finally started to bite the household began to suffer, but Jacob was unaware that it was to last seven long years. The remaining brothers had had the freedom to roam and find pasture for their flocks and had no need to venture out of the territory they knew. Therefore it was Jacob who had encouraged his sons to go into Egypt and negotiate for food as he had heard that it was plentiful there.

Benjamin was to remain with Jacob, being the only remaining son of Rachel who had died. It might also have been that Benjamin like Joseph had a mind for God.

Joseph, now a mature man of around 37 who spoke fluent Egyptian, and for seven years the Viceroy entrusted with the collection and storage of grain in Egypt, was now responsible for its distribution. It was therefore to him that all foreign buyers had to apply to purchase grain for their people.

Now fully integrated into the life of the royal family, excepting his love and willing service for the God of Abraham and in the matter of food, with an Egyptian name, a status only just short of Pharaoh himself and treated with the highest respect and honour by all who approached him, with his every command being obeyed without question, Joseph represented an awesome figure to all ordinary people and particularly those from foreign lands and nomadic people such as Jacob's family.

After about twenty years of separation Joseph's brothers were brought before this awesome ruler, separated from him by protocol, Egyptian guards, servants and an interpreter. Convinced in their minds that Joseph was long dead they would not have known, could not have known, that this high official was in fact their brother.

The Egyptians were vulnerable to attack on their North East frontier, which had been the direction from which most attacks had come, so they were very sensitive about any group of men who crossed it. It was understandable that Joseph should see these ten men as possible spies and his harshness towards them would not have raised the suspicions of the Egyptians around him.

Joseph himself had changed over the years since being sold into slavery. As his brothers were brought before him and bowed to him, he would have been reminded of the dreams God had given him, dreams that had aroused such adverse reactions from these same men all those years ago. His difficulty was to find out if they had changed in the intervening period and how they had changed. Were they still far from God? Did they still have hatred in their hearts for him?

Somehow Joseph must elicit this information without revealing who he was to his brothers or his relationship to them to the Egyptians around him.

Joseph asks, *"Where do you come from."*

They reply, *"From the land of Canaan to buy food."*

What better way of extracting further information from them but to accuse them of being spies giving as the reason for the accusation that they had passed through the vulnerable sector of the country's defenses.

Their reply that they were all the sons of one man should have been sufficient, as no one would have put at risk his entire male offspring on such a risky enterprise. But they had not mentioned Benjamin so once more Joseph accused his brothers of being spies. Suddenly put off guard they quickly try to assure the Grand Vizier that they were nothing of the sort by volunteering further information concerning their father and youngest brother and that 'one was not'.

Relieved that his brother, the son of his mother Rachel, was still alive, Joseph now had the means to demand that they bring him to Egypt. Giving the impression that their story is improbable and must be verified, his first order is that one of them be sent back to fetch Benjamin, the others being held as surety. There would have been consternation among the brothers knowing the reluctance of their father to allow this. Presumably to give them time to decide who should go back and get Benjamin they were all held in detention together.

After three days, notice the Godly number of three, they were called to appear before the same official who appears to have changed his mind in that he was prepared to allow all but one to return to their father. Because he feared God he was not willing to hold all of them on just a suspicion so he tells them to go back with food and bring their youngest brother to him; in that way he will be able to verify their story.

A sense of guilt now envelops the brothers as remembrance of their own callous behaviour towards their brother comes flooding back to haunt them. At that time they showed no mercy, being blind to his distress and deaf to his beseeching cries for brotherly love and kindness; the hatred that had permeated and built up in their minds and hearts, motivated their actions resulting in his disappearance, the manner of which was of course unknown to them and therefore a constant irritant to them.

Fortunately, as God had been in control and had arranged for Joseph to be spirited away, they did not have the added guilt of having sold him into slavery themselves, but it was the unknowing of exactly what had happened to him that played on their minds and would not go away. As it was even now they did not know for sure whether he was alive or dead so that it acted like a running sore.

Reuben, regretful that he had not been able to save Joseph from the others reminded them of his efforts to dampen their anger against him,

> *"Did I not say to you do not sin against the child but you would not hear? Therefore also behold that his blood is required".*

The day of reckoning had now arrived for the brothers as they believed in the ignorance that Joseph's blood was now being avenged, for they were morally guilty of his 'death'.

Unknown to the brothers, Joseph not only heard them discuss this matter among themselves but also understood all that they were saying. He could well be remembering, as he saw their distress at their sudden misfortune, his own sense of helplessness and hopelessness when he entered the foreign world of the pit and then slavery.

Aware that he had initiated this debate by his actions he was also able to see the outward display of remorse that revealed their broken and contrite hearts at the very thought of their callousness twenty odd years ago.

Joseph was able to stand back and watch as the brothers provided him with the evidence of their changed attitude towards him. Their hatred of him so evident the last time he saw them had been replaced with guilt. Seeing his brothers engaged in this heated discussion concerning the way they had treated him, unaware of who he was, was a new and rather bizarre experience. Overtaken with emotion, Joseph turned his back on them to regain his composure.

As the eldest it was up to Reuben to lead the brothers back to their father and give him a report of the Egyptian official's demands, thus it was that Simeon was chosen to stay. According to Rabbinic tradition it was Simeon who had counselled that Joseph be slain. The brothers saw Simeon being bound before being led away.

The Brothers Return Home without Simeon

Joseph now gives orders that their vessels be filled and every man's money restored to his sack. This was to cause consternation when they found it because of the danger of being accused of theft. Events had made them feel extremely vulnerable and in fear of their lives, just as Joseph was in fear of his life when they put him in the pit.

As it was when they stopped for one of them to give his ass some food and he saw that his money was in the top of his sack he was suddenly filled with fear and panic. Then the others also found their money in their sacks and they all wondered what such an unusual occurrence portended, *"What is this that God has done to us?"* What is encouraging is that their sense of God being part of the situation was a considerable improvement from their previously Godless behaviour.

Finally returning to their father they gave a complete account of all that had happened to them during the meeting with Joseph, referring to him as 'the man', the lord of the land, meaning a person of power and greatness.

They will have emphasize the frightening experience before the great man and his insistence that they were spies in spite of their pleading to be honest men who merely want to buy grain, their imprisonment for three days before being released and seeing Simeon being bound and led with the man telling them to bring their youngest brother to him to prove they were honest men so that they would live and not die.

It is now Jacob's turn to show remorse because this is the second time that they were together under the leadership of Reuben when one of his sons went missing. First it was Joseph, whom he loved so much, and now it was Simeon.

Such fear had gripped them now because of the money found in their sacks that Jacob saw only disaster should he allow his youngest son out of his sight. Certainly he seems to have lost complete faith in Reuben because even with Reuben putting the life of his two sons into his father's hand, (notice it was not his own life), Jacob would not give permission for his youngest son to go with them.

Thus it was when the supply of corn that they had brought back with them was beginning to run low that Judah starts to take the lead role by impressing on his father that without Benjamin with them they would not be allowed in to see 'the man' and not allowed to buy grain, therefore there was no point in going down to Egypt.

Jacob then complained about them mentioning Benjamin to this ruler, but Judah, insisted that there was no option but to go down to Egypt if they were to stay alive. What is of particular interest is that whereas Reuben was only prepare to put the lives of his children as surety, Judah put himself up as surety for the lad and offered to take full blame if he did not bring him back with them. What a contrast in attitudes.

Jacob, being more impressed with Judah than with Reuben, finally agreed to allow Benjamin to go with them, but only accompanied with double money and gifts for this man who was causing them so much grief.

It is of course reasonable to assume that at no time did the brothers admit to Jacob of their involvement in Joseph's disappearance and the fact that what had actually happened to him was unknown to them after they had put him in the pit.

Jacob naturally was grieved that they had volunteered the information that there was another son, but Judah quickly countered this with the fact that the man's questions were so searching they had had no option but to be honest. Had they given false information there could well have been retribution on an unknown scale. It was they who needed grain and the Egyptian authorities, represented by 'the man', who had the means of supplying it.

The Brothers Second Visit to Egypt

The manner in which Joseph handles his family after so many years of enforced absence is gradually being revealed. He needed to find out about them, especially their feelings about him. Had there been a complete change of heart since that hate filled day that started him on the journey to his present home in exile and the position which he knew was of God?

It is also reasonable to ask the question, in studying this particular time frame in which Joseph meets and re-establishes relationships with his family, 'Is there a picture being unfolded here of how God deals with us as He seeks to establish, or re-establish, a relationship with each one of us?'

Certainly it gives Israel an excellent picture of what is required of them to be reunited with Him as a nation. For just as the other sons had to admit that there is one that is not so the house of Israel will have to admit that there is one that they pierced (Zech, 12:10, 11 – Hadad Rimmon in the plain of Megiddo was where king Josiah was killed). There must come a time when the people of Israel acknowledge their Messiah is Jesus. Many Jews are being liberated when they recognize Jesus as their Messiah, angered by the fact that they have been misled all those years that He was an imposter. The key element in this drama is food. Without the journeys to Egypt there was only hunger and death. By this means God in His wisdom was drawing the family into a deep self-examination and true confession that would initiate a true reunion of hearts and minds that was to prove so significant in His plan for them.

Could it be that God in His wisdom has placed in our lives an element of 'hunger' or a 'desire' that is drawing us to 'Egypt' so that He can deal with us through deep self-examination and true confession to initiate a true uniting or reuniting with Him that will prove significant in His plan for our lives?

Unless the relationship between each of us as individuals and Almighty God who is seeking for us becomes evident through a dynamic life changing experience, then that relationship could well be too weak to survive trials and tribulations. It cannot be a group decision, as the scripture so clearly illustrates. Without each and every individual making his or her own true confession and act of repentance, the process of becoming wedded to the God of our salvation will be flawed and therefore will not succeed.

> *"For our gospel did not come to you in word only, but also in power,*
> *and in the Holy Spirit and in much assurance, as you know what*

kind of men we were among you for your sake. And you became followers of us and the Lord, having received the word in much affliction, with joy in the Holy Spirit." (1 Thess. 1:5-6).

The reader of scripture has the advantage of reading and understanding the drama as it unfolds, with the thoughts and feelings and conversations of both sides revealed to them, but that same information was not available to the characters in the drama at the time; nor can we shout back through the ages to give them advice.

The brothers and their father were unaware of the true identity of 'the man' who had suddenly become such a powerful force in their lives, nor the impact that he was having on them.

Joseph's inspired and patient tactics were acting as a catalyst for their soul searching and the rearranging of the relationship between the brothers and their father. The whole purpose of Joseph's disappearance, happening without the brother's knowledge, now becomes clearer.

Had they known, then this challenging process would not have been possible thereby leaving the true sin against Joseph, the hardness of heart, unbelief and hatred without cause, unrealized and an impediment to any new intimate relationship.

Reuben might have been the first born and Joseph the preferred son for succeeding Jacob had he not mysteriously disappeared, but now we see the emergence of Judah as the senior brother who commanded the respect of his father and established himself as the new potential leader; such that Jacob when blessing his sons before his death said of Judah,

"...the sceptre shall not pass from Judah, nor the ruler's staff from between his feet, as long as men come to Shiloh; and unto him shall the obedience of the people be".

It is from Judah that David and the Mashiach were to come.

Jacob, an old man mourning for the life of two of his sons, commits their journey to the God of Abraham for he realized that it was God alone who could help them now.

Obviously Jacob was unaware that God had gone before them, but in his ignorance it was important that he put his trust in God for all things. He was now of a mind that if he lost his sons then that was the will of God and he would have to accept it.

From God's point of view many of the matters we pray about have already been sorted out, but it is important that we trust God and commit everything to Him just as Jacob did. In faith we must believe in the one who is all-knowing and completely trustworthy however difficult that might seem to be at the critical time.

The anticipation experienced by the brothers as they travelled back to Egypt will have increased the nearer they got to it, especially now with Benjamin in attendance. The harshness of the treatment they experienced when being interrogated by the Viceroy was not something they wanted to remember, but they had no choice but to see him again if they wanted more grain and to see the release of Simeon.

Joseph Meets Benjamin

On reaching Egypt and being brought before 'the man' their worst fears were realized when they were told that they were to dine with this important official. Their suspicions were aroused that they might be taken as bondmen, possibly by this official because of the money found in their sacks. Before crossing the threshold of the grand house they quickly spoke to one of the stewards explaining about the money and their concern that a charge of theft might be brought against them; indeed they volunteered that they had brought that money back and additional funds to purchase more grain.

The steward was reassuring,

> *"Peace be to you, fear not; your God and the God of your father, has given you treasure in your sacks; I had your money"*

and he brought Simeon to them. Having been assured about the money in such a dramatic way it is understandable if they were confused about what was happening to them. They were not in control of events as they were in their own country which made them apprehensive. Their role during the merciless treatment of the people of Shechem and of course their treatment of Joseph was now reversed. They were the ones being threatened and on the defensive.

But more was to follow; for when they entered the great man's house they were supplied with water to wash their feet and their animals given 'provender'. They had the gift ready for the great man and all was then in readiness for his arrival. Again they bowed down to the ground before him when he appeared, such was his importance and authority, and gave him the present Jacob had insisted they bring. Once more Joseph's dreams were confirmed as being God inspired.

Joseph then asked after his father, careful not to give his identity away by speaking to them as an interested third party.

"Is your father well, the old man of whom you spoke? Is he yet alive?"

Then seeing Benjamin his immediate brother, being the son of his mother Rachel, he asked,

"Is this your youngest brother of whom you spoke to me?"

The inner emotional struggle required by Joseph to maintain his composure, not only before his brothers but also before his servants, would have been considerable. Here before him was his younger brother whom he had not seen these twenty or so long years; no longer the young boy he knew when he was taken away, but an adult, and handsome with it if, that is, he followed Joseph in good looks.

It is more than likely he had wanted to embrace his brother, but instead abruptly ended the interview. Turning in haste he left the room for his own private apartment so that he could allow his tears to flow and for his emotions to find release. In his position he fortunately did not have to give reasons for his actions.

Once he had refreshed and composed himself he went back into the room where his brethren and servants were waiting for their meal. The Egyptians would not eat with foreigners, certainly not with Hebrews, so they dined on a separate table from the brothers.

As his position prevented Joseph sitting with his servants, his brothers' suspicion of him sitting alone at a separate table would not have been aroused. In any case they were nervous and in awe of this important Egyptian official.

As they were directed to their seats they were disconcerted to find their seating arrangements exactly suited their position within the family from Reuben the first born to Benjamin the youngest. How did the Egyptian authorities know their ages? When food was taken from the official's table to theirs why should Benjamin, the youngest, have five times the quantity of food given to the others, for this was deemed a special mark of respect? All these things pointed to 'the man' being Joseph if only they had been able to understand the signs. But these things were kept from them.

Joseph Tests His Brothers

Having feasted well and after a good night's sleep they set out the following morning with their containers bulging with provisions for the family, well in excess of what they had paid for.

From Joseph's point of view he had already witnessed some outward signs of individual grief at their role in his disappearance when they were last before him. But this grief only showed a guilt complex that was more to do with the concern of each brother of their involvement in that embarrassing episode that saw the disappearance of their brother.

It was possibly more of a regret brought on by the thought that they could have been guilty of murder in the first instance, a niggling doubt about what had actually happened to Joseph than any real sense of sorrow at the result of their action.

There was also the feeling that having kept what they had done secret all these years it still had the potential to re-emerge and cause them more than just a little embarrassment.

Joseph needed to show them through experience that their real sin against him was a hardness of their hearts; their unbelief in the God of Abraham, through whom an understanding of the dreams could have been obtained had they been as close to God as Joseph was and, perhaps, most important of all, the hatred they had allowed to dwell and ferment in their hearts that had been the trigger for their actions.

As the information in chapter 8 reveals this scenario was repeated when the Messiah was rejected.

The planting of the cup in Benjamin's sack was to provide the climax to that testing experience.

The true horror came when Joseph's steward went after them and stopped them just as they cleared the city. Up to that moment they were steadily becoming more relieved to be returning home with both Simeon and Benjamin.

But when he accused them of returning evil for good by stealing his master's silver divining cup, a very important personal possession and much used in Egypt at the time, there is no doubt they would not have been able to believe what they were hearing.

In their now confused state of mind and their fear of the authorities, for them the thought that they could have done such a thing was totally out of the question, a madness. They would have ensured that they kept together; certainly Benjamin would have been properly guarded for fear of anything happening to him.

That the servant voiced the accusation in such a way that he seemed to expect them to know about this theft and admit to it was even more terrifying.

The reaction of the brothers, who were unaware of what had been going on and completely innocent of any wrong doing, will have been one of total bewilderment. The servant's suggestion was preposterous.

Believing themselves to be totally innosent of any possible charge of theft, they defensively suggested that the person found with the cup in their sack should die and all the brothers become bondmen, but the servant replied that just the guilty person should become a bondman and the rest of the brothers could go free.

Their unwitting confidence in their innocence would have been vindicated when each sack was opened and no cup found. However, when the cup was eventually found in Benjamin's sack their shock would have quickly led to despair. Benjamin was the one brother that must not be put at risk for it would mean the death of their father.

Their brother having disappeared through their actions, they could not afford to go to their father and say that the second child of his beloved Rachel was now either dead or the bondman of an Egyptian official.

The Brothers Return for a Third Meeting with Joseph

The brothers needed no persuasion, terror gripping their hearts. Packing their sacks, they returned in haste to Joseph's house to plead their case. A meeting with Joseph, significantly the third, is quickly arranged. Joseph makes out that with the cup he was well able to discover the guilty person by divination.

This is where Judah comes to the fore and concedes that they had little means of proving their innocence since the discovery of the cup in Benjamin's sack condemned them and declares, *"God has found out the iniquity of your servants",* meaning that God had found them guilty of doing wrong to their father, by the devious means they used to hide from him their involvement with the disappearance of Joseph.

Although Simeon is considered the one who counselled that Joseph be slain, it is probable that Judah was in agreement until the option of selling him became a possibility when they saw the Ishmaelite caravan.

As a natural leader, it was his hardness of heart, unbelief and hatred without cause that had encouraged his brothers at that time and it was this fact that had through the years come to haunt him. Coupled to this was the shame inflicted on themselves by the deception of their father; for by contaminating Joseph's coat with blood and having others take it to their father it gave Jacob the impression that Joseph had been killed.

They could not, in their own selfishly-minded state, have conceived the degree of distress such an event would cause their father. This too would have impacted on Judah's memory.

To compound the problem of a sense of profound guilt was the growing realisation of the wrong done to their brother Joseph. There is little doubt that over the years in their quiet moments, when they were reminded of their involvement in Joseph's disappearance, a deepening sense of guilt would have plagued them.

Judah's admission indicates that the moral regeneration of the brothers was complete. At last the admission that God had finally got the message through to him concerning his sin and as a result his willingness to give up his own life for the sake of his brother Benjamin.

So Judah said, "What can we say to my lord? What can we say in reply? Or how can we clear ourselves, since God has exposed the sin and guilt of your servants?

Behold, we are my lord's slaves, the rest of us as well as he with whom the cup was found."

But Joseph said, "Far be it from me that I should do that; but the man in whose hand the cup has been found, he will be my servant; and as for the rest of you, get up and go in peace to your father."

Joseph's insistence that Benjamin would be his bondman and that the others must return to their father spurred Judah into one final effort to secure his release. It was an eloquent and succinct account of all that had happened to them from the moment of their confession of the life of their father and the existence of a youngest brother, in response to Joseph's enquiries about their family during their first meeting, to their present situation.

18Then Judah approached him, and said, "O my lord, please let your servant say a word to you in private, and do not let your anger blaze against your servant, for you are equal to Pharaoh so I speak as if directly to him.

My lord asked his servants, saying, 'Have you a father or a brother?' We admitted to my lord, 'We have an old father and a young brother, the child of his old age.

Now that his brother is dead, he alone is left of two sons born of his mother, and his father loves him dearly.'

Then you said to your servants, 'Bring him down to me that I may actually see him.' But we said to my lord, 'The young man cannot leave his father, for if he should leave his father, his father would die.'

You then said to your servants, 'Unless your youngest brother comes with you, you shall not see my face again.' So when we returned to your servant my father, we told him what my lord had said.

When our father said, 'Go back and buy us a little food' we said, 'We can only go down to Egypt if our youngest brother is with us, then we will go down; for we told we cannot see the man's face unless our youngest brother is with us.'

Your servant my father said to us, 'You know that my wife bore me just two sons. One son went out from me, and I said, "Surely he is torn to pieces," and I have not seen him since.

If you take this one also from me, and any harm or an accident happens to him, you will bring my gray hair down to Sheol in sorrow.'

Now, therefore, when I come to your servant my father, and the young man is not with us, since his life is bound up in the young man's life, when he sees that the young man is not with us, he will die; and your servants will bring the gray hair of your servant our father down to Sheol in great sorrow.

For your servant became security for the young man to my father, saying, 'If I do not bring him back to you, then let me bear the blame before my father forever.'

Now, therefore, please let your servant remain here instead of the youth to be a slave to my lord, and let the young man go home with his brothers.

How can I go up to my father if the young man is not with me for fear that I would see the tragedy that would overtake my elderly father if he does not return?"

(Gen. 44:18 – 34)

Judah in this remarkable and passionate speech recounted the Viceroy's instructions that they would not see his face unless Benjamin was with them and Judah's warning that their father would die if anything happened to the lad.

He spoke of Jacob's reluctance in allowing the lad to come to Egypt because of the loss of the other son of his wife and that it was only on the Viceroy's insistence that he be brought, that their father finally relented.

Judah made it clear that should anything happen to Benjamin it would signal his father's death.

"And your servant my father said unto us: 'You know that my wife bore unto me two sons; and the one went out from me, and I said: Surely he is torn in pieces; and I have not seen him since; and if you take this one also from me, and harm befall him you will bring down my gray hairs with sorrow to the grave."

Now if the Viceroy's decision was final and they returned without the lad, then their father would die through sorrow having lost both sons from his wife.

Judah pointed out that as he had provided surety for the lad he would bear the blame to his father forever; it was therefore preferable that he should become a bondman in place of Benjamin.

Having seen the anguish suffered by his father after the death of Joseph he could not endure seeing the total devastation of his father should he not be able to return with Benjamin. The repetition of the phrase *'with sorrow to the grave'* and the fact that their father's soul was bound up with the lad's soul emphasized just how critical the whole matter was.

It was Judah's confession, his repentance and willingness to become a substitute for Benjamin that finally brought Joseph's emotions bubbling to the surface. Unable to contain himself any longer he ordered his staff out of the room and finally broke down in tears.

His brothers were bewildered by this sudden turn of events. One minute Judah is pleading for his brother's life, desperate for the Viceroy to change his mind regarding Benjamin, fearful that his father would die with a broken heart and the next they were alone with this powerful man crying his eyes out and telling them in their own language that he was their long lost brother Joseph. They were stunned, bewildered and confused.

"I am Joseph; does my father yet live?"

After 20 years of being separated from his kith and kin and surrounded by Egyptians, a stranger in a foreign land where God was not worshipped, having to cope with foreign customs, and with all that He had suffered before being elevated to his present position, Joseph with his brothers repentant and desperate before him needed assurance that his father, who was of a good age when he was taken away from them, should really still be alive and that he should see him once again.

Having put his brothers through such a time of testing to bring about their repentance for what they had done to him, Joseph's problem now was to assure them that he really was their brother.

Calling them near to him to give them a better opportunity to check him out he assured them that it was God's plan that he come to Egypt to preserve life. The manner of his transportation from home to Egypt had been God's method to effect his ultimate rise to his present position.

We will never be able to fathom God's methods of achieving the right end, which is why our unquestioning submission to His service is so essential.

Joseph had had time to realise just how God had achieved His purpose and that there had been no other way from the need for training for his new role and the means whereby he could be brought before Pharaoh without there being any feeling of threat.

A slave who had become the respective overseer of the Captain of Pharaoh's Personal Guard and then of the Prison Governor's estate; respected in prison; unbowed yet always helpful and supportive of those who ruled over him; practical yet clearly a man of God; worthy of trust and a man in whom full unquestioning confidence could be placed.

The butler was able to give a personal testimony to Pharaoh regarding Joseph's character and standing within the prison and his powers of interpreting dreams. Even Potiphar, who is the one most likely to have been charged with bringing Joseph before the king, will have added his weight to the butler's evidence.

From the moment he had entered Egypt, and bought from the Ishmaelites by Potiphar to the moment he was brought before the king, Joseph had been in the employ and therefore under the surveillance of senior people in the service of the king. All could vouch for his character and moral stature.

When he had given his assessment of what should be done to mitigate the effects of the seven years of drought and Pharaoh wanted to appoint Joseph as Grand Vizier, even as Viceroy, no one raised any objection, indeed the general consensus of the senior palace staff was that it was an excellent appointment. Yet moments before Joseph had been a convict. One wonders what Potiphar's wife made of Joseph's meteoric rise to power.

However necessary it was that Joseph should be taken to Egypt and sold as a slave for God's plan to become a reality, and however critical to that plan were the action of the brothers, there is no doubt that it was necessary for his brothers to realise that their attitude towards him was wrong and needed to be sorted out.

They needed to repent of their sin and seek forgiveness. God's ultimate goal had been to save life and this Joseph was at great pains to point out.

> *"And now be not grieved, nor be angry with yourselves, that you sold me hither, for God sent me before you to preserve life … and to save you alive for a great deliverance."*
>
> *"So now it was not you that sent me hither, but God; and he has made me a father (which is an exact transliteration of an Egyptian of state rank, corresponding to 'vizier') to Pharaoh and lord of all his house and ruler of all the land of Egypt."*

God had used the animosity of the brothers towards Joseph to achieve His own ends, just as He used the hatred of the Jewish religious leaders to enable His Son to die on the cross as prophesied by the prophets, but according to His timescale not theirs.

For believers in the one true God, as Abraham had been, hindsight is the one sure way to confirm that God is with them. From it God's plan and involvement in their lives can be identified to provide assurance for the future.

The son who was dead was not only alive but ruler in the land. Just as the Christ was dead yet He is alive forever more, and as head of the church, our advocate in heaven. There was clear evidence that the God who had blessed him in Potiphar's house and then in the prison, was blessing his management of the famine in Egypt.

Pharaoh, who was rejoicing in the fact that his country was being saved from starvation and disaster, on hearing that this saviour had been visited by his family in Canaan naturally offered them the best grazing land, the land of Goshen. With his full authority the brothers were to return and bring the whole family into Egypt to be looked after.

But Joseph had to warn them not to fall out along the way.

Jacob Told About Joseph

The brothers, through their traumatic meetings with, and experiences of Joseph's handling of them, had had time to come to terms with the fact that this was indeed their long lost brother whom they thought was dead. It was unlikely that the brothers would have given their father ablow by blow narrative of all that had happened but their relief that their long held belief that they had been responsible for the death of their brother and the 20 years of deception as now over. However the stain on their consciences would never be completely removed.

Jacob, who had had to rely on what his sons told him, had reached a point where he could no longer believe them. Indeed so shocked was he with their news that he almost died. The lies they had told him regarding Joseph and their untrustworthiness made it hard to accept they were at last telling him the truth.

However, it must have been the wagons Joseph had sent that finally tipped the balance and he was able to believe that his son Joseph, whom he loved so much, was indeed alive.

But it was not the descriptions of the splendour of his appearance and his life and position that enthused Jacob,

"It is enough. Joseph my son is still alive".

For Jacob, after years of mourning the death of his son Joseph, it was indeed enough that he now had proof that he was alive and he would see his son again. That was the true grandness and excitement of the occasion. The shock to his system when the truth finally fully dawned on him very nearly caused his death, but God had other plans for His servant Jacob, perhaps his greatest prophetic announcement was yet to be delivered (Gen. 49).

Jacob was a man of habit even though he had been a sojourner all his life. From an early age the accounts of how the Almighty God worshipped by his grandfather and father had spoken to them and directed them had been food to his enquiring mind.

After his first meeting with this God through the angels ascending and descending the ladder, Jacob had himself grown to know that same God, worshipped Him and ultimately served Him. Therefore, before starting the journey to Egypt, Jacob travelled to Beer-sheba, where his father Isaac had built an altar and had settled; and there Jacob offered sacrifices to his God.

During the night God appeared in a dream to Jacob giving him clearance to go down into Egypt where his offspring would be molded into a great nation in the furnace of oppression, which it was to become for his people.

His father Isaac had previously been prevented from going down into Egypt. Not only would God go with Jacob into Egypt but would also bring him back again to the Promised Land, that is at his death for burial, then his offspring would also be led back to the Promised Land when they went up to finally take possession of it as the nation of Israel, no longer to be nomads in it but possessors of it. And Joseph would perform the customary duty of putting his hands on Jacob's eyes at his death.

Having become established in the land that God was to give them, Jacob and his family were now faced with leaving much with which they had become familiar and was part of their daily life. Only transportable items that would fit on the wagons sent by Pharaoh could be taken, the remainder had to be abandoned. The total number of persons transported into Egypt was sixty-seven, but with Joseph and his sons the total was seventy.

Right up to the end of his life Rachel's name was never far from Jacob's lips. Not only had he loved her to the extent that the seven years he first worked for her seemed short, she had produced a son who had proved faithful to him and his God because he had that same desire in his heart to reach out to the Almighty God that Jacob had.

Indeed, Joseph's life seemed to mirror his own early days, for whereas he had looked heavenward, Esau looked earthward and preferred the physical attractions rather than the spiritual; now it was Joseph who looked to the spiritual and his brothers to the physical worldly attractions.

Yet it was Leah who was truly faithful to him, abandoning both her family and family gods for her husband and her husband's God. Her faithfulness was ultimately rewarded because her son Judah became the leader of the eleven brothers, and it was into his line that King David and the Mashiach were born. Leah also provided Jacob with the greatest number of sons and, through her son Levi, Moses, the greatest of all the prophets and many others were born. But her death and place of burial is only briefly recorded *("... where I buried Leah ...")* when Jacob explains to Joseph where he is to be buried. Jacob's desire was to be buried with his first and most faithful wife.

It is Judah, Jacob now sends to seek directions from Joseph for the way to Goshen, and they travelled there and set up camp in Goshen.

Now it is Joseph's turn to seek out his father whom he has not yet seen for so many years for a meeting filled with emotion. Joseph fell on Jacob's neck and the tears flowed releasing the years of homesickness and inner yearning for that essential, mutual spiritual fellowship he had had with his father from whom he had learned so much about his faith.

Joseph honoured his father and loved him. Finally Jacob was able to declare his willingness to die now that he had seen his long lost son.

Joseph, aware that the special privilege of his position was in part due to Pharaoh, now took charge of the protocol side of introducing them to the king. All that had happened as Jacob and his entourage entered the country and the emotional meeting of Jacob and Joseph will have been reported in detail to Pharaoh. All the arrangements had to be carefully made so as not to offend the royal family for shepherds were an abomination to the Egyptians.

The meeting between Pharaoh and the five selected representatives of the family was carefully choreographed with the responses to Pharaoh's questions practiced in advance. It is important to observe Joseph's loyalty to his family; that he was able to associate himself with these crude Canaanite shepherds who had done him no favours and were far removed from the grandeur of the royal palaces in which he now lived. It shows a simple nobility of character to which it is difficult to find an equal in the whole of human existence.

Joseph's one overriding foundational attribute, that allowed him to welcome such brethren with open arms and without animosity, was undoubtedly his sense of Divine appointment as the saviour of his people.

It was this total trust and faith in the wisdom and faithfulness of the God of Abraham that had initially triggered the hatred that had initiated the chain of events that brought about the present situation. Without his father he would not have acquired this faith, therefore he could deny neither his lineage nor his brethren.

Pharaoh's gratitude for Joseph's eminent services to him and his country during the famine was to give to his people the best of the land. Further to this generous offer was to appoint Joseph's relatives to the position of royal officers, superintendents to the king's herdsmen.

Joseph then introduces his father to Pharaoh. There is an interesting use of words as the two conversed for the king enquired about Jacob's age,

"How many are the days of your life?"

Jacob in reply referred to the 'days of his sojourning' as being 130 years making the point that there was a land beyond death, which would be his eternal home, a real life that could not be obtained here.

He then referred to the years of his life being few and evil, reflecting on the troubled existence he had endured, and saddened by the fact that his life had been shorter than that of his forebears. Jacob then blessed Pharaoh before leaving his presence. In this way Jacob was agreeing to come under the authority of the Pharaoh, a matter that was to play such an important part of the nation's escape from Egypt at the time of the exodus.

The family of Jacob now settled in the land, coming under the authority of Pharaoh and gaining possessions through purchase and were supported by Joseph. As for the Egyptian and Canaanite nations, they gradually paid over first their money, then their cattle and then their land to Pharaoh in exchange for food because the famine was so severe in the land, making Pharaoh the supreme lord of the whole of Egypt and everything living in it

Jacob Blesses His Sons (Gen. 49)

Jacob, having lived seventeen years in Egypt, was coming to the end of his life. Although he was not afraid to die because, as his answer to Pharaoh suggested, he was looking forward to something far greater than he could expect in this life, for God had also appeared to him on a number of occasions confirming to him his special status in God's will and plan.

However, Jacob was concerned that he should not be buried in

Egypt and to that end obtained assurances from Joseph that he would undertake the responsibility for his burial in the family burial ground.

Jacob had lived through tortuous times. Esau, Laban, Dinah and Joseph, names that trigger memories of trials and tribulations; yet it was on the anvil of affliction that the soul of this sensitive man was forged, knowing by experience that he could not travel outside of God's care and concern for him.

Such was his faith in God, tried and tested as it was, often seemingly to the point of destruction it was by that faith that he knew of a certainty that God was with him and would never leave him.

Far from being one who never made mistakes, yet he was able to rise above life's cruel reverses extracting good from each one to the end his life, blessing those around him. Jacob realized that just as he had had to face the unknown and experience danger, so would his sons.

Then Joseph, being warned of his father's poor condition, brought his two sons to him so that Jacob might bless them before he died. His father then recounted the promise God had made to him that the land of promise would be for an everlasting possession for the great nation that his offspring would become.

What is more Joseph's two sons would become as Jacob's sons and be counted within the identified tribes of Israel. Indeed, during the history of Israel the name of Ephraim is often used to identify the northern kingdom after the 2 to 10 tribal split in the time of Rehoboam (cf. 11 Chron. 25:7; Hos. 5:3;6:10;10:6; Is. 7:2;Jer. 7:15).

God is no respecter of persons. Being the first-born has no advantage as has been seen by the preference given to Abel, Abraham, Isaac, Jacob over Esau, Joseph himself, Moses and David. At this important time in his life, Jacob would have been given divine inspiration when dealing with his offspring. Although his eyes were dim his mental ability was sharp. Knowing full well how his son would have positioned his grandsons before him, Jacob placed his right hand on Ephraim's head and his left on that of Manasseh, crossing his hands over to do so.

"The God before whom my fathers Abraham and Isaac walked,

> *the God who has been my shepherd all my life long unto this day, the angel who has redeemed me from all evil, bless the lads; and let my name be named in them and the name of my fathers Abraham and Isaac; and let them grow into a multitude in the midst of the earth."*

Although Joseph tried to correct his father by changing his hands over so that the first-born would be recognized, his father protested that he was fully aware of what he was doing. It is important to consider the names of the boys. The first was named 'Making to forget' - that is for God has made me forget all my toil and all my father's house, whereas the second was named Ephraim meaning 'God has made me fruitful in the land of my affliction', which was more appropriate when the people of Israel ventured into the promised Land.

> *'I know it my son, I know it; he also shall become a people, and he also shall become great; howbeit his younger brother shall be greater than he, and his seed shall become a multitude of nations."*

There is no tribe of Joseph, the half tribes of Ephraim and Manasseh take his place in the list of the twelve tribes of Israel.

So Jacob blessed Joseph's sons,

> *"By these shall Israel be blessed, saying: God make you as Ephraim and Manasseh."*

Just as Joseph would not, could not ignore his brethren, so his sons willingly gave up a most exalted social position and an enviable political career in the Egyptian state to align themselves with their kinsmen, the despised shepherd-immigrants, such was the influence of their father and their own sense of belonging.

This unique chapter is special insofar as it contains the blessings Jacob hands out to his sons; blessing that inevitably reflect the character of each patriarch and the position God had prescribed for that tribe in the future. Speaking prophetically he says to his sons:

> *"Gather yourselves together, that I may tell you that which shall*

befall you in the end of days."

These words were to set the seal on the life of the Children of Israel to the end of time and can be seen through history and well into the future.

Reuben   his natural rights as the first-born were forfeited because he had no strength of character. Described as being as *"unstable as water"* Reuben's cardinal sin was weakness of will, lack of self-control and no firmness of purpose as could be seen when he made such a hash in trying to save Joseph. Unlike Judah, he was not willing to put himself forward to take the blame if anything should happen to Benjamin when going into Egypt to seek for food, but offered his sons instead as if killing his sons would help the loss of Benjamin should anything happen to him.

His descendents were no better, for when Deborah sought to rally the tribes in a bid for Israeli independence, in the tribe of Reuben there were deliberations, and a searching of hearts but no specific action; hence no Judges, Prophets or leaders of any kind ever came from this tribe. Indeed, after this the tribe of Reuben is hardly mentioned in Israeli history.

The three portions that he should have received as the right of the first-born were given to:

Joseph - for saving the nation,

Levi - the priesthood

Judah - kingly power or headship.

But what abhorred Jacob more than any other was the way in which Reuben *"went up to thy father's bed"* and defiled it.

Simeon and Levi   their combined action at Shechem was vicious and condemned by Jacob in no uncertain tone. *"I will divide them in Jacob"* was to mean that the tribe of Simeon was intermixed with the tribe of Judah and the tribe of Levi was to be dispersed throughout the nation of Israel. Although they were not cursed their sin was *"cursed be their anger"*

Simeon became the silent part of the nation of Judah when Israel was split at the time of Rehoboam with Israel consisting of ten tribes.

Levi was never allowed to own land. The priestly clan disappeared during the time of the Jewish revolt when Jerusalem was sacked and the Temple destroyed. It was the members of the priestly clan which shouted out *'crucify Him'* and became aggressive towards the early believers in the risen Christ.

Judah   he was not without blame when the brothers picked on Joseph, but when he finally took the lead it was he who confessed to the sin of their actions and was willing to take the place of Benjamin as a bondman.

The whole of the prophetic utterance regarding Judah is to do with his authority and kingship; the lion of Judah, the sceptre, his effervescent nature and the productivity of the land which all point to the leading tribe that has given the nation the name Jew.

Joseph the softest and most loving words are reserved for Joseph who was undoubtedly the best and noblest of the brothers. He was a man of visions, of Godly dreams combined with both moral and spiritual strength of character that was unbowed in all the vicissitudes of life.

He was the ideal son, brother, servant, administrator and the steadfast servant of the living God whom he served without question or faltering whatever the circumstances he experienced, whether apparently good or apparently bad. In him there was a consistency of spirit that is an example to all.

Jacob's blessing of Joseph surpassed that of the others for he was uniquely precious in his sight.

He was the fruitful bow by a fountain or well whose branches ran over the wall into Egypt.

So Jacob continued to bless the rest of his sons, who did not feature so strongly in the scriptural record but each one represented a twelfth part of the nation of Israel and their offspring had a part to play in the conquering of the promised land and in its history up to the present day.

When Jacob died, Joseph, promising to return to Egypt, was released to do his duty for his father. The burial of Jacob was more splendid than either of his forebears, for included in the party were the elite of Egypt, in all *"... a very great company ..."*

Unfortunately the guilty consciences of the brothers would not be silenced, nor would their willingness to manipulate totally go away. Using the name of their father they sent an unrecorded and unsubstantiated message to Joseph that he was to forgive them, then they themselves went before him, bowed low and offered themselves as bondmen to him. A clear re-enactment of the dreams he had been given by God.

Joseph's tears were for their unbelief; not just in his character but that it was God all along who had engineered the whole thing using their unwarranted hatred of him as a vehicle to initiate it.

This incident demonstrates that even with all that they had experienced, their knowledge of the one true God was at best poor and their personal relationship with Him seemingly none-existent.

> *"Fear not; for am I in the place of God? And as for you, you meant evil against me; but God meant it for good, to bring to pass as it is to this day, to save much people alive. Now therefore fear not for I will sustain you, and your little ones."*

Is this where you are with God? Even as the brothers were with Joseph? Believing yet full of unbelief? Joseph knew God. They knew God but only through Jacob and Joseph, for they lacked that one to one personal relationship with God that Jacob and Joseph had because those two men sought after Him.

Joseph, having seen the third generation of his children's children, assured the elders of Israel that God would lead them back to the land He had promised to Abraham, Isaac and Jacob, and obtained an oath that his body would be taken back to be buried with his father, at one hundred and ten years of age he died in peace.

This is merely the end of the beginning. In this day and age this same God is working His purpose out through His first born Israel and the church. Are you saying with Isaiah, *"Here am I send me"*? I am!

8 JOSEPH AND JESUS - A COMPARISON

The following text was provided freely and I was so impressed with the Jewish perception of the subject matter that I could not put it down. It has such depth of meaning and understanding that it became obvious that it needed to be included in this book. It is both profound and revealing and has a wonderful spiritual depth yet displays a simplicity so that the meaning cannot possibly be misunderstood.

Edited information © Elhanan ben Avraham

To begin with there are statements made by Rav Jesus that call to mind the Talmudic reference quoted earlier (Brachot 34B: "All of the prophets prophesied only of the days of the Messiah") "These are my words which I spoke while I was still with you, that all things which are written about me in the Torah of Moses and the Nevi'im (prophets) and the Tehilim (Psalms) must be fulfilled." (Luke 24:44), and "You search the scriptures, because you think that in them you have eternal life; and it is these that bear witness of me." (John 5:39).

These are bold statements indeed for a son of Israel to make, and yet this one born in Beit Lehem (Bethlehem) from the tribe of Yehuda (Judah) and the house of David, raised by Joseph the carpenter and his wife Miriam (Mary), did make them. But there is more to this confirmed human being that is important to our understanding.

1.   Before the world was Jesus existed (John 1:1) before Abraham was I AM (that is I have existed, I am existing and I will exist).

2. God is spirit and they who worship Him must worship Him in spirit and in truth, therefore if Jesus is begotten and not made He too must have been entirely spirit when he was with His father before the world began. Thus:
   a. the Father sent Him
   b. a body was prepared for Him (Hebrews 10:5), that is the body formed in Mary's womb.
   c. Jesus had to come down from heaven and restricted Himself initially to the body of a baby taking on the form of a human being. In the words of one hymn writer, "Our God contracted to a span incomprehensively made man".

3. Mary was a virgin when she became pregnant by the Holy Spirit, that is by the hand of the God who created all things and to whom nothing is impossible even the making of the body of a boy child initiated in Mary's womb. But why the need for her to be a virgin?
   a. Hereditary sin comes from Adam and is passed down the male line (whereas Eve was deceived, Adam sinned because to him was given the instructions regarding the Tree of the Knowledge of Good and Evil and it was he who deliberately flouted the rules).
   b. By Mary becoming pregnant by the Holy Spirit, this connection with inherited sin is broken and therefore Jesus, sinless before he entered the body remained sinless. All his half brothers and sisters, because of Joseph's involvement, were not sinless.
   c. Thus was Jesus able to take upon Himself the sins of the whole world (past, present and future).

4. He was the only eternal spirit, made truly human being who has been filled with the Holy Spirit without measure. By that means there was a continuous collaboration between the Word made flesh and God's power for miracles such as the stilling of the storm, the knowledge Jesus had as to what was going on in men's hearts and minds and His ability to cast out demons.

5.   Sent by the Father with full instruction for His ministry, empowered by the Spirit, the Word gave utterance.

Note from Peter: I have, over many years, studied scripture and God in His goodness has revealed much to me to the benefit of some. All that has been written in this book, originally called A Personal Walk Through Genesis, has been by reading and inspiration by the Holy Spirit. Unfortunately I am not a Biblical scholar and my understanding of the Word of God is limited both in detail, scale and scope. In the life of Joseph, however, I have been led to see the need for a far more profound, Jewish understanding of the text than I am able to provide. I cannot do better than to use the major part of the text on Joseph provided by Elhanan be Abraham who, in my humble and ignorant Gentile opinion, has dealt with the account of Joseph with such sensitivity that it has inspired me.

Let us now turn to the ancient texts to see if there may, or may not be, some validity to such claims. It will be beneficial to read the Genesis text along with following information.

Ref	Joseph	Jesus
37:2	A special relationship had developed between the father and this one son even as he brought bad reports about his brother.	*In several discussions with His brethren, the children of Israel, He brought before them the issue of their sins,* "Those of the Pharisees who were with him heard these things and said to him, 'We are not blind too are we?' Jesus said to them, 'If you were blind you would have no sin; but since you say we see, your sin remains'" (John 9:40-41); *and,* "If I had not come and spoken to them they would not have sin, but now they have no excuse for their sin" (John 15:22). *Jesus also said,*

Ref	Joseph	Jesus
		"But whoever shall deny me before men, I will also deny him before my Father who is in Heaven" (Matthew 10:33)
		At the age of twelve Jesus declared to Joseph and Mary, when they finally found him in discussion in the temple in Jerusalem, *"Did you not know that I had to be about the affairs of my Father?" (Luke 2:49).*

These words and acts of both Joseph and Jesus could not be, indeed were not received by their brethren without exacting a strong reaction

37:3 *"Israel loved Joseph more than all his sons."*

In the Torah (Deuteronomy 14:1) we are told that the God of Israel has many sons: "You are the sons of the Lord your God."

In Genesis 22:2,12 God tells Abraham, "Take now your son, your only son, whom you love, Isaac, and go to the land of Moriah, and offer him there as a burnt offering ..." But what of Ishmael? Therefore an "only son" here speaks of one who is chosen for a unique purpose, the only one of his kind, one through whom the covenant would be established. (Genesis 17:18-21).

In Matthew 3:17 and 17:5 it is reported that the same Lord pronounced, *"This is my beloved son, hear him."* Again, the picture of the one favoured of his Father.

Ref	Joseph	Jesus

Joseph was the son of Jacob's wife Rachel, who was buried by Bethlehem, which is where Jesus was born (Matthew 2:1).

37:4 — Joseph, being favoured over his brothers by their father caused envy and jealousy to turn to hatred, and they could not speak well of him, nor address him with shalom. It could be said that they hated him without cause.

(Psalm 69:4) "But this came to pass that the word might be fulfilled that is written in their Torah, 'They hated me without cause.'" (John 15:25). *The Rabbis have also declared that God allowed Jerusalem and the Temple to be destroyed in the first century for this same reason.*

The majority of Jewish religious authorities, both in the first century and now, cannot seem to bring themselves to speak well of Jesus of Nazareth

37:5 - 10 — Joseph recounted his dreams to his brothers, and they hated him even more. Yet the dreams were prophetic, given him by God.

Jesus made equally bold announcements before Israel: "Behold, there is one here greater than Solomon" (Luke 11:31); "But I say to you there is one here greater than the Temple" (Matthew 12:6); in order that all may honour the son, even as they honour the Father" (John 5:23); and Jesus said before the Sanhedrin, "hereafter you will see the Son of Man sitting at the right hand of Power, and coming on the clouds of heaven" (Matthew 26:64),

Ref	Joseph	Jesus
		for which his elder brethren mocked, beat, spat at him and pronounced him worthy of death.
37:11	"And his brothers were jealous of him."	"For he (Pilate) was aware that the chief priests had delivered him up because of envy" (Mark 15:10).
37:12-17	*Joseph sent by his Father to his brothers, the children of Israel who were tending the sheep at Shechem.*	"I have been sent only to the lost sheep of the house of Israel" (Matthew 15:24); *and,* "...the Father has sent me" (John 5:36)
37:18	*His brothers saw him from afar, and before he came close, plotted to kill him.*	*To this day Jesus is seen from a distance by the children of Israel through a fog of prejudice and misunderstanding, through the sins of an idolatrous religious system which misused the name "Jesus", even attempting to erase his Jewishness, and at that name (Yeshua) the Jews, for the most part, think negatively, linking it with the sufferings of the centuries, wishing to "kill" even the memory of it, that it might not come close to them, to be objectively examined (as the anagram "Yeshu", which is the common pronunciation of his name in Hebrew, is intended by some to mean "may his name and memory be erased.")*

Ref	Joseph	Jesus
37:19-20	*They mocked Joseph and plotted to kill him.*	*Then the chief priest and elders of the people were gathered together in the court of the High Priest, Caiaphas, and they plotted together to seize Jesus by stealth, and kill him." (Matthew 26:3-4).*
37:21	*Reuben rose to Joseph's defence.*	*Nicodemus arises in defence of Jesus (John 7:51).*
37:23	*They seized Joseph and stripped him of his tunic still with the intent to destroy him.*	*Jesus' garments were stripped from him before his execution, the seamless, woven tunic being of one piece, (John 19:23-24).*
37:24-25	*They threw Joseph into a pit, and they sat down to eat a meal.*	*Jesus was arrested and imprisoned when Israel reclines to eat the Passover.*
37:25-30	*Here we have the picture of Judah, one of the twelve, suggesting the selling of their brother for monetary gain.*	*Judah (Judas), one of the twelve disciples sold him to the religious authorities.*

In both cases

1. *they were turned over to the Gentiles: Joseph to the Egyptians, Jesus to the Romans (Matthew 20:18-19).*

2. *the intended sellers of their brother were unable to retain the desired money, the Midianites stealing Joseph before they could sell him, and in Judas returning the thirty pieces of silver (Matthew 27:3-7).*

   In the prophesy of Zechariah (11:13) it is written, "Then the Lord said to me, 'Throw it to the potter, that magnificent price at which I was valued by them,' so I took the thirty shekels of silver and threw them to the potter in the house of the Lord." *This sum was the value of a slave gored by an ox (Exodus 21:32).*

Ref	Joseph	Jesus
37:31	*They slaughtered a male goat in Joseph's stead, dipping his tunic in its blood.* *(It is noteworthy that there is no account of Joseph, uttering a single word.)*	"For this is my blood of the covenant, which is to be shed on behalf of many for the forgiveness of sins." (Matthew 26:28) "Behold the lamb of God who takes away the sin of the world." (John 1:29).
37:32-35	*It was reported to Jacob/Israel that Joseph was dead and he was to remain with that belief for many years, until a much later revelation, when he would again see him.*	*Jesus has been considered dead and separated from the house of Israel for two millennia. Jesus spoke a number of parables referring to a distant journey and a long passage of time, "for the kingdom of heaven is as a man travelling into a far country, who called his own servants, and delivered unto them his goods. ...Now after a long time the master of those servants came and settled accounts with them"* (Matthew 25:14-19); "For I say to you, from now on you shall not see me until you say, 'Blessed is he who comes in the name of the Lord'." (Matthew 23:38-39).
38	*This chapter is a breaking away from the account of Joseph and turning attention to Judah, who has played, and will continue to play, a key role in the fate of Joseph.* *This chapter essentially leads us to the birth of Peretz ("breach"), from whose line would come King David, and Zara ("he has shined"), sons of Judah and Tamar.*	

Ref	Joseph	Jesus

In the name Peretz we have a remez[10] regarding the later prophesy found in Micah 2:12-13, which speaks of one called "the Breaker" (poretz) who would open the way for the remnant of Israel to "break forth". It reads thus: "I will surely assemble all of you, Jacob, I will surely gather the remnant of Israel. I will put them together like sheep in a fold; like a flock in the midst of its pasture they will be noisy with men. The breaker has gone up before them, they break out, pass through the gate and go out by it, and their king goes on before them, and the Lord at their head."

This passage is reminiscent of Pesach and of the coming out of Egypt under Moses but is of course a later work, prophesying a later, yet not dissimilar, event.

39:1-6 *And Joseph was brought down to Egypt.*

Egypt in the Torah stands as the antithesis of the Promised Land, Eretz Israel. It is a land of little water and plentiful sand, filled with false religion and idolatry; an oppressive regime and a house of bondage.

It is from here that God was to deliver His people and bring them back to the land that He had promised to their fathers, "a land flowing with milk and honey," where they were to learn to serve the Living God in truth, by His Torah. They were to be "brought up" from the Land of Egypt, to

In John 6:38 Jesus declares, "For I came down from heaven not to do my own will, but the will of him that sent me." According to his words, he had left his Father's house and the glory (kvod) therein, to seek out "the lost sheep of the House of Israel" (John 14:2; 17:5).

In the first century, though Israel was in the land promised to them, yet they were under the oppressive hand of the pagan Roman Empire, and occupied by the Roman army. Religious leadership in Jerusalem was no longer truly established according to the Torah, but with those willing to compromise

---

[10]   *remez = "hint" the interpretation of Scripture at the level of allusive implication. For instance, Pidyon Haben - redemption of the first-born - is alluded to by an acronym of the letters of Bereshit, which spell "ben rishon acharei shloshim yom tifdeh" - the first son you shall redeem after thirty days.*

Ref	Joseph	Jesus

go up (to make aliyah) to the land promised to Abraham. Aliyah is the same word used today for immigration to Israel. They were not to go "back down" to Egypt (Isaiah 31:1).

with the Roman authorities. The evident corruption in the religious system was stated in the records of the Jewish sect of Qumran (Dead Sea Scrolls).

It was to this background that Jesus came and stated, "If you continue in my word, then you are my disciples indeed, and you shall know the truth, and the truth shall set you free." *To this the reply came that they are Abraham's seed and in bondage to no man.* "Jesus answered them, 'Truly, truly I say to you, Whosoever commits sin is the slave of sin. And the slave shall not abide in the house forever: but the son will abide forever. If the Son therefore shall set you free, you shall be free indeed'" (John 8:31-36).

It is written of Joseph in Mitzrayim, "that the Lord was with him, and that the Lord made all that he did to prosper in his hand." This describes a relatively short period that Joseph was a servant doing many good works in Potiphar's household, before his arrest.

And it is written of Jesus, concerning the three years before his arrest, "... all they that had any sick with various diseases brought them unto him; and he laid his hands on every one of them and healed them" (Luke 4:40)*; and,* "Go

Ref	Joseph	Jesus
		your way and tell John what things you have seen and heard, how that the blind see, the lame walk, the lepers are cleansed, the deaf hear, the dead are raised, to the poor good tidings are announced" (Luke 7:22, Isaiah 29:18-19). *Jesus also announced, "...* the Son of Man came not to be served, but to serve ..." (Matthew 20:28).
39:7-19	*Joseph was tempted by Potiphar's wife, which temptation he was able to overcome, resisting a series of opportunities; unwilling to compromise and to "sin against God."*	*Matthew 4:1-11 gives the account of Jesus' encounter with Satan (accuser, tempter), who tempted him to compromise and break the commands of God, to which Jesus resisted on every point.*
39:20	*For his moral and spiritual integrity, and refusal to compromise, Joseph was falsely accused and cast into prison. Again it is important to note that there is no record here of Joseph opening his mouth in his own defence before his accusers.*	*It is recorded in Mark 14:55-61 that many false witnesses were brought to the trial of Jesus, and that he spoke nothing in his defence, other than answering in the affirmative when asked by the High Priest as to whether he was the Mashiach. In Matthew 27:12-14 we find, "And when he was accused of the chief priest and elders, he answered nothing. Then Pilate said unto him, ' do you not hear how many things they witness against you?' And he answered him not a word,*

Ref	Joseph	Jesus
		inasmuch that the governor marvelled greatly."

The above is reminiscent of the prophesy of Isaiah (53:7-8), "He was oppressed, and he was afflicted, yet he opened not his mouth: he was brought as a lamb to the slaughter, and as a sheep before her shearer is dumb, so he opened not his mouth. He was taken from prison and from judgement, and who will declare his generation?" and, (53:12), "he was reckoned among the transgressors."

		Jesus said, "For I say unto you, that this that is written must yet be accomplished in me. And he was reckoned among the transgressors: for the things concerning me have an end" (Luke 22:37, Isaiah 53:12).
39:21-23	*The Lord was with Joseph in prison and the prisoners were given into his hand. "And whatever he did the Lord made to prosper."*	*The reference in Isaiah (53:10),* "Yet it pleased the Lord to bruise him; He has put him to grief ... and the desire of the Lord shall prosper in his hand."

The prophesy of Isaiah (61:1) reads, "The spirit of the Lord is upon me, for he has anointed me to proclaim good tidings to the humble, he has sent me to bind up the broken-hearted, to proclaim liberty to the captives, and the opening of prison to them that are bound."

40:1-22	*Here Joseph as interpreter of dreams, was able to see, not by the sight of his eyes, but discerning the judgement of God concerning who shall live and who shall die.*	

Ref	Joseph	Jesus

Isaiah 11:1-4 reads, "And there shall come forth a rod out of the stem of Jesse, and a branch shall grow out of his roots: and the spirit of the Lord shall rest upon him, the spirit of wisdom and understanding, the spirit of counsel and might, the spirit of knowledge and fear of the Lord; and shall make him of quick understanding in the fear of the Lord: and he shall not judge out of the sight of his eyes, neither reprove after the hearing of his ears: but with righteousness shall he judge the poor, and reprove with equity for the humble of the earth, and He shall smite the earth with the rod of his mouth, and with the breath of his lips shall he slay the wicked."

Jesus taught, "Judge not according to the sight of your eyes, but judge righteous judgement" (John 7:24) *and,* "And yet if I judge, my judgement is true: for I am not alone, but I and the Father that sent me" (John 8:16).

Simon Peter said of Jesus, "And He commanded us to proclaim unto the people, and to testify that it was he which was ordained of God to be judge of the living and the dead. To him give all the prophets witness" *(Acts of the Apostles 10:42:43). All of the accounts of Jesus' arrest tell of the presentation of Bar Abba and Jesus before the crowds, that by choice one would live and one would die - a reflection of this account of the butler and baker.*

Ref	Joseph	Jesus
40:23	*The chief butler did not honour Joseph's request, but forgot him when he was released, leaving Joseph imprisoned. Again we see the picture of one rejected and one abandoned, though he is righteous and correct in his judgements.*	*Barabbas was released and Jesus left in prison. Peter denied knowing Jesus three times the night of Jesus' arrest (Matthew 26:69:75). And it is written of his disciples at the time of his arrest, "And they all forsook him and fled" (Mark 14:50).*
41	*This chapter gives us the picture of a Hebrew who is able to bring a solution to an unsolvable problem, to open a way before kings and wise men of the nations who were unable to find a way.*	

Here is the prophesy of Isaiah (52:13-15), "Behold my servant shall deal prudently, he shall be exalted and extolled, and be very high. As many were astonished at thee, his appearance was so marred more than any man, and his form more than the sons of men: So shall he sprinkle many nations; kings shall shut their mouths at him: for that which had not been told them shall they see, and that which they had not heard shall they consider."

Ref	Joseph	Jesus
41:14	*The highest power (in Mitzrayim) sent and called Joseph hastily from out of the pit (the Hebrew word for pit is the same as that used to describe the hole which his brothers threw him into; it is also the same word used in the Nevi'im and the Tehilim for "the grave").* *Joseph* "shaved himself and changed his clothes,	*On the third day after the execution, the Most High revived Jesus of Nazareth from the dead, and brought him forth from the tomb.* "He is not here, but is risen: remember how he told you when he was yet in the Galilee, saying, 'The son of man must be delivered into the hands of sinful men, and be crucified, and the third day will rise again'" (Luke 24:6-7).

Ref	Joseph	Jesus

and came unto Pharaoh," is a *remez*[11] *to the messianic prophecy of* Avid Tzemach ("My servant the Branch") *in Zechariah chapter 3,* "And he showed me Joshua the High Priest standing before the angel of the Lord, and Satan standing at his right hand to accuse him. And the Lord said unto Satan, "The Lord rebuke you, Satan, even the Lord which has chosen Jerusalem rebuke you: is not this a brand plucked out of the fire?"

In Luke 10:18, Jesus said, "I beheld Satan as lightning fall from heaven."

It is described in Matthew 17:1-2, "And after six days Jesus took Simon Peter, James and John his brother, and brought them up to a high mountain apart, and he was transfigured before them: and his face did shine as the sun, and his clothes as white as the light." (see: Isaiah 61:10, "for he hath clothed me with the garments of salvation, he has covered me with the robe of righteousness").

"Now Joshua was clothed with filthy garments, and stood before the angel. And he answered and spoke unto those that stood before him, saying, Take away the filthy garments from him. And unto him he said, Behold, I have caused your iniquity to pass from you, and I will clothe you with a change of clothing". And he said, Let them set a pure mitre upon his head, and clothe him with garments. And the angel of the Lord stood by. And the angel of the Lord testified unto Joshua, saying, Thus says the Lord of Hosts, if you will walk in my ways, and if you will keep my charge, then shall you also judge my house, and shall also keep my courts, and I will give you places to walk among these that stand by. Hear now, Joshua the Chief Priest, you, and your friends that sit before you: for they are a sign: for behold, I will bring forth my servant, the Branch." (Zechariah 3:14-16).

---

[11]   *remez = "hint" the interpretation of Scripture at the level of allusive implication.*

Ref	Joseph	Jesus
41:15-16	"And Joseph answered Pharaoh, saying, It is not in me; God shall give Pharaoh an answer of peace."	*Jesus said,* "The son can do nothing of himself, but what he sees the Father do: for what things so ever He does, these also does the son likewise. For the Father loves the Son, and shows him all things that He does: and He will show him greater works than these, that you may marvel" (John 5:19-20).

Joseph and Jesus claimed to speak for God ("the word which you hear is not Mine, but the Father's which sent Me" - John 14:24).

Ref	Joseph	Jesus
41:17-36	*Joseph* "the dreamer of dreams," *again correctly interprets dreams, now doing that which the magicians and wise men could not. According to Jewish sources, the Mashiach is to give correct interpretation to the Torah (Genesis Raba 98.9.), which is to fulfil the Torah.*	*In Matthew 5:17, Jesus said,* "Think not that I come to destroy, but to fulfil." *The Mashiach was to unlock the mysteries of the Torah and the Prophets.*

An event is described in Isaiah 29:9-14, "For the Lord has poured out upon you the spirit of deep sleep, and has closed your eyes: the prophets and your rulers, the seers has he covered. And the vision of all is become unto you as the words of a book that is sealed, which men deliver to one that is learned saying, Read this, I plead: and he says, I cannot, for it is sealed; and the book is delivered to him that is not learned, saying, Read this, I plead; and he says, I am not learned. Wherefore the Lord said, For as much as this people draw near with their mouth, and with their lips do honour me, but have removed their heart far from me, for their fear towards me is taught by

Ref	Joseph	Jesus

the commandments of men; therefore behold I will proceed to do a marvellous work among this people, even a marvellous work and a wonder; for the wisdom of their wise men shall perish, and the understanding of their sages shall be hidden."

Jesus, in discussing the resurrection with the Sadducees, said, "You err, not knowing the scriptures, nor the power of God" (Matthew 22:29), *and of the state of the Scribes and Pharisees, he said,* "You blind guides" (Matthew 23:16) – *[for they were spiritual blind and could therefore not know God as they should have known Him – editor]*

41:37-38

Here the Gentile king declared that the Spirit of God was in Joseph: but had not his brothers, the children of Israel, mocked him for his visions?

Much the same has occurred during the last millennia, with many from among the Gentiles declaring that the Spirit of the Lord is in Jesus, while much the opposite has been said by the people of Israel.

Jesus had said, "The Spirit of the Lord is upon me." *But the Pharisees said,* "This fellow does not cast out demons but by Ba'al Zevuv, prince of the demons" (Matthew 12:24); *and* "Then answered the Jews, and said unto him, 'Do we not say well that you are a Samaritan, and there is a devil within you?'" (John 8:48).

Ref	Joseph	Jesus
		Peter's note: This is the way Satan hides himself. He creates confusion about his very existence by calling others Satan and being possessed by demons through his unwitting servants, in this case the Jews. The Ayatollahs of Iran refer to America as the great Satan, when they represent one of the centres of Satanic worship and power.
41:39-41	*Joseph, the insignificant servant, was brought forth from the prison and obscurity and raised above the heads of both the Gentiles and his own brethren, to sit at the right hand of power of the king, Pharaoh. The king said to him "according unto your word shall all my people be ruled," giving him full authority.*	*Jesus lay in the confines of the tomb and death, utterly defeated in Israel's eyes and in that of the Romans (the Egypt of its day), suddenly brought forth from obscurity and raise up from death, conquering the most unconquerable of all in resurrection. He was raised up to the right hand of the throne of power (g'vurah) of HaShem HaMevurach. Psalm 110:1 states,* "The Lord said unto my lord, Sit at my right hand, till I make your enemies your footstool" *(Yalkut interprets this as "King Messiah"). Jesus stated,* "All authority has been given unto me in heaven and on earth ," *(Matthew 28:18) and,* "Henceforth you shall see the son of man sitting at the right hand of power,

191

Ref	Joseph	Jesus

and coming on the clouds of heaven" (Matthew 26:64).

The prophet Daniel thus describes the Mashiach (as interpreted by Rashi and Metzudat David, this is Melech HaMashiach). "I saw in the night visions and behold, one like unto a son of man came with the clouds of heaven, and came unto the Ancient of Days, and they brought him near before him. And there was given unto him dominion, and glory, and a kingdom, that all people, nations, and languages should serve him: his dominion is an everlasting dominion, which shall not pass away, and his kingdom that which shall not be destroyed" (7:13-14). *From the Talmud we have described one called "Metatrone" (i.e. one next to the throne), in the story of "Four entered paradise" and saw there one seated next to the throne of the Most High (Hagiga 14:B).*

41:42   *Again here the image of the changing of garments; Joseph was adorned with the outer garments and symbols of Egyptian royalty - certainly styled from head to foot - in Gentile garb. He became totally unrecognisable to his Hebrew brothers.*

After the first century CE, Jesus was to be taken and as it were, made "King of the Gentiles," wrapped in the garments of foreign custom, and in time even hidden under the heavy accoutrements of idolatrous religion (which would turn his light to darkness) which essentially forgot that "King of the Jews" was written above the execution stake upon which he suffered death. All the above helped serve to blind the eyes of his own nation and brethren, Israel, who have even lost sight, to a high degree, of his being indeed a Jewish rabbi of our own.

Ref	Joseph	Jesus
41:43-44	*Joseph had been called by the king himself to reign with him over all the land, giving Joseph equal authority. They cried before Joseph, "Bow the Knee."*	*In John 5:23 Jesus said,* "He who honours not the Son, honours not the Father who sent him." *The King Messiah would reign over the earth with God:* "It is a light thing that you should be my servant to raise up the tribe of Jacob, and to restore the preserved of Israel: I will also give you for a light to the Gentiles, that you may be my salvation unto the ends of the earth," (Isaiah 49:6), *and,* "Yet have I set my king upon my holy hill of Zion. I will declare the decree: The Lord has said unto me, You are my Son, this day I have begotten you. Ask of me, and I shall give you the nations for an inheritance, and the uttermost parts of the earth for your possession" *(Tehilim [Psalm] 2:6-8 which Yalkut and Metzudat David interpret as referring to Mashiach).*

Joseph, rejected by the children of Israel, became king over Mitzrayim; Jesus, officially rejected by Israel, became king over Gentiles.

41:45	*Joseph received a new name, of the Gentiles.*	*Jesus received, through translation, the Greek name "Yesous," becoming "Jesus" in English; losing its original Hebrew meaning of "salvation" (Matthew 1:21). In the Revelation to John 3:12,*

Ref	Joseph	Jesus
		Jesus says, "and I will write upon him my new name." (In Jeremiah 23:5-6, the name of "Branch" - Messiah - is to be "the Lord our Righteousness".
	Joseph married the daughter of the Gentile priest.	*Jesus' "bride" (Revelation 19:7-9) would also be those Gentiles called out from and cleansed of idolatry, being taught of the God of Israel and His Torah ("until the fullness of the Gentiles be come in" - Paul's letter to the Romans 11:25).*
41:46	*Joseph was thirty years old when he stood before Pharaoh. This is the age according to the Torah (Numbers 4:3) that a man may begin priestly service in the Tabernacle.*	*Jesus, when he began his works in Israel, was* "about thirty years old" (Luke 3:23).
	Two sons were born to Joseph, Menashe (Manasseh) and Ephraim. When Jacob blessed the two children, he laid his right hand on the head of Ephraim, the younger, again the reversal of roles with the first born, and declared that "his seed shall become the fullness of the goyim (Gentiles)" *(Genesis 48:19). He also said that Joseph's two sons were as his own two firstborn sons, Reuben and Simeon. Thus these two were later to become half-tribes,*	*Jesus chose twelve intimate Talmidim (disciples) according to the number of tribes of Israel, himself separate, the thirteenth.*

Ref	Joseph	Jesus
41:50-52	*numbered among the twelve in the inheritance of the Land of Israel, causing the name of Joseph to rest in a separate and unique position, further fulfilling Jacob's prophesy over him that he would be* "separate from his brethren" (Genesis 49:26).	
41:55	"and Pharaoh said unto all Egyptians, 'Go unto Joseph, what he says to you, do." *In Deuteronomy 18:15 Moses states,* "The Lord your God will raise up unto you a prophet from amongst you, of your brethren, like unto me; unto him you shall hearken." *Also in 18 and 19 of the same chapter, the Lord confirms,* "I will raise them up a prophet from among your brethren, like unto you, and I will put my words in his mouth, and he shall speak unto them all that I shall command him. And it shall come to pass, that whoever will not hearken unto my words that he shall speak in my name, I will require it of him." *(Later we shall see what the Talmud says regarding this passage)*	*In the new testament, the Lord declares of Jesus,* "This is my beloved son, in whom I am well pleased, hear him" *(Matthew 17:5). And Jesus clarified,* "The words that I speak unto you I speak not of myself, but the Father that dwells in me ..." (John 14:10). *Again in 5:46 of the same book,* "For had you believed Moses, you would have believed me; for he wrote of me."

Ref	Joseph	Jesus
41:56-57	*Joseph was able, through the intercession of the Lord's spirit of wisdom, understanding, counsel, knowledge, and the fear of the Lord (Isaiah 11:2) to save the land from starvation, from lack of bread.*	*In Matthew 14:15-21, Jesus blessed five loaves of bread and two fish, which were then passed out and fed five thousand people.*

The Torah tells us, "Man shall not live by bread alone, but by every word which proceeds from the mouth of God" *(Deuteronomy 8:3). In the book of Amos 8:11 it is prophesied,* "Behold the days come, says the Lord, that I will send a famine in the land, not a famine of bread, or a thirst for water, but of hearing the words of the Lord."

In the days of Jesus, it had been over four hundred years since a prophet of God had been in the land, to bring forth His word. Malachi had been the last. The nations of the world at that time were immersed in all forms of idolatry.

Jesus told his disciples, "But you will receive power after the ruach hakodesh (Holy Spirit) is come upon you: and you shall be witnesses unto me both in Jerusalem, and in all of Judah and Samaria, and unto the uttermost part of the earth" *(ACTS 1:8);* and, "Go therefore, and teach all nations" (Matthew 28:19).

In Isaiah 55:2-3 it is written, "Wherefore do you spend money for that which is not bread and your labour for that which does not satisfy? Listen diligently unto me and eat that which is good, and let yourself delight itself in fatness. Incline your ear, and come unto me: hear, and your soul shall live; and I will make an everlasting covenant with you, even the sure mercies of David."

Ref	Joseph	Jesus

Jesus said, "I am the bread of life: he that comes unto me shall never hunger, and he that believes in me shall never thirst" (John 6:35).

Thus Jesus would save the land from spiritual starvation, and bring the knowledge of God to the goyim, to a starving world; who then, knowing the ways of life and death, could choose accordingly (as it is written in the Torah, "I call heaven and earth this day against you, that I have set before you life and death, blessing and cursing: therefore choose life" - Deuteronomy).

42   *The completely natural and essential phenomenon of hunger was used here to draw Israel out to Mitzrayim toward the fulfilling of God's overall plans. Yet this speaks of a hunger of the spirit, perhaps unbeknown to them at the time.*

In Matthew 5:6 Jesus said, "Blessed are they that hunger and thirst after righteousness ..."; and "Truly, truly, I say to you, Moses gave you not that bread from heaven; but my Father gives you the true bread from heaven. For the bread of God is he which comes down from heaven, and gives life to the world" (John 6:32,33).

42:6   *Here is the eventual fulfilment of Joseph's prophetic dream, after many years; though the children of Israel did not know that they were bowing before their brother, and would not have admitted to the fact; "they worshipped him." It is the same gesture of bowing down before kings or God, as in the case of King David's dedication of Solomon in I Chronicles 29:20,*

Ref	Joseph	Jesus
	"And all the congregation blessed the Lord God of their fathers, and bowed their heads and worshipped the Lord and the king."	
42:7	"And Joseph knew his brethren, but they knew him not." *Joseph did his best to maintain that distance of non-recognition, being in full control of the situation, though his brothers were completely ignorant of the fact. In the prophet Ezekiel 39:23 it is written,* "And the nations shall know that the house of Israel went into captivity for their iniquity: because they trespassed against me, therefore hid I my face from them, and gave them into the hand of their enemies ..."	*We are reminded again of Jesus' words,* "You shall not see me again until you say, Blessed is he who comes in the name of the Lord." *So it was to be, that Jesus' identity would be hidden from Israel, yet they would be known of him, as it is written in I John 4:19,* "We love him because he first loved us," *and Paul's word in Romans 5:8,* "But God commended his love toward us, in that while we were yet sinners, Mashiach died for us."
42:17-18	*Joseph imprisoned his brothers for three days, on the third day calling them forth. This recalls the passage in Hosea 6:2,* "After two days he will revive us: in the third day he will raise us up, and we will live in his sight."	*Jesus was raised up, according to his word, on the third day, from death. In John 11:25,* "Jesus said unto her, I am the resurrection and the life ..."

Ref	Joseph	Jesus
42:21-22	*The brothers began to associate their predicament with what they had done to Joseph, though they in no way recognised him.*	*(There has been an awakening of interest of a positive sort in Jesus among a number of Jewish writers and scholars, including Martin Buber and Rabbi Eliyahu Solevitchik, who for the most part have not recognized him as the promised Messiah.)*
42:23-24	"And they knew not that Joseph understood them, for he spoke to them by an interpreter. And he turned himself about from them, and wept ..." *Joseph wept upon hearing his brothers' conversation.*	"And when he was come near, he beheld the city (Jerusalem), and wept over it, saying, If you had only known, in this your day, the things which belong unto your shalom (peace) but now they are hid from your eyes." (Luke 19:41-42)
42:25-34	*Joseph indeed answered their supplication by supplying their needs, loading their donkeys with grain, even returning their money in their sacks. This being a fine illustration of chesed (grace), that they would know that what they had obtained had not been deserved or purchased by their own earnings.*	*Though many in Israel do not recognize the validity of the Torah, nor the portion in the Rambam's statement of faith regarding the coming of Mashiach, yet is HaShem faithful to his word,* "for his chesed endures forever." *It is written in the prophet Ezekiel 36:22, regarding the regathering of Israel to the land,* "Thus says the Lord God, I do not this for your sakes, O house of Israel, but for my Holy Names sake ..."

Ref	Joseph	Jesus
42:35-38	*Israel saw no good coming from this situation, but evil only, and fear.*	*This was the deduction of the leaders in Jerusalem in the first century,* "If we let him thus alone, all will believe on him, and the Romans shall come and take both our land and our nation" (John 11:48). *A condition that exists for the most part in Israel and the Jewish people today, regarding our relationship to Jesus and the Brit Hadasha.*
43:1-7	Joseph had told them, "You shall not see my face, except your younger brother be with you." *He would eventually gather all his brothers together before him, while his true identity was yet hidden from them. It is thus prophesied in Ezekiel chapter 39:28-29,* "Then shall they know that I am the Lord their God, which caused them to be led into captivity among the nations and I have gathered them unto their own land, and have left none of them any more there. Neither will I hide my face any more from them: for I will pour out my spirit upon the house of Israel, declares the Lord God."	

Ref	Joseph	Jesus
	The reader is given to understand that Joseph knows more about the children of Israel than they know of him, as they are completely in the dark regarding him. Today the average Jew knows little or nothing of Jesus of Nazareth, other than distortions and preconception.	
43:11	*Offerings were to be given to this unknown "man", the same who had angered them when told that they would make obeisance to him. At that time, had they known that it was Joseph to whom they were offering mincha, it would have been a mighty shock to them.*	
43:14	*Here Israel called for God's mercy in the situation, neither knowing nor understanding that Joseph is in fact God's instrument of mercy.*	*This according to the Brit Hadasha account, is the exact parallel to the work of God in Jesus towards Israel (see Paul's letter to the Romans chapter 11). For God has concluded them all in unbelief, that he might have mercy upon all."*
43:15-16	*This is the second time the brothers appeared before Joseph, the king. He commands, "Bring these men home and slay an animal, and make ready, for these men shall dine with me at noon."*	*In the period of the second national return to the Land of Israel (the first being from Egypt, the second from Babylon), which is the time of the second temple, Jesus appeared to Israel, in fact dining with his brethren.*

Ref	Joseph	Jesus
		In Luke 22:15 Jesus says, "How greatly I have desired to eat this Passover with you before I suffer." *In Isaiah 53:7 it is written,* "He was brought as a lamb to the slaughter." It is the same Hebrew word used in Joseph's command. As Joseph fed his brothers, so Jesus said, "I am the bread of life: he that comes to me shall never hunger, and he that believes on me shall never thirst," (John 6:35).
43:18-25	"And the men were afraid, because they were brought into Joseph's house." *The closer they came to Joseph, the more uncomfortable they grew, in effect experiencing their transgression (as we shall see later), though not yet knowing why.* *In 43:23 the fact is here spoken that Joseph's generosity, which put fear in their hearts, was the work of the God of Israel. Though his brethren had betrayed him and cast him out, yet did he repay them with goodness, in fact fulfilling Jesus' teaching,* "But I say unto you, love your enemies, bless them that curse you, do good to them that hate you ..."	*Jesus said,* "If I had not come and spoken unto them, they had not had sin: but now they have no cloak for their sin," (John 15:22). *Jesus' ultimate function was to deal with the matter of sin:* "For this is my blood of the new covenant, which is shed for many for the remission of sins" (Matthew 26:28).

Ref	Joseph	Jesus
	(Matthew 5:44). *In 43:18 we see that Joseph's generosity has been interpreted as malicious, and as yet is Jesus' kindness often spoken evil of amongst our people*	
43:26-28	"And bowed themselves to him to the earth." *Again we see the literal fulfilment of Joseph's dream, confirming the prophetic nature of it.*	*It is written in the revelation of John 5:12,* "Worthy is the lamb that was slain to receive power and riches, and wisdom, and strength, and honour, and glory, and blessing."
43:13-31	*We witness the depth of Joseph's feeling, expressed in tears hidden from his gathered brothers, along with his identity.*	*Jesus wept over Jerusalem, and said,* "O Jerusalem, Jerusalem, you that kills the prophets, and stones them which are sent unto you, how often would I have gathered your children together, even as a hen gathers her chicks under her wings, but you would not" (Matthew 23:37).
43:34	*Joseph fed his brothers in his own home*	*In Luke 22:30 Jesus said,* "That you may eat and drink at my table in my kingdom ..."
44:1-12	*Again Joseph provides sustenance and returns their money, the picture of chesed (grace). But this time by design, he will use another tactic to make them aware of that chesed. A false accusation is*	*As we shall see shortly, the betrayal and turning over of Jesus to the Roman authorities for execution was not in the essence of crime, for his death was of Divine intention, for he highest purpose.*

Ref	Joseph	Jesus
	levelled against them as a means of drawing out the nature of their actual transgression: hardness of heart and unbelief and hatred expressed those many years earlier. As God, the righteous judge, will not allow transgression to go undealt with at some point, so are the children of Israel taken in this trap, arrested and hindered from returning to the Land of Israel. A parallel to this is the accusation often levelled at Jews: "Christ killers."	*t Jesus said concerning his life,* "No man can take it from me, but I lay it down of myself" (John 10:17-18). *The transgression according to the prophets, including Moses, was hardness of heart, unbelief and "hatred without cause."*
44:13-34	*Here the sons of Israel tear their garments in dismay as their worst fears come upon them and all hope of success appears to be lost. The above principle is well illustrated in Judah's expression of his deep guilt (it was he who had wished to murder and later sell Joseph), realising that, "God has found out the iniquity of your servants." He confessed, "What shall we say unto my lord? What shall we speak? Or how can we clear ourselves?"*	
	We may recall the words of Isaiah 53:8, "And who shall declare his generation?" *Judah brings forth to Joseph his long harboured anguish of spirit for his crimes against Joseph himself (as yet unrecognised) and the pain which*	

Ref	Joseph	Jesus

this had caused to their father;
wishing now to repent by laying
down his own life for the sake of
his younger brother Benjamin. It
is noteworthy that the rejection of
Joseph had caused such profound
grief to Israel, the father, as
Jesus' rejection has been the
anguish of Israel.

But it is in the return, the
repentance of Judah here that we
see before us the prophesy, "For
the redeemer shall come to
Zion, and unto them that
turn from transgression in
Jacob, declares the Lord"
(Isaiah 59:20). *(It is from his*
name, Judah, that we get the
word, Yedhudi, or Jew.)

Jesus declared, "Greater love has
no man than this, that a man
lay down his life for his friends"
(John 15:13). At that moment,
Judah, in his desire to cover his
own sin against Joseph and his
father by laying down his life for
Benjamin, did not understand
that Joseph's life had already been
given to redeem not only Judah,
but all his brothers and their
families. This is much th e same
principle seen in the Akeda that
God himself provided a life in the
place of Yitzhak's on the

Ref	Joseph	Jesus
	sacrificial altar. This is also seen in the sin sacrifices in the later temple system ("A life for a life").	
45:1-2	*It is Judah's broken-hearted confession that finally tears the curtain of separation and their redeemer is revealed before their eyes.* "The sacrifices of God are a broken spirit: a broken and contrite heart, O God, you will not despise" (Telehim 51:17-19 in Hebrew). *Here is the essence of t'shuva shlemah (perfect repentance). How deep is the feeling in the breast of Joseph and the love he had for his brothers. He can no longer contain the feeling and cries aloud. The Gentiles hear the weeping, though he has sent them out, making this a private family matter. Is not the gathering of Israel back to the land again, in our days, separating them from the nations, for a purpose?* *In Ezekiel 36:24-26 it says,* "For I will take you from among the nations, and gather you out of all the countries, and will bring you into your own land. Then I will sprinkle clean water upon you, and you shall be	

Ref	Joseph	Jesus

clean from all your filthiness and from all your idols, will I cleanse you. A new heart will I give you, and a new spirit will I put within you, and I will take away the stony heart out of your flesh, and I will give you a heart of flesh."

Jeremiah, describing the gathering of Israel to her land, brings the prophesy, "Behold, the days are coming, declares the Lord, that I will make a new covenant (brit hadasha) with the house of Israel, and with the house of Judah, not according to the covenant that I made with their fathers in the day that I took them by the hand to bring them out of the land of Egypt, which my covenant they broke, although I was a husband unto them, declares the Lord. But this shall be the covenant that I will make with the house of Israel, after those days, declares the Lord, I will put my Torah in their inward parts, and write it in their hearts, and I will be their God, and they shall be my people. And they shall teach no more every man his neighbour, and every man his brother saying, "know the

Ref	Joseph	Jesus

Lord, for they shall all know me, from the least of them unto the greatest of them, declares the Lord, for I will forgive their iniquity, and I will remember their sins no more" (31:31-34).

By design this, the third time that his brothers appear before Joseph, he chooses to reveal his identity to them. Today is the third national gathering from exile of the Jewish people back to the Land of Israel. As stated earlier, the first was from Egypt, under Moses; the second, the return from Babylon; now the third, from all the nations of the world. The prophesy in Jeremiah 16:14-15 states, "Therefore behold, the days come, declares the Lord, that it shall no more be said, the Lord lives, that brought up the children of Israel from the land of Egypt; but, the Lord lives, that brought up the children of Israel from the land of the north, and from all the lands where he has driven them: and I will bring them again into their land that I gave unto their fathers." *The intent here, is to gather Israel together again to speak to them privately, in their own language.*

208

Ref	Joseph	Jesus
45:3	"And Joseph said unto his brethren, I am Joseph; does my father yet live? And his brethren could not answer him, for they were troubled at his presence."	

Allow me again to refer here to the passage which the Rabbis state speaks of "Mashiach ben Joseph", Zechariah 12:10-14, "And I will pour upon the house of David, and upon the inhabitants of Jerusalem the spirit of grace and supplication: and they shall look upon me whom they have pierced, and they shall mourn for him as one mourns for his only son, and shall be in bitterness for him, as one that is in bitterness for his firstborn. In that day there shall be a great mourning in Jerusalem, as the mourning in Hadadrimon in the valley of Megiddon. And the land shall mourn, every family apart; the family of the house of David apart, and their wives apart; the family of the house of Nathan apart, and their wives apart; the family of the house of Levi apart, and their wives apart; the family of the house of Shimei apart, and their wives apart; all the families that remain, every family apart, and their wives apart." *Here is one presumed dead by Israel, torn by a wild beast, suddenly appearing alive in the most unexpected form, time and place, asking if his father Jacob lives, the answer to which he already knows.*

Joseph's brothers cannot answer his question, for they are deeply troubled, as the tribes and families of Israel shall mourn, husbands and wives not able to look into each other's eyes, or speak, as they behold the Mashiach ben Joseph.

In Matthew 24:30 Jesus states, "And then shall appear the sign of the son of man in heaven: and then shall all the tribes of the land mourn, and they shall see the Son of Man, coming in the clouds of heaven with power and great glory."

Ref	Joseph	Jesus
45:4-6	*Mourning is for a limited period of time, as Joseph speaks kindly unto them,* "Please come unto me". *Jesus said,* "Come unto me you who are weary and heavy laden, and I will give you rest" (Matthew 11:28). *In another place, John 5:40, he says,* "And you will not come unto me, that you might have life." *Joseph tells them,* "I am Joseph, your brother whom you sold into Egypt." He comforts his brothers with great love and tenderness, explaining that this was all the work of God, for the salvation of their lives (and of course the lives of the Gentiles, who would receive his counsel and teachings), literally "to bring to life".	
45:7	"And God sent me before you to preserve you a prosperity in the earth, and to save your lives by a great deliverance."	
	Joseph was God's tool used in fulfilling the promise to Abraham of making his seed a great nation (Genesis 12:2).	
	Joseph had gone before Israel as a shepherd before his flock, bringing them to food and water, even if his sheep were reluctant ("Give ear, O Shepherd of Israel, you	

Ref	Joseph	Jesus
	that leads Joseph like a flock" - *Tehilim 80:1*).	*In John 14:2-3, Jesus' words are,* "In my Father's house there are many dwellings ... I go to prepare a place for you. And if I go and prepare a place for you, I will come again, and receive you unto myself, that where I am, you may be also." *He speaks here of his death and its special significance, that his provision would not be only a temporary one, but an eternal place of glory in the kingdom of heaven.* *Jesus, who declared,* "I am sent to the lost sheep of the house of Israel" (Matthew 15:24), *also said,* "I am the good shepherd: the good shepherd gives his life for the sheep ... No man takes it from me, but I lay it down of myself" (John 10:11, 18). *Unlike Joseph, here is one who has voluntarily taken the role of outcast, for the salvation of the flock of Israel.*
45:8	*Joseph reiterates that it had all been the outworking of God and declares his lordship over the house of Pharaoh and the land of Egypt.*	*Jesus said,* "All authority has been given to me in heaven and on earth" (Matthew 28:18).

Ref	Joseph	Jesus
45:9	Joseph commands his brothers to tell Israel the good tidings ("gospel") of their deliverance, that they must come to him to receive it.	Jesus commissioned his twelve disciples (and others) to declare the b'sorah (good news) to Israel, and to all nations (Mark 28:19).
45:10-13	Joseph tells them, "You shall be near unto me," in the place he had prepared.	Jesus said, "Father, I will that they also whom you have given me, be with me where I am, that they may behold my glory, which you have given me ..." (John 17:24).
	Joseph said, "And you shall tell my father of all my glory in Egypt, and all that you have seen." In Matthew 11:4-5	Jesus said, "Go and tell John that which you hear and see; the blind receive their sight, the lame walk, the lepers are cleansed, the deaf hear, the dead are raised up, and the poor have good news brought to them."
45:14-15	This is one of the most touching moments in all Bible history, as the children of Israel receive their brother and deliverer who had been hidden from their eyes, embracing each other with profound tears of joy.	Such joy will be at the revelation of the Mashiach.
45:16	The Gentiles heard of this and were pleased. In Psalm 126:1-2 it is written, "When the Lord returned the captivity of Zion, we were like them that dreamed. Then was our mouth filled with laughter, and our tongue with singing:	

Ref	Joseph	Jesus
	then said they among the Gentiles, the Lord has done great things for them."	
45:17-20	*With the suggestion and authority of the king, Pharaoh, Joseph gathers his people together. In Matthew 24:31* *Moses promised,* "If any of yours be driven out unto the utmost parts of heaven, from there will the Lord your God gather you, and from there will he fetch you" *(Deuteronomy)*	Jesus said, "and he shall send his malachim[12] with the sound of a great shofar, and they shall gather together his elect from the four winds, from one end of heaven to the other."
45:21	*Upon this joyous occasion Joseph gave his people gifts.*	*Paul stated in the letter to the Ephesians, quoting Psalm 68:18 and 68:19 in Hebrew,* "You have ascended on high and returned the captivity and took gifts for men."
45:22	*Joseph gave his brothers new clothing. Isaiah 61:10 says,* "For he has clothed me with the garments of salvation, wrapped me with a robe of righteousness."	*In Revelation 6:11 we find,* "And white robes were given unto every one of them."
45:24	*Joseph told his brothers not to become angry at each other on the way.*	Jesus told his Talmidim[13], "Whoever is angry with his brother without cause shall be in danger of judgement," *and,* "Love one another" *(Matthew 5:22, John 13:34)*

[12]   *Messenger*
[13]   *Disciples*

Ref	Joseph	Jesus
45:26	*The centre of Joseph's message to Jacob here was:* "Joseph is alive," *but he did not believe them.*	

Luke 24:11 describes how when it was first reported to Jesus' eleven disciples that he was alive, "They believed them not." *The Brit Hadasha report that Jesus is alive, has been, for the most part, disbelieved by Israel. The prophesy of Isaiah 53 begins,* "Who has believed our report, and to whom has the arm of the Lord been revealed?"

Ref	Joseph	Jesus
45:27	*When Israel finally did believe the report, before actually seeing Joseph,* "the spirit of Jacob their father revived", *literally,* "Jacob's spirit came back to life."	*Paul states, regarding Israel's return and their relation to Jesus, that it will be* "life from the dead" *(Romans 11:15).*
46	*Here we see the gathering of Israel to Joseph in Mitzrayim, for the purpose of making there "a great nation."*	

In the prophesies of Ezekiel we see that the gathering of the Jewish people to King Mashiach will in fact be in the Land of Israel, for a similar purpose, "For this declares the Lord God, 'Behold, I, even I, will both search for my sheep, and seek them out. As a shepherd seeks out his flock in the day he is among his sheep that are scattered, so will I seek out my sheep, and will deliver them out of all the places where they have been scattered, in the cloudy and dark day. And I will bring them out from the people, and gather them from the countries, and will bring them to their own land, and feed them upon the mountains of Israel by the rivers, and in all the inhabited places of the country ... Therefore will I save my flock, and they shall no more be prey, and I will judge between lamb and lamb. And I will set up one shepherd over them, and he shall feed them, even my servant David, he shall feed them, and he shall be their shepherd. And I the Lord will be their

Ref	Joseph	Jesus

God, and my servant a Prince among them; I the Lord have spoken it'" (Ezekiel 34:11-13, 22-24).

And in Ezekiel 37:24-26, "And David my servant shall be king over them, and they shall all have one shepherd: they shall also walk in my judgements, and observe my statutes, and do them. And they shall dwell in the land I have given unto Jacob my servant, wherein your fathers have dwelt, and they shall dwell therein, even they and their children, and their children's children forever: and my servant David shall be their prince forever. Moreover I will make a covenant of peace with them; it shall be an everlasting covenant with them: and I will place them, and multiply them, and I will set my sanctuary in the midst of them forevermore."

46:27 *Seventy souls in the house of Jacob. Seventy, in Judaism, is the traditional number of the nations, probably coming from Deuteronomy 32:8,* "When the Most High divided to the nations their inheritance, when he separated the sons of Adam, he set the bounds of the people according to the number of the children of Israel." *The prophesy of the prophet Isaiah 49:6 states,* "It is a light thing that you should be my servant to raise up the tribes of Jacob, and to restore the preserved of Israel, I will also give you for a light to the nations that you may be my salvation unto the end of the earth."

In Matthew 28:19 Yeshua said, "Go therefore, and teach all nations." *The Hebrew letter ("y" ayin) is the number seventy. This is the last letter in the name Yeshua. Amongst the Jewish people for two millennia, the last letter in his name has been traditionally dropped, making Yeshu. Ayin ("y") also the Hebrew word for "eye".*

In Paul's letter to the Romans, chapter 11:25-26 we find, "that blindness in part is happened to Israel, until the fullness of the Gentiles be come in. And so all Israel shall be saved, as it is written, There shall come out of Zion the deliverer, and shall turn away ungodliness

Ref	Joseph	Jesus
		from Jacob: for this is my covenant unto them, when I shall take away their sins."
	Joseph was sent forth by God for the salvation from hunger of both the Gentiles and Israel.	*It is written in Isaiah 42:6-7,* "I the Lord have called you in righteousness, and will hold your hand, and will keep you, and give you for a covenant of the people, for a light to the nations, to open the blind eyes ..." *In Luke 4:20-21 it is recorded that Yeshua read these words in the beit knesset (synagogue) after which* "the eyes of all of them that were in the synagogue were fastened on him. "And he began to say unto them, this day this scripture is fulfilled in your ears." *In numerous places it is recorded that Yeshua also healed the physically blind.*
46:28	*Judah was sent first to direct Israel unto Joseph in Goshen. This interplay between Judah and Joseph and the dynamic between them in the entire account, plus the prophesy given by Jacob over Judah (Genesis 49:8-12), is a remez to the Mashiach ben Joseph coming forth ultimately from the tribe of Judah. The name Judah in Hebrew actually contains the*	*The inheritance of the tribe of Judah - the Land of Judah (Judah) - therefore actually does contain the name of the Lord. David ("beloved") ben Ishai, from whose seed was to arise the "son of David", or "Mashiach ben David", was born from the tribe of Judah, in the Land of Judah, in the town of Beit Lehem, all of which is true also of Yeshua*

Ref	Joseph	Jesus

four letters of the tetragrammaton, or the name of the Lord, plus one letter "d", from which comes David. In Deuteronomy 12:11 we find, "Then there shall be a place which the Lord your God shall choose to cause his name to dwell there."

(Luke 2:1-7; Matthew 2:1-6). In Micah 5:2 it is prophesied, "But you Biet Lehem Ephrata, though you be little among the thousands of Judah, yet out of you shall come forth unto me that is to be ruler in Israel, whose goings forth have been from old, from everlasting." We read in Sh'mot 23:20-21, "Behold I send a malach before you, to keep you in the way, and to bring you into the place which I have prepared. Beware of him, and obey his voice, provoke him not, for he will not pardon your transgressions: for my name is in him."

In Jeremiah 23:5-6 it appears, "Behold, the days come, declares the Lord, that I will raise unto David a righteous branch ... and this is his name by which he will be called, 'the Lord (the tetragammaton) our righteousness' ". *Is it not possible, therefore, that Mashiach ben Joseph and Mashiach ben David, are in fact one and the same person, an individual in whom the Holy One, blessed be he, has chosen to place his name?*

Ref	Joseph	Jesus
46:29	*Israel embraces his son whom he thought was dead, after a long passage of time, with tears of joy. First we saw the reunion of the brothers, now of the old father, with Joseph. The coming together of Israel with her Mashiach will be the fulfilment of the dreams, visions and hopes of our fathers, indeed of all the prophets of Israel.*	Yeshua said, "... when you shall see Abraham, Isaac and Jacob and all the prophets in the malchut haElohim (kingdom of God) ..." (Luke 13:28), *and in John 8:56,* "Your father Abraham rejoiced to see my day: he saw it and was glad."
46:30	"And Israel said unto Joseph, now let me die because I have seen your face, because you are yet alive."	*In Luke 2:28-32 we see the aging Shimon hatzadik in the Temple at the time of the brit mila/ circumcision of Yeshua, when he took the infant up in his arms and said,* "Now let your servant depart in peace according to your word, for my eyes have seen your salvation which you have prepared before the face of all people; a light to illuminate the Gentiles, and the glory of your people Israel." *Luke 24:5-6 reports of Yeshua at the tomb in which he had been placed,* "Why do you seek the living among the dead? He is not here but is risen."
47	*This portion deals with the situation of Israel as shepherds and their flocks. And yet through the Tenach the people of Israel are referred to as sheep, as the flock of the Lord, as in Psalm 79:13,* "So we your people, and sheep of your pasture will give you thanks	

Ref	Joseph	Jesus

forever," *and in Jeremiah 50:6,* "My people have been lost sheep."

Likewise, God himself is called a shepherd, "The Lord is my shepherd" (Psalm 23:1) *and* "Give ear, O shepherd of Israel" (Psalm 80:1).

As a good shepherd leads his flock to grazing, God, through Joseph, has led Israel from famine to fullness and rest, as we read in 47:12, "And Joseph nourished his father, and his brethren, and all his father's household, with bread, according to their families."

In the Brit Hadasha, Yeshua is described, like Israel, as both lamb and shepherd, "Behold the lamb of God, who takes away the sin of the world" (John 1:29), *and* "They overcame him by the blood of the Lamb" (Revelation 12:11), *and,* "I am the good shepherd: I lay down my life for the sheep." (John 10:14-15).

The name Judah in Hebrew actually contains the four letters of the tetragrammaton, or the name of the Lord, plus one letter "d", from which comes David. In Deuteronomy 12:11 we find, "Then there shall be a place which the Lord your God shall choose to cause his name to dwell there."

The inheritance of the tribe of Judah - the Land of Judah - therefore actually does contain the name of the Lord. David ("beloved") ben Ishai, from whose seed was to arise the "son of David", or "Mashiach ben David" was born into the tribe of Judah, in the Land of Judah, in the town of Beit Lehem.

All this is true of Yeshua (Luke 2:1-7; Matthew 2:1-6). In Micah 5:2 it is prophesied, "But you Biet Lehem Ephrata, though you be little among the thousands of Judah, yet out of you shall come forth unto me that is to be ruler in Israel, whose goings forth have been from old, from everlasting."

9 A JEWISH UNDERSTANDING OF THE CREATION

The Evolutionists like to quote figures, indeed the time scale of the various aspects of the evolution of man at least is very important, particularly with the advent of carbon dating when the discoveries of archeologists can be given a date the being lived and the place where it lived, in defining the advancement of mankind from the prehistoric caveman/ape-man up to the current edition.

But the theory of evolution is restricted by its inability to explain firstly what went before the big bang and the sequence of events that occurred immediately after the big bang and prior to the appearance of our close ancestors, the upright being described by them as man.

This article explains the biblical account very well.

Edited information © Gerald Schroeder

One of the most obvious perceived contradictions between Torah and science is the age of the universe. Is it billions of years old, like scientific data, or is it thousands of years, like Biblical data? When we add up the generations of the Bible, we come to 5700-plus years. Whereas, data from the Hubbell telescope or from the land based telescopes in Hawaii, indicate the number at 15 billion years.

In trying to resolve this apparent conflict, it's interesting to look historically at trends in knowledge, because absolute proofs are not forthcoming. It is interesting to see how science has changed its understanding of the world over the years, but the record in the Torah remains fixed because the Torah doesn't have the option of changing. (I refuse to use modern Biblical commentary, because modern commentary is already too influenced by modern science.)

The only data that can be therefore be used with any degree of safety as far as Biblical commentary goes is ancient commentary. That means the:

- ext of the Bible itself (3300 years ago),
- translation of the Torah into Aramaic by Onkelos (100 CE),
- Talmud (redacted about the year 500 CE),
- three major Torah commentators.

There are many, many commentators, but at the top of the mountain there are three, accepted by all:

- Rashi (11th century France), who brings the straight understanding of the text,
- Maimonides (12th century Egypt), who handles the philosophical concepts,
- Nachmanides (13th century Spain), the earliest of the Kabbalists.

This ancient commentary was finalized hundreds or thousands of years ago, long before Hubbell was a gleam in his great-grandparent's eye. So there is no possibility of Hubbell or any other scientific data influencing these concepts. That's a key component in this attempt to keep the following discussion objective.

A Universe With a Beginning.

In 1959, a survey was taken of leading American scientists. Among the many questions asked was,

"What is your concept of the age of the universe?"

Now, in 1959, astronomy was popular, but cosmology - the deep physics of understanding the universe - was just developing. The response to that survey was recently republished in Scientific American - the most widely read science journal in the world. Two-thirds of the scientists - an overwhelming majority - gave the same answer which was,

"Beginning? There was no beginning. Aristotle and Plato taught us 2400 years ago that the universe is eternal. Oh, we know the Bible says

'In the beginning.' That's a nice story, it helps kids go to bed at night. But we sophisticates know better. There was no beginning."

In 1965, Penzias and Wilson discovered the echo of the Big Bang in the black of the sky at night, and the world paradigm changed from a universe that was eternal to a universe that had a beginning. Science had made an enormous paradigm change in its understanding of the world.

It is essential to understand the impact of that dramatic and far reaching change of thinking. Science, which had said that there was no beginning, now said that our universe had a beginning, proving that the first words of the Bible *"In the beginning ... "* were correct after all. The importance of that scientific "discovery" cannot be overstated. Evolution, cave men, these are all trivial problems compared to the fact that we now understand that we had a beginning.

Of course, the fact that there was a beginning does not prove that there was a beginner. Whether the second half of Genesis 1:1 is correct, we don't know from a secular point of view. The first half is "In the beginning;" the second half is *"G-d created the Heavens and the Earth."* Physics allows for a beginning without a beginner. I'm not going to get into that today, but my new book, "The Science of G-d," examines this in great detail.

It all Starts from Rosh Hashanah.

The question we're left with is:
"how long ago did the "beginning" occur?"

Was it, as the Bible might imply, 5700-plus years, or was it the 15 billions of years as is accepted by the scientific community?

The first thing we have to understand is the origin of the Biblical calendar. The Jewish year is figured by adding up the generations since Adam. Additionally, there are six days leading up to the creation to Adam. These six days are significant as well.

Of course, what the question would be is where we make the zero point. On Rosh Hashanah, the Jewish New Year, the Shofar is blown three times during the Musaf service. Immediately upon blowing of the Shofar, the following sentence is said:
"Hayom Harat Olam - today is the birthday of the world."

This verse might imply that Rosh Hashanah commemorates the

creation of the universe but it doesn't. Although Rosh Hashanah does commemorate a creation, it is not the creation of the universe.

The Shofar is blown three times to commemorate the last of the three creations that occurs in the Six Days of Genesis. First, there is the creation of the entire universe and the laws of nature. Then on Day Five, there is the creation that brings us the Nefesh, the soul of animal life. Finally, at the end of Day Six, there is a further creation that brings us the Neshama, the soul of human life.

Rosh Hashanah commemorates not the first or the second of the creations, but the third only, that is the creation of the Neshama, the soul of human life. This means that the counting for the 5700-plus years of Jewish history starts from the creation of the soul of Adam. Thus the clock that begins with Adam is separate from the six days. This means that the Bible has two clocks.

This might seem like a modern rationalization, if it were not for the fact that Talmudic commentaries 1500 years ago record this information. In the Midrash (Vayikra Rabba 29:1), an expansion of the Talmud, all the Sages agree that Rosh Hashanah commemorates the soul of Adam, and that the Six Days of Genesis are separate.

Now 1500 years ago, when this information was first recorded, it wasn't because one of the Sages like Hillel was talking to his 10-year-old son who said, "Daddy, you won't believe it but we went to a museum today and learned all about a billions-of-years-old universe," and Hillel says, "Oh, I better change the Bible, let's keep the six days separate." That wasn't what was happening.

It is essential in this situation to use the mind frame of 1500 years ago, when people travelled by donkeys and electricity or even zippers were yet to be invented. Why were the Six Days taken out of the calendar? At the time, there was no need to make them separate.

The reason they were taken out was because they came to realise that time is described differently in those Six Days of Genesis. To say, "There was evening and morning" is an exotic, bizarre and unusual way of describing time even at that time.

From Adam, the flow of time is clearly in human terms. Adam and Eve lived 130 years before having children! Seth lived 105 years before having children, etc. From Adam forward, the flow of time is totally human in concept. But prior to that time, it is an abstract concept: "Evening and morning." It is like looking down on events from a viewpoint that is not intimately related to them.

Looking Deeper Into the Text.

In trying to understand the flow of time here, it is important to remember that the entire Six Days of Creation in Genesis are confined to 31 sentences! This has given people so many headaches in trying to understand science and relate it to the Bible, At MIT, in the Hayden library, there were about 50,000 books that dealt with the development of the universe: cosmology, chemistry, thermodynamics, palaeontology, archaeology and the high-energy physics of creation. Up the river at Harvard, at the Weiger library, they probably have 200,000 books on these same topics. Yet the Bible gives us just 31 sentences. So don't expect that by a simple reading of those sentences it is possible to know every detail that is held within the text. It is obvious that there is a need to dig deeper to get the information out.

The idea of having to dig deeper is not a rationalization. The Talmud (Chagiga, ch. 2) tells us that from the opening sentence of the Bible, through the beginning of Chapter Two, the entire text is given in parable form, a poem with a text and a subtext. Now, again, think according to the mindset of 1500 years ago, the time of the Talmud. Why would the Talmud think it was parabolic? Is it possible that 1500 years ago they thought that G-d couldn't make it all in 6 days? It was a problem for them? People have a problem today with cosmology and scientific data. But 1500 years ago, what's the problem with 6 days? No problem.

So when the Sages excluded these six days from the calendar, and said that the entire text is a parable, it wasn't because they were trying to apologize away what they'd seen in the local museum. There was no local museum. No one was out there digging up ancient fossils. The fact is that a close reading of the text makes it clear that there is information hidden and folded into layers below the surface.

The idea of looking for a deeper meaning in Torah is no different from looking for deeper meaning in science. For those who get up early in the morning, look over and there comes the Sun, rising in the east. Wait a few hours and the Sun sets in the west. The simple "reading" is "there's the Sun again going around the Earth." But there is much more to it. How about the Earth rotating on its axis? And neglecting the rest of the universe and just considering the Sun-Earth system, it is not the Sun that is moving, although that is every perception of human perception.

In the Sun-Earth system it is the Sun that is standing still, and the Earth that is rotating on its axis which means that at this moment, even sitting down, people are moving about 800 miles an hour. There go the clouds. Look at them zooming by. No, that's not what's happening, because we're all moving together. It cannot be felt because it is inertial motion, there is no acceleration. So it feels like we're standing still. But in fact we are moving at 800 miles an hour as we rotate around to get a day and a night out of that one 24-hour day.

The Earth is moving around the sun at about 20 miles a second. And the entire Solar System is moving around the centre of our galaxy at about 250 miles a second. That is per second. Do we feel any of it? No. So when Galileo argued and claimed that Earth is not standing still, he got put under house arrest.

Just as we look for the deeper readings in science, we need to look for the deeper readings in text. Thousands of years ago we learned that there are subtleties in the text that expand the meaning way beyond. It is those subtleties we need to see.

Natural History and Human History.

There are early Jewish sources stating that the calendar is in two parts (even predating Leviticus Rabba which goes back almost 1500 years and says it explicitly). In the closing speech that Moses makes to the people, he says that if you want to see the fingerprint of G-d in the universe, "consider the days of old, the years of the many generations" (Deut. 32:7). Nachmanides, in the name of Kabbalah, asks, "Why does Moses break the calendar into two parts -

'The days of old, and the years of the many generations?'

Because,

'Consider the days of old' is the Six Days of Genesis.

'The years of the many generations' is all the time from Adam forward."

Moses says it is possible to see G-d's fingerprint on the universe in one of two ways. Look at the phenomenon of the Six Days and the development of a universe which is mind-boggling. Or if that doesn't impress, then just consider society from Adam forward - the phenomenon of human history. Either way it is possible find the imprint of G-d.

I recently met in Jerusalem with Professor Leon Lederman, Nobel Prize winning physicist. We were talking science, obviously. As the conversation went on, I said, "What about spirituality, Leon?" And he said to me, "Schroeder, I'll talk science with you, but as for spirituality, speak to the people across the street, the theologians." But then he continued, and he said, "But I do find something spooky about the people of Israel coming back to the Land of Israel." Interesting.

The first part of Moses' statement, "Consider the days of old" - about the Six Days of Genesis - didn't impress Prof. Lederman. But of the "Years of the many generations" - human history - that impressed him. Prof. Lederman found nothing spooky about the Eskimos eating fish at the Arctic circle. He found nothing spooky about Greeks eating Musika in Athens. But he finds something really spooky about Jews eating falafel on Jaffa Street. Because it shouldn't have happened. It doesn't make sense historically that the Jews would come back to the Land of Israel. Yet that's what happened.

And that is one of the functions of the Jewish People in the world. To act as a demonstration. We don't want everyone to be Jewish in the world, just to understand that there is some monkey business going on with history that makes it not all just random. That there's some direction to the flow of history and the world has seen it through us. It is not by chance that Israel is on the front page of the New York Times more than anyone else.

What Is A "Day?"

Let's jump back to the Six Days of Genesis. First of all, it is known that when the Biblical calendar says 5700-plus years, to that must be added "the six days."

A few years ago, I acquired a dinosaur fossil that was dated (by two radioactive decay chains) as 150 million years old. (If you visit me in Jerusalem, I'll be happy to show you the dinosaur fossil - the vertebra of a plesiosaurus.) So my 7-year-old daughter says, "Abba! Dinosaurs? How can there be dinosaurs 150 million years ago, when my Bible teacher says the world isn't even 6000 years old?" So I told her to look in Psalms 90:4. There, you will find something quite amazing. King David says, "1000 years in Your (G-d's) sight are like a day that passes, a watch in the night." Perhaps time is different from the perspective of King David, than it is from the perspective of the Creator. Perhaps time is different.

The Talmud (Chagiga, ch. 2), in trying to understand the subtleties of Torah, analyses the word "choshech." When the word "choshech" appears in Genesis 1:2, the Talmud explains that it means black fire, black energy, a kind of energy that is so powerful you can't even see it. Two verses later, in Genesis 1:4, the Talmud explains that the same word - "choshech" - means darkness, i.e. the absence of light.

Other words as well are not to be understood by their common definitions. For example, "mayim" typically means water. But Maimonides says that in the original statements of creation, the word "mayim" may also mean the building blocks of the universe.

Another example is Genesis 1:5, which says, "There is evening and morning, Day One." That is the first time a day is quantified: evening and morning. Nachmanides discusses the meaning of evening and morning. Does it mean sunset and sunrise? It would certainly seem to.

But Nachmanides points out a problem with that. The text says "there was evening and morning Day One... evening and morning a second day... evening and morning a third day." Then on the fourth day, the sun is mentioned. Nachmanides says that any intelligent reader can see an obvious problem. How do we have a concept of evening and morning for the first three days if the sun is only mentioned on Day Four? We know that the author of the Bible - even if you think it was a bunch of Bedouins sitting around a campfire at night - was smart. He or she or it produced a best-seller. For thousands of years! So it is not possible to attribute the sun appearing only on Day Four to foolishness. There is a purpose for it on Day Four. And the purpose is that as time goes by and people understand more about the universe, you can dig deeper into the text.

Nachmanides says the text uses the words "Vayehi Erev" - but it doesn't mean "there was evening." He explains that the Hebrew letters Ayin, Resh, Bet - the root of "erev" - is chaos, mixture, disorder. That's why evening is called "erev", because when the sun goes down, vision becomes blurry. The literal meaning is, "there was disorder." The Torah's word for "morning" - "boker" - is the absolute opposite. When the sun rises, the world becomes "bikoret", orderly, able to be discerned. That's why the sun needn't be mentioned until Day Four. Because from erev to boker is a flow from disorder to order, from chaos to cosmos. That's something any scientist will testify never happens in an unguided system. Order never arises from disorder spontaneously. There must be a guide to the system. That's an unequivocal statement.

Order can not arise from disorder by random reactions. (In pure probability it can, but the numbers are so infinitesimally small that physics regards the probability as zero.) So you go to the Dead Sea and say, "I see these orderly salt crystals. You're telling me that G-d's there making each crystal?" No. That's not what I'm saying. But the salt crystals do not arise randomly. They arise because laws of nature that are part of the creation package force salt crystals to form. The laws of nature guide the development of the world. And there is a phenomenal amount of development that's encoded in the Six Days. But it is not included directly in the text, otherwise creation would be in every other sentence!

The Torah wants people to be amazed by this flow of order, starting from a chaotic plasma and ending up with a symphony of life. Day-by-day the world progresses to higher and higher levels. Order out of disorder. It is pure thermodynamics. And it is stated in terminology of 3000 years ago.

The creation of time.

Each day of creation is numbered. Yet there is discontinuity in the way the days are numbered. The verse says: "There is evening and morning, Day One." But the second day doesn't say "evening and morning, Day Two." Rather, it says "evening and morning, a second day." And the Torah continues with this pattern: "Evening and morning, a third day... a fourth day... a fifth day... the sixth day." Only on the first day does the text use a different form: not "first day," but "Day One" ("Yom Echad"). Many English translations make the mistake of writing "a first day." That's because editors want things to be nice and consistent. But they throw out the cosmic message in the text! Because there is a qualitative difference, as Nachmanides says,

THE ORIGIN OF LIFE

between "one" and "first." One is absolute; first is comparative.

Nachmanides explains that on Day One, time was created. That's a phenomenal insight. Time was created. I can understand creating matter, even space. But time? How do you create time? You can't grab time. You don't even see it. You can see space, you can see matter, you can feel energy and you can see light energy. I understand a creation there. But the creation of time? Eight hundred years ago, Nachmanides attained this insight from the Torah's use of the phrase, "Day One." And that's exactly what Einstein taught us in the Laws of Relativity: that there was a creation, not just of space and matter, but of time itself.

Einstein's Law of Relativity.

We look at the universe, and say, "How old is the universe? Looking back in time, the universe is about 15 billion years old." That is our view of time. But what is the Bible's view of time? How does it see time? Maybe it sees time differently. And that makes a big difference.

Albert Einstein taught us that Big Bang cosmology brings not just space and matter into existence, but that time is part of the nitty gritty. Time is a dimension. Time is affected by your view of time. How you see time depends on where you're viewing it. A minute on the moon goes faster than a minute on the Earth. A minute on the sun goes slower. Time on the sun is actually stretched out so that if you could put a clock on the sun, it would tick more slowly. It's a small difference, but it's measurable and measured. If you could ripen oranges on the Sun, they would take longer to ripen. Why? Because time goes more slowly. Would you feel it going more slowly? No, because your biology would be part of the system. If you were living on the Sun, your heart would beat more slowly. Wherever you are, your biology is in synch with the local time.

If it were possible to look from one system to another, time would be seen very differently. This is because time, depending on factors like gravity and velocity, is perceived very differently.

For example: One evening we were sitting around the dinner table, and my 11-year-old daughter asked, "How could you have dinosaurs? How could you have billions of years scientifically - and thousands of years Biblically at the same time? So I told her to imagine a planet where time is so stretched out that while we live out two years on Earth, only three minutes will go by on that planet. Now those places actually exist, they are observed. It would be hard to live there with their conditions, and you couldn't get to them either, but in mental experiments you can do it. Two years are going to go by on Earth, three minutes are going to go by on the planet. So my daughter says, "Great! Send me to the planet. I'll spend three minutes there. I'll do two years worth of homework. I'll come back home, no homework for two years."

Nice try. Assuming she was age 11 when she left and her friends were 11. She spends three minutes on the planet and then comes home. (The travel time takes no time.) How old is she when she gets back? Eleven years and 3 minutes. And her friends are 13. Because she lived out 3 minutes while we lived out 2 years. Her friends aged from 11 years to 13 years, while she's 11 years and 3 minutes.

Had she looked down on Earth from that planet, her perception of Earth time would be that everybody was moving very quickly. Whereas if we looked up, she would be moving very slowly.

Which is correct? Is it three years? Or three minutes? The answer is both. They're both happening at the same time. That's the legacy of Albert Einstein. It so happens there are literally billions of locations in the universe where if you could put a clock there it would tick so slowly that from our perspective (if we could last that long) 15 billion years would go by... but the clock at that remote location would tick out six days. Nobody disputes this data.

Time Travel and the Big Bang.

But how does this help to explain the Bible? Because the Talmud and commentators seem to say that Six Days of Genesis were regular 24-hour periods!

Let's look a bit deeper. The classical Jewish sources say that before the beginning, we don't really know what there was. We can't tell what predates the universe. The Midrash asks the question: Why does the Bible begin with the letter Bet? Because Bet (which is written like a backwards C) is closed in all directions and only open in the forward direction. Hence we can't know what comes before - only after. The first letter is a Bet - closed in all directions and only open in the forward direction.

Nachmanides the Kabbalist expands the statement. He says that although the days are 24 hours each, they contain "kol yemot ha-olam" - all the ages and all the secrets of the world.

Nachmanides says that before the universe, there was nothing... but then suddenly the entire creation appeared as a minuscule speck. He gives a dimension for the speck: something very tiny like the size of a grain of mustard. And he says that is the only physical creation. There was no other physical creation; all other creations were spiritual. The Nefesh (the soul of animal life) and the Neshama (the soul of human life) are spiritual creations. There's only one physical creation, and that creation was a tiny speck. The speck is all there was. Anything else was G-d. In that speck was all the raw material that would be used for making everything else. Nachmanides describes the substance as "dak me'od, ein bo mamash" - very thin, no substance to it. And as this speck expanded out, this substance - so thin that it has no essence - turned into matter as we know it.

Nachmanides further writes: "Misheyesh, yitfos bo zman" - from the moment that matter formed from this substance-less substance, time grabs hold. Not "begins." Time is created at the beginning. But time "grabs hold." When matter condenses, congeals, coalesces, out of this substance so thin it has no essence - that's when the Biblical clock starts.

Science has shown that there's only one "substanceless substance" that can change into matter. And that's energy. Einstein's famous equation, $E=MC2$, tells us that energy can change into matter. And once it changes into matter, time grabs hold.

Nachmanides has made a phenomenal statement. I don't know if he knew the Laws of Relativity. But we know them now. We know that energy - light beams, radio waves, gamma rays, x-rays - all travel at the speed of light, 300 million metres per second. At the speed of light, time does not pass. The universe was aging, but time only grabs hold when matter is present. This moment of time before the clock begins for the Bible, lasted about 1/100,000 of a second. A miniscule length of time. But in that time, the universe expanded from a tiny speck, to about the size of the Solar System. From that moment on matter exists, and time flows forward. The clock begins here.

Now the fact that the Bible says there is "evening and morning Day One", teaches us time from a Biblical perspective. Einstein proved that time varies from place to place in the universe, and that time varies from perspective to perspective in the universe. The Bible says there is "evening and morning Day One".

Now if the Torah were seeing time from the days of Moses and Mount Sinai - long after Adam - the text would not have written Day One. Because by Sinai, millions of days had already passed. Since then there was a lot of time with which to compare Day One, it would have said "A First Day." By the second day of Genesis, the Bible says "a second day," because there was already the First Day with which to compare it. You could ask on the second day, "What happened on the first day?" But you could not say on the first day, "what happened on the first day?" because "first" implies comparison - an existing series. And there was no existing series. Day One was all there was.

Even if the Torah was seeing time from Adam, the text would have said "a first day", because by its own statement there are six days. The Torah says "Day One" because the Torah is looking forward from the beginning. And it asks, "How old is the universe? Six Days" (that is just taking time up until Adam). Six Days. We look back in time, and say the universe is 15 billion years old. But every scientist knows, that when we say the universe is 15 billion years old, there's another half of the sentence that we never say. The other half of the sentence is:

"The universe is 15 billion years old as seen from the time-space coordinates that we exist in."

That is Einstein's view of relativity.

The key is that the Torah looks forward in time, from very different time-space coordinates, when the universe was small. But since then, the universe has expanded out. Space stretches, and that stretching of space totally changes the perception of time.

Imagine in your mind going back billions of years to the beginning of time. Now pretend way back at the beginning of time, when time grabs hold, there's an intelligent community. This is totally fictitious but, for the sake of this experiment, let us imagine that the intelligent community has a laser which is going to shoot out a pulse of light every second. Every second -- pulse. Pulse. Pulse. It shoots the light out, and then billions of years later, way far down the time line, we here on Earth have a big satellite dish and we receive that pulse of light. On that pulse of light is imprinted (printing information on light is called fibre optics - sending information by light), "I'm sending you a pulse every second." And then a second goes by and the next pulse is sent.

Now light travels at 300 million metres per second. So the two light pulses are separated by 300 million metres at the beginning. Now they travel through space for billions of years, and they're going to reach the Earth billions of years later. But wait a minute. Is the universe static? No. The universe is expanding. That's the cosmology of the universe. And that means it's expanding into an empty space outside the universe. There's only the universe. There is no space outside the universe. The universe expands by space stretching. So as these pulses go through billions of years of travelling, and the universe is stretching, and space is stretching, what's happening to these pulses? The space between them is also stretching. So the pulses really get further and further apart. Billions of years later, when the first pulse arrives, we say, "Wow - a pulse!" Written on it is "I'm sending you a pulse every second." You call all your friends, and you wait for the next pulse to arrive. Does it arrive another second later? No! A year later? Maybe not. Maybe billions of years later. Because depending on how much time this pulse of light has travelled through space, will determine the amount of stretching that has occurred. That's standard cosmology.

15 billion Years or Six Days?

Today, time is observed looking backwards, that is 15 billion years. Looking forward from when the universe is very small - billions of times smaller - the Torah says six days. In truth, they both may be correct.

What's exciting about the last few years in cosmology is we now have quantified the data to know the relationship of the "view of time" from the beginning, relative to the "view of time" today. It is no longer a matter of science fiction. Any one of a dozen physics text books all use the same number. The general relationship between time near the beginning and time today is a million million. That's a 1 with 12 zeros after it. So when a view from the beginning looking forward says "I'm sending you a pulse every second," would we see it every second? No.

We'd see it every million million seconds because that is the stretching effect of the expansion of the universe.

The Torah doesn't say every second, does it? It says Six Days. How would we see those six days? If the Torah says we are sending information for six days, would we receive that information as six days? No. We would receive that information as six million million days. Because the Torah's perspective is from the beginning looking forward.

Six million million days is a very interesting number. What would that be in years? Divide by 365 and it comes out to be 16 billion years. Essentially the estimate of the age of the universe. Not a bad guess for 3000 years ago.

The way these two figures match up is extraordinary. I'm not speaking as a theologian; I'm making a scientific claim. I didn't pull these numbers out of a hat. That's why I led up to the explanation very slowly, so you can follow it step-by-step.

Now we can go one step further. Let's look at the development of time, day-by-day, based on the expansion factor. Every time the universe doubles, the perception of time is cut in half. Now when the universe was small, it was doubling very rapidly. But as the universe gets bigger, the doubling time gets exponentially longer. This rate of expansion is quoted in "The Principles of Physical Cosmology," a textbook that is used literally around the world.

(In case you want to know, this exponential rate of expansion has a specific number averaged at 10 to the 12th power. That is in fact the temperature of quark confinement, when matter freezes out of the energy: 10.9 times 10 to the 12th power Kelvin degrees divided by (or the ratio to) the temperature of the universe today, 2.73 degrees. That's the initial ratio which changes exponentially as the universe expands.)

The calculations come out to be as follows:

- The first of the Biblical days lasted 24 hours, viewed from the "beginning of time perspective." But the duration from our perspective was 8 billion years.
- The second day, from the Bible's perspective lasted 24 hours. From our perspective it lasted half of the previous day, 4 billion years.
- The third day also lasted half of the previous day, 2 billion years.
- The fourth day - one billion years.
- The fifth day - one-half billion years.
- The sixth day - one-quarter billion years.

When you add up the Six Days, you get the age of the universe at 15 and 3/4 billion years. The same as modern cosmology. Is it by chance?

But there's more. The Bible goes out on a limb and tells you what happened on each of those days. Now you can take cosmology, palaeontology, archaeology, and look at the history of the world, and see whether or not they match up day-by-day. And I'll give you a hint. They match up close enough to send chills up your spine

ABOUT THE AUTHOR

After an electrical engineering apprenticeship in the Royal Navy, Peter went on to serve on a number of ships in different parts of the world, finally being responsible for the weapons maintenance department of a frigate and lecturing to trainee officers on weapon systems. He also spent two years at the Royal Navy's training college in Fareham, Hampshire instructing on underwater weapon and defence systems.

Leaving the service at 30 in 1969, Peter worked as a quality engineer for the British Aircraft Corporation at Filton, Bristol on spacecraft and guided weapon systems before moving to R. A Lister (Diesels) where he became a technical writer in 1984. He then worked as a contract author, mostly in the nuclear industry, writing instructional and training documentation before finally retiring in 2011.

For over 20 years, Peter was a Methodist Local Preacher before becoming an official prison visitor on January 1st 1990 and from 1994 worshipping with his wife at the prison he visits in order to focus on supporting prisoners who wanted to change their lives around which he did for almost twenty six years.

Peter met a Jew named Derek who had become a Christian in prison. On his release to the local community, Peter was able to help him adjust to a new life of going straight.

It was Derek who first asked Peter to write on scripture in 2002, after which Derek's brother Aaron, a rabbi serving in the USA, came under the influence of Peter's writing and became a Christian. Aaron asked him to write first on the book of Revelation and then on the subject of Moses' Tent of the Meeting, which he self-published early 2011.

Peter was married in December 1961 and has three sons and six grandchildren. His autobiographical book explaining how he came to write his books is called "A Tale of Three Men".

MORE FROM

Peter Russell-Yarde

www.ingramcontent.com/pod-product-compliance
Lightning Source LLC
Chambersburg PA
CBHW021617120626
46545CB00001B/271